The Great Game of Politics

The Great Game of Politics

WHY WE ELECT WHOM WE ELECT

Dick Stoken

A Tom Doherty Associates Book

New York

A Forge Book
Published by Tom Doherty Associates, LLC
175 Fifth Avenue
New York, NY 10010

www.tor.com

Forge® is a registered trademark of Tom Doherty Associates, LLC.

ISBN 0-765-30732-4

First Edition: January 2004

Printed in the United States of America

0 9 8 7 6 5 4 3 2 1

To my mother,

"Sarah" Ogens Stoken,

who set my course

Acknowledgments

Thanks to my assistant, Robin Kramer, for tidying up many loose odds and ends in preparation for publication.

I am indebted to Joel Weisman and Richard Ellis for reading parts of the manuscript and offering many helpful suggestions.

To William Gianopulos, whose editorial advice, along with broad critical observations, has left footprints throughout this book, many thanks.

United States—1788

Contents

Introduction

Not only do men move about on a charted landscape. The
landscape itself is in constant motion, and men best be quick
enough to move about with it. When they aren't, they go through
the cracks that open under their feet.

PROBABLY SOPHOCLES, AROUND 450 B.C.

I was young and cocky once. I had mastered the way the world
worked . . . or so I thought. No Sir-ee! The earth was not going to
open up under my feet. But, during the 1980s and after, I saw old
familiar patterns, based on a world that focused on avoiding
danger, shrinking in the rear-view mirror. Suddenly, like many in my
generation, I realized "I" was a stranger in a profoundly different
place. And then I heard the deafening rumble of the ground shaking
beneath my very feet.

DICK STOKEN, A CONFESSION, SOMETIME IN THE EARLY 1990S

This book is about the **constant motion** in American society
and politics.

Every generation or so there is an upheaval in the political and
social life of the American people. Not to be alarmed! This is not a

major transformation on the order of the American, French, or Russian revolutions. Nor is it a total change in the nature of a society, or a shift in America's basic ideology. Rather, it is mini-revolution, a "little" upheaval, within the bounds of the greater American tradition. It becomes a new subculture in which people view their central ideology differently, a different variation of the same major theme.

Every so often a society that focuses on achieving high public purpose—ranking people by the depth of their devotion to the public good—is supplanted by one that dances to the music of a money culture, wherein wealth becomes the chief means of distinguishing one person from another. And then . . . after people have adapted and become acclimated to the new money culture, it's back again to a "little" world that centers on devotion to the public good. Our sub-cultures, "little" worlds, are in constant motion. An old one dies; a new one is born.

Each mini-revolution, the shift from old to new, marks a break in the continuity of American society. A nation of people is suddenly required to turn and march in another direction. The rules by which society operates change. Familiar institutions become inexorably twisted into unrecognizable shapes. Core social arrangements take on new patterns. And by the time the tectonic plates of society stop shifting, the mini-transformation will have evolved into a new political model—a **paradigm.**

These paradigms are terribly important. In each there is a fresh way in which people view reality. In each there is a new mode of behavior, fresh habits of thought, and a new order of values. A paradigm is the "given," the lens, through which we all view the world, and it has a subtle, but significant, effect on the way we act.

Yet most people are so busy adjusting their lives to the new conditions that they are only dimly aware of these mini-transformations that come about every 20 years or so, just as predictably as winter follows summer. Most are caught off guard, as if they had neglected to stock up on warm clothing, fuel to heat their homes, and shovels to dig themselves out of deep snowfalls, before wintertime arrived. They fall through the cracks that open up under their feet.

This constant motion, these shifting paradigms, have been the puzzle of "mankind." Can we avoid those cracks, which open under our feet?

The answer is **YES!**

Politics serves as the ideal conduit for making sense out of most of these shifts going on in our world. Through the realm of politics we can understand how the world works and how we fit in. As we shall see, the American political process is not chaotic or random. There is an essential shape to it. Some presidents have had a huge impact on the course of American history. Others have not; they have merely followed in the footprints of the giants. The great leaders are the transmission mechanism to the mini-revolutions. By focusing on them we make the American story coherent.

How do we assess who were the important presidents? Ask a true liberal and you will get one set of great presidents, while a conservative surely has another. This story of politics is *not* based on another subjective opinion of who might be the better leader, Democrat or Republican. It differs from most others in that it relies on criteria that are quantifiable to determine which presidents had the greatest impact on their times and in whose path a generation of Americans followed.

It is based on listening to the American people, that is, interpreting "the will of the people." When they march off to the polling booths every four years to register their opinion, we learn a great deal about how they feel about the prior four. Election results are not subjective; their readings are crystal clear. Even close contests tell you something: that there was no strong preference for either candidate.

Our founders, who were not fools, built the political system of democracy on the very idea that the people are sovereign, that their collective wisdom outranks that of any political scholar, any TV commentator, or the highest-standing intellectual. More on that in the following chapter. If we let the American people provide the verdicts, we get a pretty good reading of the political tea leaves.

There have been nine great presidents, one who set the course of American history and eight who played a major role in altering that course. *Each presided over and directed "fundamental," as opposed to "incremental," political changes in American society.*

A pattern-setting president arrives on the scene and pursues policies that undermine the old political model and begin the transformation to a new one. As the mini-revolution takes on its primary shape it becomes a new paradigm. Presidents who follow the model builders, especially those of the same party, govern according to the core political doctrine laid down by the paradigm leader. For example, Democratic presidents Harry Truman, John Kennedy, Lyndon Johnson, and Jimmy Carter all remained true to the primary New Deal agenda set by Franklin Delano Roosevelt. And even minority presidents Dwight Eisenhower, Richard Nixon, and Gerald Ford did not stray too far from the New Deal's basic tenets.

So this book is about politics, about America's important political leaders. But it is also about the "little" transformations that follow in their wake, providing the constant motion with the cracks that open under people's feet; it is about the mini-revolutions being shaped into new paradigms. Each is part of the other. Together they make an essential whole. The story of politics is central because it is the vehicle by which we can recognize the transformations to a new paradigm.

Using the mini-revolutions as reference points we are going to take a journey going back in time to the American Revolution. American history should no longer appear as a patternless swirl of events. It has been a series of shifting political models. When we penetrate these little worlds the nation's past takes on an essential form.

Interestingly, this pattern could have helped make sense of the recent bizarre Bush-Gore election, which seemed so unlike all the others. But to students of **The Great Game of Politics** it wasn't. As far back as the spring of 1999 this election appeared to be shaping up much like three others in the past. In all three the majority party, of those eras, was trying to win back the White House after a period of minority party rule. Each time they succeeded—even though a shift of only a handful of votes in one or a few states could have changed the outcome—but only after applying every bit of political muscle available. Normally the majority party has control of the election apparatus, the majority of state election boards, along with the Supreme Court. And in close contests against an incumbent minority party, this generally proves to be the decisive factor. The paradigm wins out. Just as an immune system protects the body by attacking alien organisms, a political paradigm, when it can (in close calls), rejects the candidate who is dangerous to its longevity. Gore versus Bush: another example of a majority party restoration.

Throughout American history there have been two great parties engaged in an ongoing duel. Each is convinced it has accumulated most of the wisdom in the United States and wants to be the major author of the American story. Many Americans have come to identify themselves with one of the two, and the basic agenda and mission of the other is simply not an acceptable vehicle for their hopes and dreams.

Yet unbeknownst to ourselves we are usually selecting, voting for, one of two main Western worldviews. As we shall see, both major parties' main agenda has remained remarkably consistent since the beginning of the republic. Each represents a great tradition that has played, and still is playing, an important role in the making of the modern world. Both parties are part of a single whole.

Then there is the "why" of these mini-revolutions. Why do political models change? As we shall see, it is because of a law of social nature. Human beings are part of a catching-on process, which affects what goes on in the real world and sows the seeds for these mini-transformations.

A brief note on the uniqueness of the American political revolution. Major political revolutions rarely succeed. Since the mid-1600s there have been five earthshaking revolutions in Western societies and all but one now lie in the ash heaps of history. England's mid-seventeenth-century attempt to establish a republic failed; the grand French Revolution was the poster boy for "how not to do a revolution"; the German Revolution, which according to the Nazis was going to last a thousand years, hardly made it to 12; and the Russian Revolution, which was going to bury capitalism, barely made 74 years before imploding.

Only the American one, now over 200 years old, still flourishes. It is the lone success and, as we shall see, much of the credit may derive from its ability to steer from one side of the political spectrum to the other—from right to left—and back again.

Why do I call politics, which to many is a deadly serious business, a game?

In politics there are winners and there are losers; there are rules, both implicit and explicit; and there is a prize, which is simply enormous, the right to shape public and foreign policy so as to influence events for four years. It is a game of both skill and chance, although some may play for fun and frolic. Any citizen over the age of 18 years has the right to play. All get a chance to impose their own particular view of what they think the "world" should be like upon that world.

Most important, "all of us," those who choose to participate and those who don't, have a great stake in the outcome. Thus no other game, from basketball to baseball, from charades to scrabble, rivals politics in importance. Not the "money" game! Not the "sex" game! Nor even the "love" game! Politics is simply the biggest and most important game of all; it is the **"Great" Game.**

In the end, making sense of the Game of Politics is the way to avoid those cracks that open under our feet. It is the way to unravel the riddle of mankind.

—⊸⊷⊶⊷⊸—

I

Political Paradigms

During the 1980s something new and unusual was afoot in America's political culture. Prior to that time society had built its political-economic foundation upon "big" and intrusive government, around legislation to regulate business, around policies to provide security and protect people from danger. But with a suddenness unseen in half a century that foundation was toppled and a new one erected based on business deregulation, on creating avenues of opportunity, and on encouraging competition. This shift from seeking security to taking risks was part of a mini-revolution in the social and intellectual climate that altered views on nearly everything from business to family life, from work to religion.

Moreover, a new entrepreneurial spirit was visible throughout the land. During the placid 1950s, David Riesman, in *The Lonely Crowd*, reported, college students considered business "dull and disagreeable as well as morally suspect." Businesspeople back then were generally considered vulgar and greedy, besides being wicked oppressors of the working class. But by the turn of the century college students obsessed over internships, the proletariat had taken up day-trading, and governments everywhere had put business at the top of their agendas. The business culture was triumphant.

What happened? Why such a profound shift?

A new political "**PARADIGM**" was born. It was a fresh American era.

What Is a Political Paradigm?

A paradigm is a set of compatible political, economic, and social beliefs related to a central theme and accepted by most members of society. Underlying this theme is the way people view risk. When the majority of men and women see their world as fraught with risk they will endorse ways of thinking that promise to avoid danger. They are likely to approve of government attempts to intervene in the economy, to provide security, a safety net to protect the weak and elderly. Reducing risk becomes the frame of reference by which other things, such as the role of government and individual careers, are tacitly interpreted, evaluated, and judged. Ideas or proposals that fly in the face of this underlying assumption are not likely to receive much of a following.

On the other hand, let a people witness a long run of peaceful prosperity and they are likely to adopt a view that sees their world as relatively risk-free. When this underlying assumption is in place, men and women will be amenable to placing more trust in markets, to accepting a greater degree of competition, and to assuming more risk in their individual life. In this atmosphere, ideas to privatize a portion of Social Security, to institute school vouchers, and to cut back on welfare will reach a more receptive audience.

These underlying perceptions of risk implant filters in the mind—which we are not totally aware of—that act as an inner beacon to guide us in making choices. They provide the cement that binds a nation's political, economic, and social thinking into a unified whole so that it forms a **paradigm,** that is, a political model, which develops its own set of unstated rules, its own culture, its own expectations for the American people, and its own vision of where the nation is headed. The paradigm becomes the lens through which most people view their world, and it affects the way they think and act.

When perceptions of risk shift, a mini-revolution in a nation's social, economic, and political views ensues. A new mindset forms, and with it comes a different way of behaving, from risk avoidance to risk taking or from chance taking to caution. A people who had viewed political and economic occurrences through a lens that favored big government action to solve societal problems might put on a different pair of glasses and begin to appreciate the market as the best way to tackle the nation's headaches. Those same people who formerly had been suspicious of business and its merchant class, might begin to adopt an entrepreneurial spirit and worship at the altar of money.

A new political paradigm does not mean that the basic nature of the American political ethic is changing. Rather, it is a smaller change within a much grander tradition. Take two different business organizations, both of which operate in America's capitalistic economy and share the same basic business profit objectives. Scratch beneath the surface and you might notice different cultures, different rules, and different worker expectations. One company might have a "laid-back" business structure and look to the outside world as a source of opportunity, while the other may view the outside world as threatening and maintain a formal organization. Both are practicing different variations of the same general American business culture. In much the same way, America's political models are variations around a more general American ethic. If you don't like the one you are in, wait a generation or so and another more to your liking may come along.

As in the culture of a business, where the direction is set by the owner, the CEO, or perhaps a previous owner of the company, the **president of the nation** sets the course, which turns a new mass-risk perception into a political paradigm.

Before modern times, kings set the tone of a nation or society.

In those premodern eras, the very important events were the coronation of a new king. The nobility, who usually resided at the royal court for part of the year, would listen very carefully to what the new king was saying, trying to draw a bead on whether vast and far reaching changes were in the wind. They would observe how strong a leader he was likely to be, what his agenda was, and which groups he was going to favor. And when they returned to their castles in the heartland, they were likely to emulate the king's behavior, his manner and direction of governing, in their own dealings with the common folk; thus a style and course to the country's political, economic, and social affairs set by the ruler flowed throughout the nation and set the mood of everyday society.

However, not all kings set a tone of governing much different from their forebears. In fact, most followed along the same pathways as the prior king; so too with America's presidents. Most follow along the course launched by some predecessor, perhaps two or three removed. Only a few have torn up the existing way of doing things and implemented vast new political changes, a mini-revolution, that reverberated throughout the nation for years to come. Those few who broke the mold became paradigm-setting presidents. They planted the roots, which defined their parties and the nation's political culture for years to come. **They had the biggest impact on American society and politics.**

The important paradigm shift prior to the one in the 1980s began in 1933. During the most chilling depression in our nation's history dispirited voters marched off to the polls to cast their ballot for Franklin Delano Roosevelt, giving him one of the largest landslides in American history. Roosevelt stirred up a mini-revolution that was to lead to a new political model, wherein government became responsible for its citizens' well-being. To understand the FDR paradigm *think*: BIG GOVERNMENT, SOCIAL JUSTICE, and RISK AVOIDANCE.

The citizens of America struck a bargain with the federal government. The state got an immense amount of power, and in return the public received protection; "big" government would provide a safety net and bring about a fairer and more just society. This idea of government intervention in the economy was able to fly because it was related to the underlying assumption that favored risk avoidance.

Presidents who followed in FDR's wake governed with this paradigm leader's shadow looming over their shoulder. They compared themselves with Roosevelt and believed in the things FDR believed in. Their agendas did not deviate too far from the course he had set. They continued down his path of greater government involvement in the economy, introducing more and more regulations and controls and additional programs to help the poor and the elderly. Big government came to be viewed as the answer to the nation's problems. It had, under Roosevelt's guidance, cured the depression, won a war, and produced economic stability. No doubt it could also tackle other big societal shortcomings, like poverty, racism, and crime. Any problems, no sweat; the government with its vast resources would handle them. Just pass another bill and spend more money from the public purse.

A "New Deal" was followed by a "Great Society." Under the government's prodding, social innovation followed social innovation, pressuring society to open up its doors to make room for more and more diverse groups of people. Laborers burst through first, but women and "blacks" soon followed.

It was a time when the "devotion to the public good" spirit ruled. People were encouraged to serve others, to commit to causes greater than their own self-interest. Societies' helpers, doctors, educators, members of the Peace Corps, and public servants, garnered respect and status. These do-gooders became the country's popular idols. And by God, if you were Mother Teresa or a Nobel Prize laureate you were guaranteed to ride at the head of the parade.

Meanwhile, the entrepreneurial spirit was at a low ebb. To be sure, there were people who were able to find a special niche in the economy and carve out a small piece of the American business pie. But for the most part, big corporations held sway over the American economy, and for those who chose business for their livelihoods, jobs with the big companies were worth dreaming about. They offered security, comfortable working conditions, and a wide rage of financial benefits, all without unduly encroaching on the employee's home life.

Throughout this era the "liberal" outlook reigned supreme. The people of America believed well-meaning and well-educated men and women could engineer the nation's social problems from Washington. But beginning in the late 1960s it was becoming glaringly evident that the well-meaning policies were creating an inflationary bias in our economy and spawning a "let the government take care of you" dependency. Throughout the 1970s the economy was in a rut, vacillating between deep recession and galloping inflation, social breakdown became increasingly visible as the incidence of crime, illegitimacy, and drug usage exploded through the roof, and traditional American values were melting away, while new ones that glorified narcissism, hedonism, and an "anything goes" culture were becoming embedded.

By 1980 popular discontent had reached very high levels. Yet Democrats, including members of President Jimmy Carter's inner circle, were confident that the country would never buy the policies of Ronald Reagan, who, four years earlier, was seen as a "right-wing" ideologue, sadly out of step with the central direction of our society. But in November of that year this ex–movie actor, espousing ultra-conservative policies, swamped Carter.

The "New Economy" Paradigm

When Ronald Reagan took his position as head of state in January of 1981 he set in motion new policies and a style of governing that was to shake the foundations of the existing order. It was to be another bloodless mini-revolution, which would continue to alter the landscape of the country until a fresh political paradigm was firmly in place.

Reagan's revolution was based on a new way of perceiving risk. Depression and full-scale war were far removed from the experience of the Yuppies and generation X'ers who came of age during the late 1970s, 1980s, and 1990s. Their world appeared a lot less risky than that of the men and women who reached maturity around mid-century. Under Reagan's guidance this new perception of risk bred a fresh appreciation for the workings of the marketplace and undermined the devotion a former generation held for big and intrusive government. The Reagan political model is based on a different mindset from the one in the prior model and to make sense of it *think*: FREE MARKETS, INDIVIDUAL RESPONSIBILITY, and RISK TAKING. (See table 1.)

According to Reagan, the government was taking away too much decision-making power from its citizens. The Reaganites deliberately set out to give people more control over and responsibility for their own lives and initiated policies to remove the constraining forces of market regulation and unleash the power of competition so as to lift the nation's economy out of its stagflation rut of the 1970s.

And it worked!

A sleeping economy was awakened and ignited the greatest business boom in American history, which, with but one tiny bump in 1990, continued on till century's end and reestablished the nation as the world's preeminent economic power. And better yet, inflation receded. The way people looked at government programs changed; instead of viewing Social Security as protecting people, many men and women now see it as interfering with their ability to build a bigger nest egg for retirement. Instead of regulations being seen as a necessary adjunct to a modern economy, people now view them as binding the economy in a straitjacket. The phones? Deregulate and let the people choose their own

TABLE I

Two Types of Paradigms

Some Event Sets Off Underlying Mass Perception

A. Event Creates Unanticipated Pleasure People See Very Little Risk	B. Event Creates Unanticipated Pain People See a Great Deal of Risk
Behavior	
risk taking	risk avoidance
pursuing pleasure / taking chances	avoiding pain / cautious
seeking adventure	seeking security and safety
opportunistic	rule-abiding
having fun / tending toward hedonism	serious / leaning toward Puritanism
materialistic	purposeful social action or spiritual
Cultural Type	
entrepreneurial	devotion to the public good
money culture	social betterment culture
economic future appears glowing	economic future looks bleak
intensely competitive / focus on winning	cooperative / weekly "paycheck" mentality
individual freedom	community spirit
people want more	people satisfied with less
individuals know what's best	individuals can't be trusted
Attitudes	
outrageous maverick "standout" behavior applauded	modesty / a "melt in with the crowd" conventional behavior appreciated
"flamboyant," colorful dress	appropriate but drab "uniform" dress
Government Role	
leaves people alone to make own decisions	in control / protects people
reduces business regulations	increases business regulations
creates more opportunity	fosters stability
Status (Based on)	
individual success	service to causes or to others
bigger homes and grander cars	higher intellectual and cultural achievements, philanthropy
The emphasis on these traits shifts—they are not necessarily all or nothing.	

desired combination of services. A problem with the airlines? Open them up to competition.

America became a land of entrepreneurs. Anyone with an idea and the willingness to put in long hours had a chance for the brass ring. The prestige of business reached heights never seen in the past century, not even during the 1920s. The stock market replaced baseball as our national pastime. It was OK—no, make that "glamorous"—to be a businessman. Public servants fled government jobs in droves to seek their fortune in the new economy. Chance-taking businesspeople became society's new celebrities, while the high-status public service people of the former paradigm were now seen as a bunch of wimpy, misguided do-gooders. Those professions had lost their cachet and were on the decline income- and status-wise. "The Donald" (Trump) replaced Mother Teresa as society's top role model.

Attitudes about wealth clearly changed as people either experienced more of it or hoped to do so in the future. Americans had a sense that income and wealth distribution was fairer than it had been, even though in actuality the gap between rich and poor was becoming wider than it had been in decades. According to New York University economist Edward Wolff, the wealthiest 1 percent of American families held 21.8 percent of the nation's net worth in 1976. But 22 years later that same category had amassed 38.1 percent of the nation's wealth. Yet, according to the University of Chicago's National Opinion Research Center, fewer people in 1998 thought "the government should try to reduce income differences between rich and poor" than thought so in 1978.

When the Democrat Clinton became president, he did not challenge the primacy of the marketplace in American life. Instead he satisfied his constituency by making spending cuts a bit more humane. His lone effort to establish an old style "big government" policy, a national health program, smacked of another government scheme to remove control and responsibility from people's lives. Within this political model built around risk acceptance this program was predictably unable to attract public support. In fact, it provoked a big public backlash. In the following mid-term elections the Democrats lost both houses of Congress for the first time in 40 years.

During this paradigm the word "liberal" has become a nasty label. Contemporary Americans are more conservative; the young—especially the young—are a lot more conservative politically. In the Era of Reagan the Berlin Wall came down, the incidence of crime fell, and even the Chinese Communist Party came to put its trust in the market place, rather than Chairman Mao. In the words of the late Chinese Communist leader Deng Xiaoping, "To get rich is glorious." Naturally, Reagan was not responsible for all of those vast changes. Many shifts were already afoot before he set foot in the White House. However, as other pattern-setting presidents had before him, he set a tone that validated those already emerging and that led to still others. In so doing, he set a direction for our nation that would long outlive his time in office.

Shifts in the American landscape of this magnitude come about at intervals ranging from 12 to 48 years. Each has its own central political and cultural theme, which is quite different from the one that preceded it.

How Do We Recognize a New Paradigm?

Who were the important paradigm-setting presidents? Most historians and political pundits have a ready list of presidents whom they deem important or great. Yet those lists are usually quite subjective, reflecting the political bias of the observer. Instead, why not pay attention to the people who lived during the time? Remember, one of the principal assumptions of a democracy is that the people as a whole, the body politic, are wiser than any individual, no matter the education, intellectual credentials, or social position.

To begin with, it is necessary to recognize that American elections are mainly a referendum on what has gone on during an administration's prior four years. If the voters are pleased with the "state of the Union," they will return the leader or a stand-in from the same party to office. Of course, this does not mean that all voters take that approach. Obviously some are issue-oriented and look at the contenders' views on matters they deem important. However, there are issue people on both the left and the right and to a large extent they cancel each other out, so there is only a small difference between those who view one of the candidates as the best choice and those who favor the other.

A much larger group is the "go with what is working" crowd, and because their voting is usually more uniform they overwhelm the issue people. When the country appears to be in good shape and peace and prosperity reign, current policies seem to be working and this group will not see a need for change. On the other hand, should things go wrong, large numbers of this group will be unhappy with the direction in which the country is traveling and willing to bet on a new set of policies.

When a new president arrives on the scene and puts forward a bold and far-reaching program that challenges the prevailing political orthodoxy it may be the beginning of a new mini-revolution. The test of whether this president will become a pattern-setter is his ability to attract followers on the new path he has charted. Can he lead his party into becoming the majority party, attracting new groups of voters, and changing voting patterns for years to come? Will succeeding presidents remain true to his basic philosophy and political agenda? Fortunately, there is a way to see if this is occurring. There are two requirements and both are measurable.

First, and most important, a paradigm-setting president must easily win reelection, capturing an *absolute majority* (more than 50 percent) of all votes cast. Fifty percent indicates an unarguable general agreement among the nation's citizens. Their preference is clear. Before popular voting began in 1824, a majority of the Electoral College sufficed. A majority endorsement, after a new set of policies has been put in place, is the preliminary sign that the mini-revolution is well on its way to becoming a new paradigm. Example: Ronald Reagan took office in 1981 and immediately changed the direction of government. In 1984 he went before the voters as a sitting president, to ask approval for this new course he set. Over 58 percent endorsed it, suggesting a new paradigm had begun. Usually this is all the evidence required.

Since the beginning of the republic 28 sitting presidents have gone before the voters seeking ratification of their policies (table 2). FDR, who broke tradition and ran for two additional terms, is counted only once. In each case the public had a chance to evaluate the president and his policies *after* they had been put into practice. Voters knew what they were getting before they marched off to the polls to affirm or reject. Fifteen sitting presidents were reelected with a majority of all votes cast.

However, only eight had stirred up a mini–political revolution before seeking a second term. George Washington, Thomas Jefferson, Andrew Jackson, Abraham Lincoln, Teddy Roosevelt, Calvin Coolidge, Franklin Delano Roosevelt, and Ronald Reagan each initiated a bold new program that was to change the face of American political life. They were pattern-setters. (See table 3.)

Yet sometimes a president dies in office or begins a mini-revolution late in his reign, and that complicates matters, but just a bit. Warren Harding took the helm of government in 1921 and immediately began to change the political landscape but died in 1923, before receiving voter approval for his new agenda. Not to worry, Vice-president Calvin Coolidge stepped into Harding's shoes, adopted his program, making it his own, and took it before the voters. Coolidge gets the nod as pattern-setter because he, not Harding, owned the program at the time the voters first gave endorsement.

TABLE 2

Election Results: 1788–2000

Election of	Winner	Party	% of electoral votes	Loser	Party	% of electoral votes	Difference
1788	G. Washington	Federalist	85.2	unopposed		0	85.2
1792	**G. Washington**	**Federalist**	**97.8**	unopposed		0	97.8
1796	J. Adams	Federalist	51.4	T. Jefferson	Republican	49.3	2.1
1800	T. Jefferson	Republican	52.9	**J. Adams**	**Federalist**	**47.1**	5.8
1804	**T. Jefferson**	**Republican**	**92.0**	C. Pinckney	Federalist	8.0	84.8
1808	J. Madison	Republican	69.3	C. Pinckney	Federalist	26.7	42.6
1812	**J. Madison**	**Republican**	**58.7**	D. Clinton	Federalist	40.8	17.9
1816	J. Monroe	Republican	82.8	R. King	Federalist	15.4	67.4
1820	**J. Monroe**	**Republican**	**98.3**	unopposed		0.4	97.9

Election of	Winner	Party	% of Popular Vote	Loser	Party	% of Popular Vote	Difference
1824	J. Q. Adams	National Republicans	30.9	A. Jackson	Republican	41.3	10.4
1828	A. Jackson	Democrat	56.0	**J. Q. Adams**	**National Republicans**	**43.6**	12.4
1832	**A. Jackson**	**Democrat**	**54.2**	H. Clay	National Republicans	37.4	16.8
1836	M. Van Buren	Democrat	50.8	W. Harrison	Whig	36.6	14.2
1840	W. Harrison	Whig	52.9	**M. Van Buren**	**Democrat**	**46.8**	6.1
1841	J. Tyler fills in for W. Harrison						
1844	J. Polk	Democrat	49.5	H. Clay	Whig	48.1	1.4
1848	Z. Taylor	Whig	47.3	L. Cass	Democrat	42.5	4.8
1850	M. Fillmore fills in for Z. Taylor						
1852	F. Pierce	Democrat	50.8	W. Scott	Whig	43.9	6.9
1856	J. Buchanan	Democrat	45.3	J. Frémont	Republican	33.1	12.2
1860	A. Lincoln	Republican	39.8	S. Douglas	Democrat	29.5	10.4
1864	**A. Lincoln**	**Republican**	**55.0**	G. McClellan	Democrat	45.0	10.0
1865	A. Johnson fills in for A. Lincoln						
1868	U. Grant	Republican	52.7	H. Seymour	Democrat	47.3	5.4
1872	**U. Grant**	**Republican**	**55.6**	H. Greeley	Democrat	43.8	11.8
1876	R. Hayes	Republican	48.0	S. Tilden	Democrat	51.0	(3.0)
1880	J. Garfield	Republican	48.3	W. Hancock	Democrat	48.2	0.1
1881	C. Arthur fills in for J. Garfield						
1884	G. Cleveland	Democrat	48.5	J. Blaine	Republican	48.2	0.3
1888	B. Harrison	Republican	47.8	**G. Cleveland**	**Democrat**	**48.6**	(0.8)
1892	G. Clevelnd	Democrat	46.1	**B. Harrison**	**Republican**	**43.0**	3.1
1896	W. McKinley	Republican	51.0	W. Bryan	Democrat	46.7	4.3
1900	**W. McKinley**	**Republican**	**51.7**	W. Bryan	Democrat	45.5	6.2

*Bold = sitting presidents

*T. Roosevelt running as a progressive actually came in second with 27.4 percent of the vote, 14.4 percent less than Wilson.

Election of	Winner	Party	% of Popular Vote	Loser	Party	% of Popular Vote	Difference
1901	T. Roosevelt fills in for W. McKinley						
1904	**T. Roosevelt**	**Republican**	**56.4**	A. Parker	Democrat	37.6	18.8
1908	W. Taft	Republican	51.6	W. Bryan	Democrat	43.0	8.6
1912	W. Wilson	Democrat	41.8	**W. Taft**	**Republican***	**23.2**	18.6
1916	**W. Wilson**	**Democrat**	**49.2**	C. Hughes	Republican	46.1	3.1
1920	W. Harding	Republican	60.3	J. Cox	Democrat	34.1	26.2
1923	C. Coolidge fills in for W. Harding						
1924	**C. Coolidge**	**Republican**	**54.0**	J. Davis	Democrat	28.8	25.2
1928	H. Hoover	Republican	58.2	A. Smith	Democrat	40.8	17.4
1932	F. Roosevelt	**Democrat**	**57.4**	**H. Hoover**	**Republican**	**39.6**	17.8
1936	**F. Roosevelt**	**Democrat**	**60.8**	A. Landon	Republican	36.5	24.3
1940	**F. Roosevelt**	**Democrat**	**54.7**	W. Willkie	Republican	44.8	9.9
1944	**F. Roosevelt**	**Democrat**	**53.4**	T. Dewey	Republican	45.9	7.5
1945	H. Truman fills in for F. Roosevelt						
1948	**H. Truman**	**Democrat**	**49.5**	T. Dewey	Republican	45.1	4.4
1952	D. Eisenhower	Republican	55.1	A. Stevenson	Democrat	44.4	10.7
1956	**D. Eisenhower**	**Republican**	**57.4**	A. Stevenson	Democrat	41.9	15.5
1960	J. Kennedy	Democrat	49.7	R. Nixon	Republican	49.5	0.2
1963	L. Johnson fills in for J. Kennedy						
1964	**L. Johnson**	**Democrat**	**61.0**	B. Goldwater	Republican	38.5	22.5
1968	R. Nixon	Republican	43.4	H. Humphrey	Democrat	42.7	0.7
1972	**R. Nixon**	**Republican**	**60.7**	G. McGovern	Democrat	37.5	23.2
1974	G. Ford fills in for R. Nixon						
1976	J. Carter	Democrat	50.1	**G. Ford**	**Republican**	**48.0**	2.1
1980	R. Reagan	Republican	50.7	**J. Carter**	**Democrat**	**41.0**	9.7
1984	**R. Reagan**	**Republican**	**58.8**	W. Mondale	Democrat	41.0	17.8
1988	G. H. Bush	Republican	53.4	M. Dukakis	Democrat	45.6	7.8
1992	W. Clinton	Democrat	43.0	**G. H. Bush**	**Republican**	**37.4**	5.6
1996	**W. Clinton**	**Democrat**	**49.2**	R. Dole	Republican	40.7	8.5
2000	G. W. Bush	Republican	47.9	A. Gore	Democrat	48.4	(0.5)

First nine elections were before there was a popular vote; the figure is the percentage of the vote in the Electoral College. Does not necessarily equal 100 percent as some electors didn't cast their vote.

The 1796 election totals more than 100 percent because a vice-presidential vote was counted for president.

Source: www.uselectionatlas.org

TABLE 3

The Nine Paradigm-Setting Presidents

Paradigm-setter	Begin Presidency	1st Reelection	% of Votes	Successor	2d Reelection	% of Votes
1. George Washington	1789	1792	97.8	John Adams	1796	51.4
2. Thomas Jefferson	1801	1804	92.0	James Madison	1808	69.3
3. James Madison*	1809	1816	82.8	James Monroe	1820	98.3
4. Andrew Jackson	1829	1832	54.2	Martin Van Buren	1836	50.8
5. Abraham Lincoln†	1861	1864	55.0	Ulysses Grant	1868/1872?	52.7/55.6
6. Teddy Roosevelt	1901	1904	56.4	William Taft	1908	51.6
7. Calvin Coolidge**	1923	1924	54.0	Herbert Hoover	1928	58.2
8. Franklin Roosevelt	1933	1936	60.8	Franklin Roosevelt	1940	54.7
9. Ronald Reagan	1981	1984	58.8	George H. Bush	1988	53.4

The Six Contenders/Failed Legacy

Paradigm-setter	Begin Presidency	1st Reelection	% of Votes	Successor	2d Reelection	% of Votes
1. James Monroe	1817	1820	98.3	J. Q. Adams	1824	30.9
2. Ulysses Grant	1869	1872	55.6	Rutherford Hayes	1876	48.0
3. William McKinley	1897	1901	51.7	Teddy Roosevelt‡		
4. Dwight Eisenhower	1953	1956	57.4	Richard Nixon	1960	49.5
5. Lyndon Johnson	1963	1964	61.0	Hubert Humphrey	1968	42.7
6. Richard Nixon	1969	1972	60.7	Gerald Ford	1976	48.0

*Madison was both a successor to Jefferson and a paradigm-setting president. Launched a mini-revolution in late 1815. Therefore 1st voter endorsement is in 1816.

†Interrupted 1865–1869 by Andrew Johnson, an accidental president.

‡Teddy Roosevelt took over from McKinley but did not follow his agenda/began his own mini-revolution.

**Calvin Coolidge inherited Harding's policies and made them his own.

All eight presidents set government on a new course shortly after taking office and in the following election received voter permission to keep proceeding in that direction. This procedure was reversed just once. James Madison won reelection as a sitting president in 1812 before initiating a major change in the direction of government. But then during his second term he challenged the political creed of his day and launched a new mini-revolution. However, Madison, like most presidents, adhered to a two-term limit and was unable to get the electorate's green light for his new agenda. In this case, James Monroe, Madison's political ally, picked up his predecessor's baton and espousing his policies ran as his heir. Monroe's landslide victory indicated preliminary approval for the new set of policies. So who gets the nod as paradigm-setter: Madison or Monroe?

Monroe, unlike Coolidge, was *not* a sitting president and therefore did not own the record when he asked for voter approval. Madison's responsibility for the new policies was much clearer to the electorate in 1816 than Harding's role in agenda setting was to those who went to the polls in 1924. Ownership is important. Also, Madison had already been reelected as a sitting president. Although voters had not been aware of the fact that he would adopt a new program, the win did give him a certain legitimacy to put forward a new agenda. Add Madison to the eight previous pattern-setters and we end up with nine.

The second requirement is repeating the majority win four years later. If there is any doubt about whether a paradigm has begun, this second back-to-back majority win should settle the matter. It means that after having witnessed a president and his new policies—appraising how well they have worked—through two presidential terms, American voters have given another thumbs-up, confirming the mini-revolution has become a new political model. Furthermore, by that time the president's party will have become firmly entrenched as the new majority party. Usually a political legacy is also created at the same time the second requirement is fulfilled. That is, someone from the model builder's own party, a successor, embraces his agenda and wins the paradigm endorsement with a majority of the votes cast. Example: After two Reagan terms George H. Bush took the paradigm mantle and went before the voters for their blessing. Over 53 percent gave it, indicating their belief that the course Reagan had set was the true and correct direction of government. On the other hand, FDR, while still occupying the White House, went before the electorate three times, achieving majority wins each time. This second requirement was met, and then some, before an heir was anointed.

All nine pattern-setting presidents met the second requirement also; a successor (or FDR himself) ran on the pattern-setter's program four years after preliminary approval and won another election with a majority of all votes cast. Monroe's second win fulfilled the back-to-back electoral victory requirement for the Madison paradigm. Also, even FDR finally got his heir, albeit when the paradigm was growing weary. Harry Truman was elected in 1948, though without a majority of all ballots cast.

Lincoln's assassination shortly after he was reelected also muddies the waters, but not much. This was because Vice-president Andrew Johnson did not follow the Lincoln agenda. Johnson had been a Democrat when chosen for the second spot and tilted back in that direction after attaining high office. A Republican Congress blocked him and ultimately impeached him, failing to convict by one vote but making sure he could not claim Lincoln's mantle. In the following election the Republicans nominated Ulysses S. Grant, Lincoln's favorite Civil War general, who returned the nation to Lincoln's model-building policies. Grant became "Honest Abe's" true heir, and his big 1868 win for the Republicans can be considered the second back-to-back victory, erasing any doubt about Lincoln being a pattern-setting president. Or, if one prefers to make allowance for the Johnson interruption, Grant's huge 1872 win may be regarded as fulfillment of the second requirement (two terms of mini-revolution, interrupted by one Johnson term). Either way, Lincoln gets a paradigm-setting role.

Those nine were America's important paradigm-setting presidents. All stirred up a mini-revolution, which was followed by back-to-back majority wins. All left a political legacy. The great English playwright William Shakespeare said, "All the world is a stage, and we are the actors." If that be so, it has been these model-building presidents who wrote the scripts.

The remaining six reelected sitting presidents—Monroe, Grant, McKinley, Eisenhower, L. Johnson, and Nixon—did not attempt to take the nation down a new path either before or after reelection. Nor were they able to create a legacy. After two terms of living with those presidents, there was insufficient voter enthusiasm to elect a successor with more than half of all votes cast. All failed the second test. (By the way, so too did the three sitting presidents who were reelected *without* a majority of all votes cast).

However, Hayes, who might have been a Grant successor, did make it to the White House, but he collected fewer votes than his opponent. Teddy Roosevelt could not be considered McKinley's heir, as he scuttled his predecessor's program and began his own model-busting mini-revolution. When the public went to the polls in 1904 they were rendering judgment on Roosevelt's agenda; McKinley's had long been left in the dust.

Dwight Eisenhower came closest to meeting this second test. He won reelection with a landslide 57.4 percent of the popular vote. But in 1960 Richard Nixon, Eisenhower's heir apparent, received only 49.5 percent of the popular vote, losing the election by a measly 120,000 votes amidst claims of widespread voter fraud. Interestingly, this is another example of how a paradigm builds in its own immunity system, which helps protect it and perpetuate its longevity. Normally, the majority paradigm party is able to get hold of the election machinery, the boards and commissions, in a majority of the states, and as a result fraud usually favors the majority party. In 1960 the Democrats and John Kennedy benefited; in 1876 the Republicans with Rutherford Hayes were able to overrule the will of the majority. A candidate of the minority party oftentimes has to overcome voter fraud, and this provides a further hurdle against change that is built into the system.

After a pattern-setting president's program is endorsed by the electorate, his policies become the political *glue* that will perpetuate the political model. Think "tax and spend" and government reform during the FDR paradigm. Focus on "tax cuts" and deregulation during the Regan era. The initial success of the pattern-setter in solving the nation's main problems leads others to adopt his approach. It becomes the model of how to face up to new problems. A set of chief executives steeped in mainstream paradigm thinking follow and practice common policies until a fresh political mini-revolution begins.

The followers are tweakers, who reinforce and refresh the essential agenda or try to manage it better, but essentially they stay within the limits of the political model. They will not try to, nor are they likely to be able to, change the existing paradigm. Even presidents from the opposing party fall into line. They are not able to set bold new courses of action. Eisenhower and Nixon, Republicans during the FDR political culture, accepted the welfare state, trying to make it a bit more responsive to market signals, and sought to differentiate themselves mostly on foreign policy. And the Democrat Bill Clinton, operating within the "New Economy" paradigm, moved toward the center and adopted important parts of Reagan's program.

A paradigm, once set in motion, tends to persist. Consensus is reached that these policies and ways of thinking are the orthodox way to deal with the world; they become the political creed of that era. The party of the model-building president dares not challenge those beliefs. They become embedded as institutions in society. After a while, even the press, or much of it, comes under the spell of the new outlook. They view the political landscape through the same lens as the rest of the people do and adopt the paradigm mindset. If they don't, they are likely to lose their following and be replaced or supplemented by others more in tune with mainstream model thinking (e.g., Rush Limbaugh and other commentators with a rightest slant gained larger and larger audiences during the conservative 1980s). Either way, the media's coverage unintentionally slants to favor those more in tune with the paradigm, and the stars of TV, radio, and the press act as attack dogs against those who stray too far out of the mainstream. This, of course, further constrains politicians who follow on the heels of the legendary leader from wandering off course.

If we examine this nation's past through the prism of its nine mini-revolutions, rather than by scrutinizing each and every little four-year piece, we get an entirely different picture of our country's political culture. Let us return to 1789, when the nation's first president was inaugurated, and uncover the grand pattern in the American story.

—∞∞∞—

II

The Federalists

Near the end of the 1700s a struggling group of colonies on the North American continent broke a five-thousand-year mold of civilization and began a unique experiment in self-government. Up until that time, the overwhelming majority of mankind had been governed by rulers, kings and emperors, determined by heredity or selected by a powerful aristocracy. Let us go back to the beginning of civilization and briefly summarize how we got from there to here, the beginning of the American Republic.

Backgound

About ten thousand years ago, some men and women began to exchange a nomadic existence based upon hunting and gathering for a life built around the growing of crops and the domestication of animals. Historians call this great transformation the "Agricultural Revolution." During that time people gained mastery in cultivating crops and domesticating animals. But it was not only a revolution in agriculture; it was a dual revolution. The other half was a revolutionary change in social organization, which also was to alter the character of human lives and the history of the human species as a whole.

Archeologists tell us men and women in hunting and gathering societies lived at a basic subsistence level. The efforts of all members went into acquiring enough food to sustain the group. There was a leader, but his (it was a he) privileges or perks were rather modest. There seems to have been very little social differentiation; people shared more or less equally. But once our ancestors settled down to raise crops, that all changed profoundly.

An agricultural people, unlike hunters and gathers, were able to accumulate a surplus. Groups of people were able to grow more food than needed for subsistence. This surplus became the key to the great social transition. The important, though probably unarticulated, question of that time was (and, for that matter, still is) **who got the surplus?** Naturally it went to those people who had the skills, or whose fathers or grandfathers had the skills, that the group deemed important to guide and protect the members. These people got the wealth and power, set the tone and direction of society, and provided the authority necessary to maintain social order.

They became the top layer in the societies that were forming and set up an "aristocracy." Beneath them was a small middle class, usually merchants and artisans, who played a lesser role. Still further down the totem pole was an enormous lower stratum, who did the menial work and in return were rewarded with the crumbs. And usually at the very bottom were the slaves, who handled the degrading work. These societies were highly stratified, with great distinctions between the rulers and the ruled. Families also took on a hierarchal order. Men became the undisputed heads of households and wives and children were treated as their property, obeying their every command.

People of that time were bound together in a set of immutable relationships: a father to family, master to servant. Those relationships were based upon a set of informal and unarticulated mutual obligations that one could not easily walk away from. The end result was a fixed social system wherein individual yearnings and talents were subordinated to the needs of one's social superiors.

According to historians, it took about five thousand years of wrenching change before the agricultural societies acquired their essential shape. And during the whole of that transformation it is highly unlikely contemporaries could recognize the revolutionary nature of what they were going through or foretell where society was ultimately headed.

Four major civilizations emerged: Western, Chinese, Indic, and Near Eastern (to become Islamic). Other civilizations followed, such as the Japanese and Byzantine, but they were satellites, or offshoots, of one of the big four. All the major civilizations were of the same general mold. All were based on agriculture; all had quite similar social structures wherein people's lot in life depended upon the social strata of the family they were born into. To be sure, there were exceptions, such as the Greeks or early Romans, but they did not endure. After a historically brief period of time society reverted back to its fundamental mold. During the approximately five thousand years from the dawn of civilization until the beginning of the eighteenth century nothing much changed.

But somewhere around the 1680s it did. Sir Isaac Newton, capitalizing on a long line of growing scientific findings, formulated laws of the universe, with the law of gravity sitting at the apex. It was a great step forward for mankind, as it implied that man could master his universe. The enthusiasm that followed set in motion a beehive of activity in Western society that, by the early 1700s, was especially ferocious in both Great Britain and France.

Britain became one great workshop as men throughout the nation began to tinker in their sheds. By the middle of the eighteenth century some had come up with a way to harness steam power and were using it to substitute machine for human labor. At the center of this mighty revolution was cotton. As colorful cotton garments became cheaper they replaced drab, scratchy, and difficult to wash woolen clothes. Cheap, mass-produced cotton products enabled the masses to imitate the upper classes and brighten their spirits by brightening their dress. The new entrepreneurs who fashioned this Industrial Revolution, those who made the machines and built the factories to produce cotton fabrics, became fabulously wealthy, muscled their way to the top of the social heap, and attained status. Although this revolution in industry had begun and was taking place mostly in England, across the Atlantic, in parts of New England, some businesspeople soon began emulating them.

Meanwhile, something quite different was going on in France. There the ferment following the great scientific discoveries was taking place in the salons of the larger cities. Men were questioning the legitimacy of their political and social organization. Many of those thinkers felt that the scientific discoveries had shown that progress was inevitable, **that all problems could be solved by reason,** and that mankind would forever be chipping away at new frontiers. The more optimistic of these French rationalists thought human nature perfectible and hence a utopia here on earth attainable, or, at the very least, that human life was capable of great improvement. These were new and quite different assumptions from those mankind had previously been operating under, and would bring into question the power of the few over the many, the implicit social contract between ruler and ruled. Why must men and women, who have the natural capacity to take care of themselves, have to submit to a ruling class?

This French version of the Enlightenment articulated a fresh set of principles about people's rights and liberties, which set in motion a profound change in the way Western societies organized themselves. It provided the intellectual underpinnings to the American Revolution of 1776. Then, in the summer of 1789, Frenchmen, following America's example in self-government, overthrew their rulers. The French, in entrusting political control to the masses, were to push much further than the American colonists dared go.

This great upheaval in social organization, while less recognized than the industrial transformation, has been, perhaps, even more far-reaching. Building on the ideas of the French rationalists, Americans have created a society unlike any that existed before. In Western societies today, individuals are no longer doomed to be what their fathers or mothers were. Their place depends more on merit, talent, and "hard work" than upon the social strata they were born into. Yes, distinctions and inequities based on class have not totally disappeared; there is a still an upper crust. But those on the top layer are no longer able to lord it over the lower orders as they once did. The privileges of the few are well on the way to becoming the rights of the many. The middle class is huge, growing in economic and political clout, and has the freedom to challenge the actions of the socially powerful. And the bottom layer no longer functions merely to serve the upper stratum. The have-nots have graduated into a have-less crowd and have a multitude of options to choose from. This class, in fact, sets many of our social codes and standards of everyday conduct. And lowbrow culture dominates much of our TV programming and music.

We are in the midst of reordering the social relationships of society. Traditional rules no longer constrain the choices of women, blacks, gays, and other groups who had been marginalized in the past. Institutions are no longer authoritative and set in concrete. Today members of the clergy confess doubts about the existence of God. Generals put their troops through sensitivity training. Relationships are no longer thought of as immutable. If they are no longer fulfilling, one may walk away. Women are no longer expected to get fulfillment chiefly in marriage and the family. Families are child-centered, wherein the young are not so obedient and from teenagedom on deference often runs from parents to child.

Yet Americans are scarcely aware of the revolutionary nature of the social changes they have been experiencing. Each change of the past two hundred years was viewed by the generation going through it as the end product of a one time change, while, in fact, these changes were but way stations to further change. Each new crop of young adults makes its own demands, pushing the social transformation a step further. Yet no sooner do they settle in thinking their world has finally achieved social harmony when, lo and behold, their children rise up and rebel, taking this revolution to yet another level. This is, of course, unsettling to many in the older generation, who at one time thought themselves the new "modernists." Where it will end, when, and whether or not our children's children will be comfortable with the outcome, no one knows. But this we know: Humans are still in the process of rewriting the rules of social structure so as to accommodate the maximum amount of "individual freedom." This revolutionary transformation in the way society organizes itself, set in motion by the political changes occurring in France and America at the end of the eighteenth century, has taken on a life of its own. Mankind, once more, is in the midst of a dual revolution, as the Industrial Revolution, like the Agricultural Revolution before it, is being accompanied by a great social transformation.

During the eighteenth century mercantilism was the prevalent economic dogma in the Western world. Governments of mercantilist countries were heavily involved in the commerce of the nation. They sought to direct the development of commerce through subsidization of industry and infrastructure. Usually at the top of the list was a high tariff designed to protect domestic industries from cheap foreign imports.

And then there was that matter of money. You needed it to conduct business and to store wealth. Earlier mercantilist nations had viewed money simply as gold and silver, and the more you could accumulate the better. As time went on they learned that banks could create money by issuing notes that they promised to redeem for the gold or silver in their vaults. However, at times they would issue notes way beyond the hard money stored in their basements. Once holders of the currency got wind of it, they would rush to redeem these notes and their value would fall. The likely outcome was the bank going bust and the notes becoming worthless. How to deal with this? Well, England had come up with a way a hundred years earlier.

She created a national bank, which was responsible for keeping the flow of money circulating in the economy—neither too little nor too much. By letting a national bank, acting as an agency of the government, control the amount of money and credit in the nation, chances for a sound currency improve. First, political leaders become responsible for selecting responsible men or women to act in a responsible manner. Yet this too can go awry, because responsible people, as the world has seen, can err—or act in a nonresponsible manner. Fortunately, there was a second line of defense. Because governments could stand behind their notes by relying on their power to tax their citizens, if need be, the likelihood of bankruptcy became minimal.

This issue of money and how much of it a nation should have is very, very important, and especially so for a commercial nation. If you don't have enough money, it becomes difficult to grow your economy. Prices fall and people become disinclined to hang on to goods they do not need for immediate consumption. Without the confidence to hold capital goods, such as factories and machines, the supply of manufactured goods is likely to fall. In fact, without enough money it is difficult to keep your economy from contracting. On the other hand, increase the supply of it too much (easy money)—that is, beyond the ability of producers to increase the supply of goods so as to keep pace—and prices will rise. This is inflation and has untoward implications. In an inflationary economy prices are rising rapidly on most all fronts, although, and keep this in mind, the various price rises are not likely to be equal. For instance, wages might very well be escalating at levels way beyond the prices manufacturers can get for their goods and profits plummet, creating a disagreeable situation for businesspeople and investors.

When prices are soaring, paper money has an uncertain future value. People will choose hard assets, such as gold and silver, which appear to be sensitive to inflation, as a store for their wealth. But unfortunately, those items don't produce further wealth. So once again people become discouraged from holding capital goods; only this time the reason is because there are much better alternatives available.

This issue of a national bank and what constitutes the nation's currency became an important political issue in the nineteenth century. As we shall see, some people—the creditor class and merchants, for instance—prefer a sound money policy, while others, debtors and farmers, see an easy money policy as being in their best interests.

The American Republic

After the Revolutionary War, the United States was less than a third its present size. (See page 9.) The original thirteen colonies were situated east of the Appalachian Mountains, extending from Maine (which was then part of Massachusetts) down to the southern edge of Georgia. Florida belonged to Spain, and western Florida stretched all the way to the Mississippi River, blocking access to the Gulf of Mexico. The areas just west of the Appalachians, up to the Mississippi River, were territories of the United States, just opening up to settlement. However, that land was still heavily populated by Indians, who at times could be quite unfriendly. There were still lingering memories of 1763, when Pontiac, chief of the Ottawa, and his warriors went on a rampage, from Niagara to Virginia, wiping out hundreds of pioneer families.

Already there were three distinct regions of the country, each with its own economy and culture. The New England area around

Boston was highly commercial and, to a large extent, modeled on England. The Northern "Yankees" got their living mainly from shipping, fishing, and whaling. Much like their Puritan forefathers, they were morally righteous, earnest, and hardworking. They were also quite democratic, both socially and politically.

The people of the South—Virginia, North Carolina, and the area around Charleston—were less religious, more fun-loving, and wealthier. The Southerners were devoted to their land, which was both a source of security and a means to independence. Large plantation owners dominated this section, and of particular significance was their peculiar institution of slavery, which New Englanders frowned upon. These sectional differences would make it difficult to find a common purpose around which to build the Union.

Luckily, there was a third area. The middle states of New York and Pennsylvania were dominated by the rapidly growing urban trading centers of Philadelphia and New York City, which were already more worldly and cynical than the towns in the other sections. This middle area, which was more flexible politically and socially, held the balance of political power.

When the colonists met in the mid-1770s to draft the Articles of Confederation, there was a deep hatred of crown authority. The delegates aimed to destroy government's overreaching power and lead the world in rooting out tyranny once and for all. They were determined to end government's authority to squeeze money from people, shore up religious establishments, and, above all, grant offices, honors, and favors. The delegates thought the best way to prevent excessive government power and preserve their liberty was to place as many constraints as possible on federal authority.

Inspired by the idealism emanating from the French Enlightenment, they created a Confederation with a weak central government, one that did not have the power to maintain its territorial integrity, to conduct war, to regulate trade, or even to fund its own expenditures. Naturally, a host of problems arose. Without adequate taxing power, the government was starved for revenues and on the brink of defaulting on its financial obligations. When the British ignored its treaty obligations to evacuate their posts in the Northwest Territory, the government was unable to respond. But most prominent was an uprising known as Shays's Rebellion, which symbolized the Confederation's inability to maintain civil order. In 1786 Daniel Shays and a group of impoverished farmers in western Massachusetts sought to protect their farms from mortgage holders who were suing to foreclose. The farmers closed a county courthouse and at one point threatened to seize a federal arsenal. Massachusetts appealed to the Confederation for help. But Congress, lacking sufficient funds to support an army, was unable to do anything. Luckily, a group of wealthy Bostonians raised an army of four thousand troops to put down the insurrection, or the arsenal might have fallen.

Fear of incipient anarchy, along with the impotence of the Confederation, swayed the colonists into a 180-degree turn in support of a strong federal government. A new constitutional convention was called and this time the Federalists, a group of people who thought a more robust national government would save the revolution from its excesses, prevailed. A Constitution was ratified and the first election was held in late 1788. George Washington, the hero of the Revolutionary War, received the unanimous support of the Electoral College.

When Washington arrived in New York City in April of 1789 to become the nation's first president, he bore a great responsibility. The political stability of the new republic depended on how he would define and invent his role of chief executive. Fortunately, he had the dignity, patience, and restraint that the potentially powerful office needed. Washington, whose strengths resided in character and judgment, rather than intellectual brilliance, set a standard: that the chief executive of a self-governing nation should act with efficiency and honesty. This was in sharp contrast to the corruption in contemporary European governments and in many state governments. Washington left no doubt that he alone made policy but included both Alexander Hamilton and Thomas Jefferson, the chief architects of competing visions of America's mission, in his cabinet.

The Great Debate

Hamilton, the leading Federalist theoretician, thought the national government should be committed to creating an environment conducive to the growth of commerce. The three key ingredients in Hamilton's economic blueprint were: a national bank on the order of the successful bank of England, which would allow the government to pay its debts and prevent currency inflation; a stiff tariff, to protect infant industries; and a strong national government that would provide incentives and bounties to promote the development of manufacturers. This was, in short, standard mercantilist policy of the late eighteenth century. The focus on commerce, he argued, would make the country rich and prosperous, as was already happening in Great Britain. According to Hamilton, the people best suited for leadership roles in this commercial society were the rich, educated, and wellborn. But in time the wealth would trickle down from class to mass and all would benefit.

Alexander Hamilton was skeptical of the popular ideas of the Enlightenment and disgusted by the bloody excesses of the French Revolution, especially its Reign of Terror, in which thousands of aristocrats, priests, and others were guillotined for political offenses. His chief worry was that our "Republican" form of government would degenerate into unchecked rule by the masses, a "mobocracy," which would appropriate the property of the merchant class. "The people," he once said, "are a great beast." It was not surprising that he considered the right to hold and dispose of property to be paramount among our liberties; and in his scheme of things the maintenance of public order was far more important than individual freedom. This vision of encouraging an environment favorable to economic growth is the core belief of today's Republican Party. And if forced to make a choice, conservatives today would choose order over the rights of individuals.

On the other side of the debate was Thomas Jefferson, the chief advocate of a faction that called themselves Democratic-Republicans, or "Republicans" for short. The party of Jefferson has long since transmuted into the Democratic Party and should not be confused with the Republican Party of today. Jefferson believed that society should be reorganized so as to ensure the maximum amount of individual freedom. His enemy was the privileged aristocrat, who because of his wealth and power was able to exploit the masses. According to Jefferson, "the mass of mankind has not been born with saddles on their backs, nor a favored few booted and spurred, ready to ride them." An admirer of the French Revolution ("the French revolution is the most sacred cause that man was ever engaged in"), he believed in the ideas of the Enlightenment, especially in the perfectibility of men and their innate virtue. He thought human nature could be shaped by experience and external circumstances, which a corrupt, rank-conscious Old World society had not permitted. Furthermore, he disdained commerce, because he assumed the merchants and bankers who achieved prominence would set up a monetary aristocracy, which would be every bit as antidemocratic as the blood aristocracies of Europe.

In Jefferson's view, America's strength lay not in its industrial potential but in its agricultural productivity. Creating a nation of farmers, an agrarian society, would be the best way to guarantee the maximum amount of individual freedom. The mass of people tilling the soil would have the opportunity to use their own ingenuity and energy to share in the nation's wealth and thus become self-sufficient, independent, and incorruptible. While this alternative vision of an agrarian society has long since passed from view, Jefferson's dream of individual "freedom" remains as the Democratic Party's chief article of faith, although its boundaries have been extended to include more and more areas, from religion to personal habits, and more and more people, from blacks and women to gays and Native Americans. And for liberals in today's world, the rights of individuals come well before the rights of property, no question about it.

These two clashing world visions have dominated American politics since its beginnings. During most of the ensuing two centuries **one party has stood for economic growth and public order, while the other has emphasized social equality along with individual freedom.**

President Washington attributed the failure of the prior Confederation to a weak executive branch and, favoring the Federalists, sought strong powers for the central government. He adopted Hamilton's extraordinary financial program, tilting the young nation in a commercial direction. To send a signal to European bankers, who controlled much of the available investment capital, that the United States was solvent and a reliable credit risk, the government paid off the Revolutionary War debt at par and set up a national bank, which ingrained fiscal discipline in the nation. In order to raise revenues for the government, Washington's administration imposed a tariff of approximately 5 percent on imports. Because they thought federal law more sympathetic than state laws to commerce and the protection of property rights, the Federalists enacted a judiciary bill, which established an elaborate federal court system, including a Supreme Court. Washington's administration also tackled the issue of a national land policy. They enacted the Land Act of 1796, which stipulated that federal lands in the new territories be sold in bundles of 640 acres but set the prices high enough to discourage western land development.

In 1792 Washington agreed to stand for another term and was unanimously reelected. It was the preliminary indication that a first political paradigm had begun. Soon afterwards the general's attention turned to foreign affairs. In 1793 French armies took to the highways to spread their "war of all peoples against all kings" across Europe. England, who had just awakened to the possibilities of creating an industrial empire, was frightened by those revolutionary ideas and joined hands with a changing coalition of threatened monarchs to stop the French. During much of the next 22 years, until 1815, the French and the English were in a fight for their respective lives. Both would reject America's liberal interpretation of neutral rights on the high seas and render all neutral commerce illegal and liable to seizure. This presented a problem to the new American Republic.

There was no way the people of the 13 colonies, most of whom were descendants of Western Europeans, could ignore what was going on across the ocean. Americans lined up on either side. Those more enamored of the commercial-industrial possibilities the invention of the steam engine promised were usually sympathetic to England and horrified by what was going on in France. They were in the Federalists' camp and looked to Hamilton for leadership. On the other hand, those whose imagination had been fired by the idea of a community of men and women, bound together as equal participants, without a privileged group sitting on the top layer, looked to France as their beacon of light. They were the Republicans, and naturally Jefferson became their leader.

Washington, recognizing the fragile nature of the new nation, proclaimed American neutrality in the struggle between the two European powers. However, Great Britain was treating its former colony with disrespect. The British were seizing American ships on the high seas in total disregard of the United States' liberal interpretation of neutral shipping rights. Furthermore, the British refused to leave their frontier posts in the Northwest Territory and were encouraging local Indians to attack settlers and traders. Washington thought a show of force was necessary to convince Great Britain and the rest of the world that the new American nation was serious about supporting its government and its laws. He reorganized the army into a national military force and sent General Wayne to a smashing victory over the Indians at Fallen Timbers, which helped secure the West for the next decade. At about the same time, Washington raised about fifteen thousand militia to put down a rebellion by a group of western Pennsylvanians in protest of the federal excise tax on whiskey.

This display of colonial power seems to have impressed the British. In 1795 John Jay was able to negotiate a treaty whereby Great Britain agreed to evacuate the Northwest posts and open up part of its empire to American commerce. Although the treaty secured America's territorial integrity, a vocal group of Republicans thought the nation had been shortchanged. They were appalled that Jay had not won British approval of America's conception of neutral rights on the high seas. However, Washington and his advisors realized that, given the disparities of power between the two nations, Jay had gained as much as could be expected. Congress, under Republican prodding, attempted to intervene, demanding Washington show the state papers relating to Jay's mission. The general refused, thereby setting a precedent for executive secrecy in the interest of national security, which most subsequent presidents have upheld. The treaty also provided a model for settling grievances with other nations without resorting to war. Washington, in his famous farewell address to the nation, would also warn Americans to steer clear of permanent foreign entanglements, and this bit of fatherly advice served the country well for many years to come.

When Washington's second term was up in 1796 he chose not to run again, beginning a voluntarily two-term tradition for America's head of state. Washington made it clear that he favored Vice President John Adams, a Federalist, as his successor. Despite an attempt by the French minister to influence the outcome of the election in favor of the Republicans, Adams, who vowed to follow in Washington's big footsteps, won handily. The Washington-

Hamilton mini-revolution had passed its second test, confirming a political paradigm had successfully taken root. Adams retained Washington's cabinet, hewed to the course his predecessor had set, and tried to maintain neutrality in the struggle between Britain and France.

Meanwhile, France had interpreted Jay's treaty as a U.S. tilt toward Great Britain, and relations between France and the United States steadily deteriorated. French privateers began attacking American ships on the high seas, and French provocateurs on American shores plotted mischievous intrigues with the Indians. In hopes of resolving the conflict, Adams sent a three-man negotiating team to Paris. However, the French foreign minister, Talleyrand, shunted them off to his lackeys, who demanded a huge bribe as a precondition to negotiations. The Americans refused to play the game—negotiator Pinckney's response was "no, no, not a sixpence"—and left in a huff. When word of this diplomatic humiliation reached the nation, it set off a domestic political explosion and led to the revocation of the Franco-American peace treaty forged during the American War of Independence. America and France were soon fighting an undeclared "quasi-war" on the high seas.

This created an opportunity for some of the extreme Federalists, led by Hamilton's crowd, to call for a strengthening of the central government. With large segments of the American public egging him on, Adams prepared the nation for war. There was a general rearmament, which included new fighting ships, additional harbor fortifications, and a greatly expanded U.S. Army, along with additional taxes to fund the military buildup. Although Adams had no prior military experience, he began to appear in public in full military dress, including a sword strapped to his side.

Republicans were horrified. They thought the possibility of a land invasion by French forces remote and feared the real reason for the army buildup was to silence them. Moreover, they believed the Federalists, by fostering a privileged and arrogant ruling class, "a new aristocracy," had betrayed the spirit and intent of the original revolution. So they began a full-scale attack on the Federalists carried on through newspapers and pamphlets.

The Federalists, on the other hand, believed the coarse language and slander of those publications were destroying the governing gentry's personal reputation for character and poisoning relations between rulers and ruled, thereby undermining the essential respect necessary for political order. Then they made a fatal mistake by resorting to desperate repressive measures. To stop the flow of Republican literature they enacted the Alien and Sedition Acts, which made criticism of the government a crime punishable by fine or imprisonment. Many well-known Republicans were convicted and conveniently silenced before the next election, nearly all on flimsy charges, some of which were downright feeble or silly.

In the midst of the turmoil, Adams decided to make another stab at peace negotiations. He appointed a new envoy and sent him on a peace mission to France. The French, now under the direction of Napoléon, agreed to make terms and bring the "quasi-war" to a close. But on this side of the Atlantic it backfired. After all the taxation, after the military buildup based on the threat of a war that never came, the electorate was unsettled.

In the election of 1800 Jefferson challenged Adams, dubbing the Federalists the party of tyranny, militarism, and taxation. He accused Adams of expanding the powers of the federal government too far, of instituting "a reign of terror." Adams was defeated and for the first time in modern history an incumbent ruling group handed over the reins of government to their opponents. Yet there was no rioting in the streets, no military coup, no secession from the Union.

Those 12 years of consistent economic and political policies constituted the first American political paradigm. During that span the Federalists set the course of government in the commercial direction Hamilton had recommended. They founded a national bank, established the credit of the United States at home and abroad, and provided for a revenue-raising tariff. Furthermore, the government of Washington set an example of honest administration, added a Bill of Rights to the Constitution, secured the territorial integrity of the new nation, avoided entry into the European War, and harnessed the exuberant energies released in the Revolution of '76, and this enabled the new nation to begin on a firm footing.

However, the Federalists had clung to the orthodox eighteenth-century view of a hierarchical world, which "was swimming against the tide of the revolutionary ideology of the time." Nor did they properly understand that in a democracy it is necessary to acknowledge the opinions of the masses. This disregard of the popular will was telling in Adams's hasty "midnight appointments," of a slew of Federalist judges, the Judiciary Act of 1801, made after his electoral defeat. These assignments, along with the appointment of John Marshall as Chief Justice of the Supreme Court, were done in a last-ditch effort to thwart the Republicans for years to come.

TABLE 4

First Political Paradigm (1789–1801), 12 Years

Election of:		Majority Paradigm Party		Minority Paradigm Party	
		Federalists		Democratic-Republicans	
Paradigm			Electoral votes		Electoral votes
1788	Begins	**George Washington***	69	unopposed	0
1792	Preliminary	**George Washington**	132	unopposed	0
1796	Confirmed	**John Adams**	71	Thomas Jefferson	68
1800	Ends				
***Bold** = winner.					

Congress		Federalists		Democratic-Republicans	
		House	Senate	House	Senate
1st	1789–1791	**38***	**17**	26	9
2d	1791–1793	**37**	**16**	33	13
3d	1793–1795	48	**17**	**57**	13
4th	1795–1797	**54**	**19**	52	13
5th	1797–1799	**58**	**20**	48	12
6th	1799–1801	**64**	**19**	42	13

***Bold** = in control of House or Senate

Source: Composition of 1st–6th Congress: *Encyclopedia of American History*

Years in the White House with control of at least one house of Congress:

  Federalists: 12
  Democratic-Republicans: 0

Economic Policies
- Establishment of national bank
- Establishment of tariff
- National debt paid off
- Taxes collected

Other Important Events
- Bill of Rights ratified by the states
- Army and navy established
- Neutrality proclamation in European War
- Whiskey Rebellion put down
- War with England sidestepped: Jay's treaty
- Quasi-war with France on high seas settled before it became "hot" war
- Alien and Sedition Acts
- Virginia and Kentucky Resolutions to protest the Alien and Sedition Acts
- Washington's farewell address

Agrarian Policies
- Land Act of 1796 (parcels of 680 acres at $2 per acre high enough to discourage western development)
- Indians defeated in old Northwest in battle of Fallen Timbers

The Democrats: The Age of Jefferson and Jackson

In 1801 Thomas Jefferson, the staunch supporter of the French Revolution, took the helm of government and northeasterners quaked in their boots waiting for the mob-inspired revolution to begin. But there was no reenactment of the French Revolution. Rather, Jefferson and his Republican followers sought to carry out what they thought was the original aim of the Revolution of 1776: limiting the power of the national government and putting the humanitarian hopes of the Enlightenment into practice. They wanted to create a national government that would rule without the traditional attributes of power and leave the care of persons and property to the states.

The Republicans allowed the sedition laws to lapse and adopted a new liberal naturalization law. They cut the military budget in half, believing that the benefits of a standing army were not worth the cost in either money or the threat to liberty it posed. A majority of the navy's warships were retired. The Republicans also jettisoned the Judiciary Act of 1801, eliminated all federal internal taxes, pared federal expenses to the bone, and paid off about one-half of the national debt in 10 years.

Jefferson and his allies were appalled by the elitism of the Federalist era and sought to break up the politically supported privileges of the New England gentry. The most glaring was the Nation's Bank, which, under the Federalists' stewardship, had become a tool to confer privileges on a New England "commercial aristocracy" while discriminating against Republican borrowers. The Republicans allowed the bank charter to lapse and turned the nation's money system over to state banks, which they thought would better serve their purposes. But they were ignorant of the inflationary potential those banks, without restraints on the amount of paper currency they could issue, might create.

Jefferson sought to turn the United States away from becoming a nation of commerce. He thought the chief asset of the nation was its abundant land. The Republicans pursued an aggressive agrarian program, which included expanding the frontier, shuffling the Indians farther back into the interior, and reducing the price of a homestead. For two decades the Republicans lowered the price of a homestead, reducing the minimum size of purchasable tracts and relaxing terms of credit, making it easier and yet still easier to move public lands into the private hands of ordinary citizens. As early as 1804 upward of 4 million acres were passing annually into private hands, up from a few hundred thousand in 1800.

Jefferson also set out to put an end to social hierarchy and extinguish a world of powdered wigs and knee breeches. Once in office, he removed the customary props to social rank. White House protocol was banished, including the rules for honoring dignitaries, American or foreign. At his parties, those standing nearest the dining room when the meal was announced went in first. He adamantly refused to make any distinctions that might separate him from his fellow citizens, even on a personal level. If Jefferson happened to be near the front door of the White House, he would often answer it himself, even when attired in a lounging robe.

In 1803, over the Federalists' objections, Jefferson purchased the Louisiana Territory, which extended from the Mississippi

River to the Rockies, from France for $15 million, a paltry three cents an acre, perhaps the greatest bargain in American history. It was the most popular and momentous event of his presidency. In one fell swoop, it doubled the land size of the country, creating immense opportunities for further settlement, assured control of the Mississippi River, the main artery of traffic in the nation's interior, and paved the way for eventual dominance of the United States in the Western Hemisphere.

During Jefferson's tenure hordes of pioneers streamed across the Appalachians, pushing the Indians farther back toward the Mississippi River. Shawnee Chief Tecumseh and his brother the Prophet formed an Indian confederacy to resist the steady encroachment of settlers, and Tecumseh's warriors began attacking settlers in the Mississippi and Ohio valleys. Frontier violence would continue until General William Henry Harrison, governor of the Indiana territory, with 1,000 army regulars, routed Tecumseh's warriors and destroyed their village at the battle of Tippecanoe in 1811. From that time on Indians would be only a minor obstacle to white settlement east of the Mississippi, and Harrison became a national hero.

By 1804 Jefferson was at the apex of his popularity. Gone was the semblance of a classical republic led by a traditional gentlemanly elite; in its place a democratic, egalitarian society of ordinary men and women filled with the great possibilities that lay before them was taking shape. Old encrusted habits and relationships were being destroyed and new opportunities were being created, especially for the middle and lower stratum of the population. No wonder Jefferson was reelected in 1804, and by a huge margin. The people had provided a preliminary sign that a new "Jefferson" paradigm was forming.

Shortly thereafter continental war between France and England was resumed and once again the two European powers were tampering with American shipping. With foreign commerce and national honor at stake, Jefferson was pressured to do something. However, the military and naval strength of the country had declined to such a level that making war was impractical. Instead Jefferson imposed an embargo on trade with Britain and France. It was a liberal experiment in what he called "peaceful coercion." He felt he could bring the British and French to terms by keeping our ships in port and depriving the British and French of food and other resources. "Our commerce is so valuable to them," he declared, "that they will be glad to purchase it when the only price we ask is to do us justice." But the embargo proved to be worthless. While the two European powers showed few ill effects, it delivered a staggering blow to American foreign trade, bringing economic paralysis to the trading cities of the Northeast and the farms and plantations of the West and South. To make matters worse, many American shippers were ignoring the embargo and the Republicans found it necessary to pass a series of enforcement acts that grew increasingly harsh. Finally, in a move that Alexander Hamilton would have applauded, Jefferson was forced to call out the army to uphold the regulations.

In 1808 Jefferson favored his friend and secretary of state, James Madison, to succeed him. American voters, still intoxicated with the smell of freedom, were willing to overlook the embargo issue and provided Madison with a clear-cut electoral victory, confirming the existence of a Jefferson paradigm. Madison continued on the course set by his predecessor. He took a bite out of Spanish West Florida, claiming it was part of the Louisiana Purchase, and appended it to the nation. Rather liking it, he took a second bite, opening up a window on the Gulf of Mexico.

He replaced the unpopular embargo with a less masochistic Non-Intercourse Act, and then again with Macon's Bill Number 2, which allowed the country to resume trading with England and France but contained a curious carrot-and-stick provision. If either of the two European powers repealed restrictions upon neutral shipping, the American government would halt commerce with the other. The French took the bait and revoked their decree against neutral shipping. Madison reinstated nonintercourse with England, and this sent relations with England on a collision course. Yet, as war clouds darkened, the Republicans resisted efforts to increase the government's capacity to wage it.

In the mid-term elections a new group of Republican congressmen, unwilling to tolerate national humiliation, were elected. Many were eager for war. Some saw prime parts of Canada as ripe for the picking. Others were looking for an excuse to push the Indians farther into the backcountry. And those representing the Southern planters had their eyes on Florida. With these "War Hawks" egging him on, Madison asked Congress for a declaration of war against Great Britain.

In late 1812, before much of the fighting had occurred, Madison was reelected to another term. Soon afterward it became evident that the war was going badly. The federal government could not recruit troops, collect taxes, or borrow money. The promise of apportioning part of the Canadian lands floundered as detachments of men serving in the state militias refused to fight outside their state boundaries. On one occasion, New York militia stationed on the U.S. side of the Niagara River watched American regulars, who were attacking British troops on the Canadian side, go down to defeat rather than come to their aid. Other recruits, once their three-month enlistments were up, turned around and went home. Meanwhile, most banks south of New England teetered on the brink of bankruptcy. The New England states, still loyal to the Federalists and opposed to the war, met to discuss secession, which was narrowly voted down.

In 1814 an expeditionary force of fewer than 5,000 British soldiers marched toward Washington, D.C. The government summoned 95,000 troops, but only 7,000 showed and made a stand just outside the nation's capital. After suffering about sixty-six casualties they broke and ran, leaving a clear path to the capital city. As Madison and other key members of the government scrambled to a hastily devised defense camp outside of the city, the British pressed on and arrived in Washington, D.C., that same evening in time to dine at the White House. After dinner they set fire to the White House and other public buildings. It was probably the most humiliating episode in American history.

The situation was different in the South, where Andrew Jackson proved to be the only general who demonstrated real leadership. When a group of Tennessee militia attempted to leave, he lined the road with regulars and commanded them to shoot anyone who attempted to leave. The mutineers backed down and from that point on General Andrew Jackson, known as "Old Hickory," which his friends insisted was the "hardest wood in all creation," had total control over his men. After securing the South, Jackson marched his troops to New Orleans, where he arrived just in time to defend the city. Jackson's forces, though outnumbered two to one, routed the British. Although the fighting took place after the war had officially ended, it was the most decisive victory of the conflict and allowed the "States" to claim victory in a war in which they had barely managed to hold the English to a standoff. Andrew Jackson had rescued America's pride and was hailed a national hero.

By war's end it was apparent the Jefferson-Madison program had left key American institutions severely weakened. There was no national army worthy of the name. The banking system was a shambles and the government was near bankruptcy. So in 1815, late in his second term, Madison switched gears and set the Republican agenda in the direction of strengthening some of the key institutions. This shift in the political winds to what was generally called the "New Nationalism" ended the second paradigm.

In the first 15 years of the nineteenth century Jefferson and the early Republicans extended the boundaries of the country and adopted a federal land policy that encouraged rapid settlement of the West. They broke up artificial privileges, which had become part of the Federalist era, and showed it was possible to establish a stable and workable system of government based on the rights of the individual. But above all, in lifting the restraints to individual progress and leveling the playing field the Jeffersonians had started in motion a fundamental reorganization of American society that was to transform this country . . . and all of Western society.

New Nationalism: The Third Political Paradigm

A third mini-revolution began late in 1815, when Madison reversed course and backpedaled from many of the Republican policies. His administration chartered a second U.S. bank, initiated a steep increase in the tariff, and authorized a standing federal army of 10,000, quadruple its prewar size. Although Madison vetoed an internal improvements bill, he recommended a constitutional amendment to permit congressional action in that area. The Republicans were, in fact, embracing some of the policies of their former Federalist rivals.

In 1816 Madison passed the torch to James Monroe, who ran as a "New Nationalist" and proceeded to beat the socks off his Federalist opponent, Rufus King. This voter mandate to continue in the new direction was preliminary evidence the nation was in a new political model. The Federalist Party, which had been on the decline since their opposition to the War of 1812, was almost completely destroyed. With the Republicans now the nation's sole political organization, it appeared party strife would end, and a period of national political harmony, often referred to as the "era of good feeling," followed.

During that time the United States wrested Florida from Spain, securing all the land east of the Mississippi River. Spanish Florida had been a beehive of hostile Seminole Indians, runaway slaves, and renegade whites who were constantly making trouble along the border. In 1817 President Monroe asked Andrew Jackson to raise a force of Tennessee militia and restore order along the border. An army detachment, accompanied by women and children, on the way to join Jackson was ambushed and massacred by a tribe of Seminoles. An angry Andrew Jackson, although lacking government authorization, burst into Florida and, like an avenging demon, destroyed Seminole villages, overthrew the Spanish governor, and executed two British adventurers thought to have incited the Seminole atrocities. Once again Jackson was a national hero, and Monroe was reluctant to reprimand him, especially since the incident convinced Spain to sell Florida along with her claims to the Oregon Country to the United States for $5 million.

Following the war, stirrings of a market economy were first heard. The introduction of toll roads, canals, and steamboats had reduced the cost of transportation and opened up interior markets. In New England a baby textile industry took root. To be sure, this market economy was in an infant stage. At most about 20 percent of the nation's workers were employed in trade, factory production, transportation, and the professions. Nonetheless it enabled many newly prosperous citizens to claim their own share of social recognition, further breaking the bonds of the old fixed and stratified social order.

In the euphoria of good times America experienced its first speculative boom. It was in land. People thought that demand for it would be insatiable. Speculators, tempted by ever-rising cotton prices and the easy credit policies of the second national bank, were purchasing 160-acre blocks of land from the government for $320, putting down only 20 percent, and reselling at exorbitantly higher prices. By late 1818 land in some prime cotton areas was fetching $150 an acre. An investor who had plunked down $64 in cash was able to pocket about $24,000. But these speculators did not realize that the flip side to a speculative boom was bust.

In early 1819 America experienced its first genuine financial panic. The cotton "bubble" burst and pulled the prop out from under the land market. Soon afterwards the postwar economic boom turned to bust, leading to the bankruptcy of scores of firms and thousands of individuals throughout the United States. Large numbers of farmers lost their property and artisans their jobs. It was a cruel awakening to thousands who had hoped to become rich. To discourage land speculation, thought the chief culprit for the bust, the administration pushed through the Public Land Act of 1820, which abolished the use of credit for land purchases. But at the same time it lowered the cost of buying a homestead by about 60 percent. Nearly everyone thought that would do the trick and expected business conditions to improve soon.

In 1820 the American people were due to go to the polls again. The Republicans did not have to worry about the deteriorating business conditions, as most people felt they would soon improve. Besides, the party's shift toward nationalistic policies had awakened a new sense of pride and purpose in the American people. The party of Washington and Hamilton did not even bother to field a candidate. Monroe got all the electoral votes but one. This had not happened since the reign of George Washington and, most important, corroborated that a third "New Nationalism" paradigm was firmly in place.

Shortly after the election of 1820, the first important North–South sectional dispute surfaced. The North attempted to block Missouri's entry to the Union as a slave state. As Maine was about to be admitted as a free state, this would have left the Union with 12 free and only 11 slave states, tilting the balance of political power in favor of the North. The South, deeply disturbed about losing political influence, threatened secession. However, Henry Clay, speaker of the House, came to the rescue and brokered the famous "Missouri Compromise." Missouri was admitted as a slaveholding state, but slavery was prohibited north of the 36/30th latitude. Political equilibrium was reestablished and sectional problems were put on hold for a generation.

Meanwhile, to most everyone's surprise, economic conditions did not improve after the election. Instead they kept deteriorating and the Republicans were at a loss over what to do about it. It was the first long period of hard times that the young nation had to endure. More important, the demise of the Federalists had not led to consensus. A credible opposing party had enabled the various factions within the Republican Party to compromise so the party could stand together to ward off its challenges. The elimination of political opposition had eroded party discipline and led to "no-party rule." Disputes over tariffs, banks, and internal improvements produced wrenching strains, and the Republican Party began to split apart.

By 1824 the Republican Party had ruptured. Four candidates, representing different sectional interests and economic policies, vied for the presidency. Andrew Jackson, the hero of New Orleans and the only candidate without a conspicuous prior role in national politics, won over 41 percent of the popular vote but fell short of an Electoral College majority. John Quincy Adams, who had come in second with only 31 percent of the popular vote, won the election in the House of Representatives, after receiving the backing of Henry Clay, who had finished fourth.

Adams began his term as a minority president and lost sight of the old Republican constituency. He appointed Henry Clay secretary of state and they took on the label "National Republicans." Together they proposed a bold program, called the "American System," designed to tilt the national government much further in a pro-commerce direction. It called for government assistance in the building of roads, canals, and harbors, so as to hasten industrialization. Adams also encouraged Congress to raise tariffs and stood aside while Congress, pressured by the special interests, fixed the rates at ridiculously high levels. The result was the "Tariff of Abominations."

The Adams administration also showed considerably less enthusiasm in pursuing the traditional Republican agrarian policies. They retreated from squandering public land on shiftless squatters and dragged their feet on hustling the Indians westward. To many, it appeared that Adams and his cohorts had finally crossed the line and were now outfederalizing the old Federalists. This alienated large sections of the country, especially the "Cotton South," which viewed the policies of high tariffs and internal improvements as furthering the emerging industrialization in the North.

Meanwhile, Andrew Jackson and his followers were outraged at the outcome of the election. They charged that a "corrupt bargain" between J. Q. Adams and Clay had deprived the general of the presidency. Jackson and his allies began campaigning for the next election immediately and they threw out all prior rules on electioneering that aristocratic office seekers of the early nineteenth century had abided by. Their strategy was to go over the heads of the corrupt ruling elite and appeal directly to the people for support. They dropped the "Republican" label, called themselves Democrats, and focused on expanding suffrage. They were so successful that 55 percent of the eligible voters participated in the election of 1828, up from about 25 percent in the prior election. And Jackson received a whopping 56 percent of the popular vote, which would stand as a high-water mark for over 75 years. It was a genuine landslide.

The third political model was over, and during its 13-year span Republicans put forward programs that looked, smelled, and felt like those originally proposed by the Federalists. However, this paradigm shift, unlike the one that began in 1801, was not total. Although the Republicans had increased tariffs, rechartered a national bank, and expanded the size of the army and navy, they were not simply Federalists in disguise. Until J. Q. Adams took the helm they had not lost their core ideology. They still embraced states' rights, maintained their constitutional scruples against federally sponsored internal improvements, and did not stray from their devotion to limited government. Most important, they remained true to their basic agrarian policies. They acquired Florida, continued to encourage western settlement, and lowered the purchase price for land, making it easier for a poor man to acquire a homestead. This shift in the political model, unlike the prior two, was not a *full-scale shift* to the other side of the political spectrum.

Number Four: The Jackson Paradigm

Andrew Jackson, who was the hero of the lower and middling elements of American society, arrived in Washington, D.C., in March of 1829 to take the helm of government. A ragtag army of ten thousand well-wishers, coming from every one of the 24 states, streamed into the city to see their man inaugurated. They drank the city dry of whiskey, crammed the hotels, sleeping five in a bed, and after the inaugural followed their new president to the entrance of the White House. While the gentry looked on from the safety of their balconies, these Jacksonian ruffians proceeded to enter the White House. Mayhem followed as men with muddy boots jumped on chairs and sofas and smashed the White House's china and glassware.

Andrew Jackson steered the government back to the simplicity of earlier Republican doctrines. Following the script Jefferson had written almost thirty years prior, Jackson's administration further liberalized public land policy. After a protracted fight in the Senate the government temporarily adopted the Preemption Land Act, which gave frontiersmen who had squatted on public lands "squatters" rights: the right to purchase the land for $1.25 an acre before it was put up for sale. To further encourage settlement in the new lands, Jackson pursued a relentless policy of Indian removal. His administration called for the speedy removal of all eastern Indians to designated areas beyond the Mississippi

River. By 1833 all the southeastern tribes except the Cherokees had agreed to evacuate their ancestral homes.

Jackson's Democrats opposed internal improvements; they cut back on government expenditures, so much so that by the end of Jackson's administration the public debt was totally eliminated. This has never happened since. They also instituted a modest tariff reduction, which, however, did not satisfy the South. South Carolina, the hothead of the South, complained that the reduction was not enough and threatened to nullify the federal tariff laws. Jackson, who was a staunch Unionist, moved troops to Charleston Harbor but balanced this show of military strength by an additional cut in the tariff. This adroit use of compulsion and concession together nipped the threat of secession in the bud. Furthermore, it set a precedent of using force against states that defied federal authority.

Andrew Jackson, like Jefferson before him, went to war against privilege, especially government-granted privileges, which were seen as restricting individual opportunity. And the second Bank of the United States was the most exclusive privileged monopoly in the country. It stood as a symbol for all the others. Small businesspeople and workingmen felt that the bank restricted competition and prevented them from entering upon the avenues of enterprise. Jackson did away with the "monster" national bank once more and put the government's money in "pet" state banks, which in turn issued a flood of paper money. This fueled a speculative boom, but that comes later.

In 1832 Jackson defeated Henry Clay, the standard-bearer for the National Republicans, in another landslide. Fifty-four percent of the voters rallied to Jackson's cause, thereby signaling preliminary approval for the new course he was setting. To be sure, Jackson's reign was more than just a return to the early Republican virtues. "Old Hickory," a self-made man of immense willpower, was the most forceful and aggressive president since George Washington. Jackson became the people's champion, vetoing bills, actively intervening to secure passage of the laws he favored, and pushing Congress to do his bidding. He threw out the aged and incompetent bureaucrats of the previous administrations, replacing them with Democratic sympathizers, thus beginning the "spoils system" in the national government. When John Marshall, Chief Justice of the Supreme Court, died, Jackson appointed his crony Roger Brooke Taney to replace Marshall. Taney shifted the direction of the Court and introduced the modern doctrine of putting the public interest before the rights of private property. In the famous Charles River Bridge case, while conceding the rights of private property should be "sacredly guarded," Taney maintained "the community also has rights and . . . the happiness and well being of every citizen depends upon their faithful preservation."

When the sun finally set on Jackson's administration, it had extended the boundaries of individual freedom, further enlarging the scope of opportunity available to an expanding body of aspiring citizens, and had woven a system of political and social organization that gave the common man a chance. Pushing further than even Jefferson dared go, Jackson had made sure the "little guy" was included in the political system, and this goal of *inclusion*, for those formerly left out, has remained a central tenet of the Democrat Party throughout its history.

Although the Jackson administration moved the government back in the direction of its earlier agrarian focus, it could only temper the forces of industrialism. The seeds of industry, once planted in American soil, could not be stamped out. The Jackson agrarian paradigm, no matter its inclinations, would have to make room for the swelling force of an intractable industrialism. In fact, by removing government restrictions and privileges, and committing the nation to a currency and credit system much looser than the prior "national bank system," the Jackson administration had unintentionally helped ignite an entrepreneurial impulse, which was to give Jacksonian democracy much of its freshness and vitality.

But there was an underlying problem with the Jacksonian program. It was the inconsistency of demanding life, liberty, and happiness for white Americans while denying those "natural rights" to Negroes. Liberal ideas of abolishing slavery were already on the march throughout the rest of the Western world. Great Britain abolished slavery in the British West Indies in 1833. It was during Jackson's tenure that an abolitionist movement to free the slaves sprouted up in this country. And ironically, it put the Democratic Party, which was both the states' rights party with its major base of support in the slaveholding South and the party of individual freedom, between a rock and a hard place. Looking back, it was obvious that there was a major contradiction within the Jacksonian paradigm.

In 1836 Martin Van Buren, Jackson's vice-president and hand-picked successor, faced a crowded field of three Whig opponents. The Whigs were made up of the remnants of the Adams-Clay National Republican Party along with a coalition of others opposed to Andrew Jackson's aggressive use of executive power. Van Buren was able to capitalize on the pervasive feeling that the country was marching in the right direction and captured a clear majority of the popular vote, confirming that the fourth American mini-revolution had become the Jackson paradigm.

No sooner had Van Buren settled in as head of government than a bundle of problems surfaced, which would derail his administration. Texas, which had just recently fought its way to independence from Mexico, asked to be annexed into the Union. However, it was a slave state, and the North, fearing Texas would tilt the balance in favor of the South, protested. The issue became too hot for the cautious Van Buren to handle. Dutifully he followed Jackson's policy of Indian removal, but about one-quarter of the 15,000 Cherokee Indians marching under military guard to Oklahoma died from disease or malnutrition. This infamous march became known as the "trail of tears."

Yet, most unfortunately for Van Buren, Jackson's easy money

policies had ignited another speculative boom, which fed on get-rich-quick schemes. A financial panic in 1837 was followed by a deep and protracted depression once again. The price of cotton fell by almost 50 percent, banks across the nation suspended specie payments, and there were demonstrations of unemployed workers in several of the larger cities. Van Buren backpedaled a bit from Jackson's ill-advised financial policies and set up an "Independent Treasury." The idea was to place government funds in strong vaults or subtreasuries, to be constructed in various cities. It would bury the government's money so that it could not contribute to an overexpansion in bank credit, such as had preceded the panic of 1837. But during this long business slump the public lost its trust in the Jacksonian banking system, and this provided an opening, a mile wide, for the opposing party.

The Minority Party Takes Over

In 1840 the Whigs smelled victory in the air and selected William Henry Harrison, the "Hero of Tippecanoe," to head their ticket. The party waged one of the most colorful campaigns of all time. Men and boys rolled huge paper balls, representing their gathering majority, from village to village all the way from Kentucky to Baltimore, while chanting the catchy campaign ditty:

> "What has caused this great commotion, motion, motion,
> our country through?
> —It is the ball a-rolling on, for TIPPECANOE AND TYLER TOO:—
> Tippecanoe and Tyler too.
> And with them we'll beat little Van, Van, Van, Oh! Van is a used-
> up man."

Harrison easily beat Van Buren in an election where nearly 80 percent of the eligible voters went to the polls. However, something different happened this time. The Democratic defeat did not put an end to the Jackson paradigm. During a period when life expectancies were much shorter than now, the Whigs nominated the 68-year-old Harrison to lead them. And hoping to broaden the party's appeal they selected John Tyler, a former Jacksonian Democrat with questionable loyalty to the party, for the second spot. Harrison died a month into his term and Tyler climbed onto the saddle. However, he betrayed the economic tenets of the party, returning to his original Democratic precepts. He blocked all attempts to create a new national bank, vetoed all bills for internal improvements, and made the Jacksonian Preemption Land Act permanent. Although he accepted a slight upward revision in the tariff and agreed to repeal the Independent Treasury Act, the Whigs considered him a traitor, who had stolen victory from them.

In 1844 the Whigs chose the popular Henry Clay, who made his third stab at the presidency. The Democrats selected a dark horse candidate, James Polk, who was called "Young Hickory." Polk offered a program of territorial expansion: annexation of Texas and the acquisition of California and Oregon. His plan also included tariff reduction and the reestablishment of the Independent Treasury.

Majority Party Restoration

Polk beat Clay in a close election, restoring the Democrats to power, and publicly stated that he planned to retire after one term. Congress, responding to the election returns, voted to annex Texas three days before Polk moved into the White House. The new president immediately went to work on implementing his program to extend the borders of the United States. In an aggressive diplomacy of bluff and bluster he induced Great Britain to give up most of the Oregon Territory. Next he turned his attention to the lands west of the Louisiana Territory. The crown jewel was California, which with its fine natural harbors, fertile lands, and unsurpassed beauty promised limitless riches. He offered to purchase it, along with New Mexico, from Mexico. When rebuffed he initiated war with Mexico. It was an easy victory and in the important battle of Buena Vista Gen. Zachary Taylor emerged a national hero.

Polk achieved his objectives, probably more so than any president before or after. During his one term in the White House he had, as promised, "substantially" reduced the tariff, reestablished the Independent Treasury, and, following America's "Manifest Destiny," swallowed one-third of Mexico, pushing the American frontier as far as it could go, all the way to the sparkling blue waters of the Pacific Ocean. You would think people would be rejoicing in the streets and hoisting President Polk on their shoulders. But that was not the case. The voters, instead of rewarding the Democrats, actually threw them out of office in the next election. What went wrong?

The acquisition of the new territories brought to the surface the simmering issues of sectional balance and slavery. Were the new territories to be free or slave? In late 1846 Senator Wilmot, an antislavery senator from Pennsylvania, who spoke for the large number of Northern Democrats who felt betrayed by the "pro-Southern" tilt in their party, threw the gauntlet down and proposed a provision to bar the spread of slavery to the new territories. This Wilmot Proviso became the central issue in the following election. But was slavery the real issue?

Oftentimes just before teenage children are about to go off to college they provoke quarrels with their parents based on grievances, real or imagined. Parents find it maddening to deal with these issues. No matter how logical, how agreeable or accommodating, they are unable to get any satisfaction. Reach an accommodation and a new grievance pops up. Psychologists tell us why: This is because the issues are not the issues. Their children are experiencing what psychologists call "separation anxiety." An unexpressed, underlying anxiety about leaving their nest is provoking the children to use any possible excuse to lash out. And that is the root issue. If perchance the superficial issues the children raised were the real issues, reasonable and responsive parents would be able to deal with them. The inability to find some reasonable accommodation tells us these are not the real issues.

In much the same way, slavery was used as the cover-up for important underlying economic and political issues. As the North saw it, a recalcitrant South was blocking in Congress the policies, a protective tariff and subsidies to the railroads, necessary to feed the nation's industrial energies. If the territories were to became slave states, the South and their Democrat friends in Congress would be able to block Northern political power and check the thrust to industrialization.

As the South saw it, the North was attracting millions of immigrant wage earners, was developing vast urban centers, and was gaining mastery over the mysterious sources of credit and investment capital. If the South was denied land for expansion it would surely become a second-class colony subjected to the dictates of a tyrannical Northern government. Southerners dug in their heels and demanded the expansion of slavery into the new territories.

So it came to be: the vast addition of new lands to the American nation, which most future generations would see as a blessing, provoked a sectional quarrel over the status of slavery in those areas. And this was to become the stuff of politics during the period from 1848 to the election of Abraham Lincoln in 1860. To be sure, this is not to say that slavery was not also a real issue. It was! But perhaps it was not the root issue. Had it been, the politicians could have dealt with it. God knows they tried!

Another Minority Party Interlude

In the election of 1848, the first important third party, the "Free Soilers," with a strong antislavery platform and a slogan of "Free Soil, Free Speech, Free Labor and Free Men," attracted 10 percent of the vote, showing the appeal of the antislavery issue in the North. With many Northern "conscience" Democrats peeling off and voting "Free Soiler," the Whigs, with Zachary Taylor, the hero of the Buena Vista, as their leader, captured 47 percent of the popular vote, which was enough to beat the Democrat, Lewis Cass.

The fate of slavery in the newly acquired territories became the chief issue and the South threatened secession once more. Meanwhile, Taylor died in office and Millard Fillmore took charge. After some of the greatest senatorial debates in the nation's history, Senator Henry Clay again stepped in and, with a big assist from Senator Stephen Douglas of Illinois, brokered the "compromise of 1850." The North got California as a free state and the elimination of the slave trade in Washington, D.C. The South's prizes were popular sovereignty in New Mexico and Utah and, most important, a more stringent fugitive slave law, whereby escaped slaves who had made their way to the North would be returned to their owners. This 1850 Act did not repeal the Missouri Compromise. The earlier law had dealt only with the Louisiana land purchase, while the recent compromise of 1850 referred to the lands acquired from Mexico.

It appeared as if sectional controversy had been put on hold, at least for a while. Thanks to the rapid railroad building and the flow of gold from the newly discovered mines in California, Americans were enjoying the best economy since the panic of 1837. Despite California's admission as the sixteenth free state, as opposed to 15 slave states, tensions eased and an Indian summer of peace and prosperity followed. Yet beneath the surface the sounds of a nation splitting in two could still be heard. In a test of the Fugitive Slave Act in Boston, Anthony Burns, a runway slave whom the courts had ordered returned to his owner, was escorted to the wharf by a battalion of the U.S. Army, four platoons of marines, and a sheriff's posse through streets covered with black crepe as twenty thousand antislavers hissed and booed and every church bell along the way tolled the funeral dirge. Harriet Beecher

Stowe's *Uncle Tom's Cabin*, a moral indictment of slavery, was published and sold over 300,000 copies by the end of its first year—an unheard of amount in the 1850s.

A Second Majority Party Restoration

In 1852, with the slavery issue seemingly settled, Franklin Pierce, "Young Hickory of the Granite Hills," as he was known, won 51 percent of the vote, retrieving the White House for the Democrats. To pacify the South and rectify the political imbalance, the Pierce administration attempted to revive interest in territorial expansion. In an act of international bad manners they schemed to add Cuba as another slave state, but some opposition senators got wind of it and nipped the project in the bud.

Jefferson Davis, secretary of war, recognized that the land of Dixie still had one last card to play in order to retain its political predominance. It was the advantage a southern railroad route to the Far West had over northern and central routes. It was shorter, had better contours, and, as it led through states and territories that were already organized, the Indian menace was less pronounced. The only problem was that it had to pass through some Mexican territory. To skirt that hurdle and make sure the South retained its edge, Davis convinced Pierce to purchase what today are the southernmost parts of Arizona and New Mexico, and the race to the Pacific was on.

Senator Stephen Douglas of Illinois, probably the most popular Democratic senator and angling for the next presidential nomination, was not about to be outfoxed by Jeff Davis and his Southern brethren. Douglas was convinced that the railroad was key to the country's future prosperity and wanted the first railroad to the Far West to connect to the northern region of the nation. This meant the Indian country west of the Missouri River would have to be surveyed and opened for sale. To facilitate this, the region had to be organized as a territory. So he proposed the Kansas-

Nebraska Act, which would open up the new territory. As an inducement to win the South's approval and overcome their concern about the creation of more free states, he offered popular sovereignty, whereby any new state would be able to decide for itself whether to be admitted to the Union as "free" or "slave." Southern representatives and senators took the bait and voted as a block in favor. In 1854 the Kansas-Nebraska Act became a law. However, it violated a sacred compact, the Missouri Compromise, and appeared to be a capitulation to the "cotton snobs," setting off a political firestorm in the North. The turmoil between the states began building toward a climax.

Kansas, with the question of whether it would be admitted as a free or slave state, became the battleground. Both Northerners and Southerners tried to stack the deck by sending sympathizers into the state, and a "little" civil war broke out. In 1856 "bleeding Kansas" was the chief campaign issue. Pierce looked like a sure loser and the Democrats refused to renominate him. He became the first and only elected president denied renomination by his own party. Instead they turned to James Buchanan, who had the good fortune of having been out of the country during the bitter Kansas-Nebraska debates.

The opposition Whig Party, because of its Southern wing, was unable to seize the opportunity, provided by the confusion within the Democrat Party, and become a true antislavery party. It broke up and the bulk of its constituents, along with ex–Free Soilers and conscience Democrats from the North, formed a hothead new Republican Party, which latched onto the antislavery issue. This new party's appeal was directed solely to a Northern audience, and it refused to throw a bone to the South. Their commercial policies, which followed in the spirit of the Federalists and Whigs, included high tariffs and federal support for internal improvements. They chose John C. Frémont as their presidential candidate, and their rallying cry became "Free Soil, Free Speech and Frémont." Complicating matters, however, was a third party, the "Know-Nothing" Party, running on opposition to immigration and Roman Catholicism with ex-president Fillmore at its head. Alongside the furor over slavery there was an increasing antagonism toward foreigners, especially Catholics. These newcomers, who generally clustered in their own communities, were seen as bearers of an alien culture. The "Know-Nothings," appealing to people's baser instincts, were able to pick off 22 percent of the total vote, which enabled the Democrat, James Buchanan, to win with 45 percent of the popular vote. However, the new antislavery Republican Party had won 11 of the 16 free states. It was a remarkable showing and the South could surely feel the daggers of abolition pointing at her heart.

In early 1857 Buchanan moved into the White House, and his administration reeled from disaster to disaster. The Taney Court issued the "Dred Scott" decision, which implied that slavery was theoretically legal in every territory of the United States. This, of course, incited the North and further fueled the flames of sectional controversy. The blatant attempts by the Buchanan administration to stack the deck, bypassing the people's will, so that Kansas would be admitted as a slave state outraged Northerners. Even Stephen Douglas had enough. He broke with Buchanan and led the fight against the resolution to admit Kansas as a slave state with all the vigor at his command. Minnesota and Oregon were admitted to the Union as the seventeenth and eighteenth free states, while Kansas was denied admission as a slave state. Another financial panic hit in 1857 and was followed by a steep economic contraction that severely depressed Northern industry.

The declining power of Northern Democrats gave the Southern Democrats who dominated Buchanan's administration free rein. Demands by the northeastern industrialists for a higher tariff to ease the strain of the depression went unheeded. A new homestead law, which the westerners wanted, was blocked by Buchanan. In a desperate attempt to pacify the South the Buchanan administration tried to rekindle interest in territorial expansion. They talked of adding Cuba, invading Mexico, anything to distract the South's thoughts from secession. But these proposals were unrealistic and easily shot down.

Meanwhile, John Brown, a fierce abolitionist, thought he could take matters into his own hands. Hoping to provoke a slave uprising, he and 18 followers seized the federal armory at Harpers Ferry, Virginia. They killed the town's mayor and took some of the leading townspeople prisoner. Brown was captured and sentenced to death, but the outpouring of sympathy and admiration in the North for this man stunned the South. Listen to Ralph Waldo Emerson, the most respected poet and man of letters during the mid–nineteenth century: "Brown . . . would make the gallows as glorious as the cross." Perhaps most important was that during the depression of the late 1850s, unlike in prior economic busts, the price of cotton soared and the South's economy prospered. The land of Dixie, now exporting seven-eighths of the world's cotton, thought it was sitting on top of the economic heap and was thus emboldened to strike out on its own.

By the mid-1850s there was something else in the air, which can best be described as an *excess of democracy*. The rapid transformation of our society and economy, the abundant opportunities for self-advancement, the expansion of the frontier, the rise of the city, the rapid social mobility, had produced an excess of individualism, which eroded the values of orderly civilization. White manhood suffrage was nearly universal and new classes of society were brought in, which didn't have the self-restraint to act in a manner that made democracy work. Men and women felt completely unfettered by precedent and under no obligation to respect the important lessons of the past. A general rejection of authority spread throughout society. Traditional restraints imposed by church, community, and family to curb individual behavior in the interests of social harmony or public morality were seen as antidemocratic. Anything that smacked of legal privilege, that stacked the odds in favor of one group over another, was vulnerable to attack by the public.

Most telling was the rejection of authority in the political sphere. Large numbers of people were no longer listening to solutions proposed by men they did not respect. Again listen to Ralph Waldo Emerson, egging the people on, "Let me admonish you, first of all, to go alone; to refuse the good models; even those, which are carried in the imagination of men. . . ."

All societies require a system of rules, restraints, and limits. And in America during the 1850s breaking the rules became the rule. It undermined the sense of community, which is bound together by a shared sense of values. According to Walter Bagehot, the shrewd English journalist, writing about the situation in America, "The unpleasantness of mob government has never been exemplified so conspicuously . . ." So, the "mob," the great beast the Federalists feared, had finally shown its ugly head.

In 1860 the Republicans nominated Abe Lincoln, an obscure wanna-be senator from Illinois, who symbolized the North's growing revulsion to slavery along with its sympathetic recognition of the expanding industrial economy. The Democrats nominated Senator Stephen Douglas, also of Illinois. Southern delegates, remembering Douglas's opposition to letting "slave" Kansas into the Union, perceived this as a Northern tilt in the party and bolted. They chose their own candidate, John Breckinridge, and this virtually guaranteed a Lincoln victory.

In 1860 Lincoln's new Republican Party seized the day. Lincoln turned the tables on the Democrats and exploited its contradiction in trying to be both the party of individual freedom and the party sympathetic to slavery. He tore into their soul, taking away their core issue, "individual freedom," thus outflanking them from the left. The new Republicans combined Jeffersonian ideas of freedom with a Hamiltonian tilt toward commercialism. To further sweeten the pot they offered settlers a free homestead, 160 acres of public land, neutralizing the agrarian issue. The Republicans had co-opted both the right and the left. They had become the party of freedom . . . and the party of commerce; the party of

Jefferson . . . and the party of Hamilton; the party of the people . . . and the party of business; the party of labor . . . and the party of capital. Lincoln's Republican Party left no room for any credible opposing vision.

Although Lincoln collected only 40 percent of the vote, it was enough to swamp Douglas and two other opponents in the Electoral College. To the South the future looked bleak. With the reins of government in the hands of an antislavery party, totally unsympathetic to the land of Dixie, there appeared to be almost no chance of redressing the growing political imbalance. There would not even be attempts to try to pull a "Cuba" out of a hat. Faced with the prospect of permanent minority status in American politics, South Carolina bolted and the other Southern states soon followed. The Jacksonian paradigm split wide open and into the breach marched two rival armies—one dressed in blue and dedicated to holding the Union together and the other in gray, determined to maintain a genteel way of life—and began the longest and bloodiest war in the nation's history.

All the shouting in the 1850s, all the historians of the twentieth century, all the teachers in public school, tell us the Civil War was about slavery. Yet when someone says this is not about money . . . rest assured . . . it's about money! When someone says it's not about sex . . . you can depend on it . . . it's about sex! Let's try it the other way. When everyone tells us the War Between the States was about slavery . . . think again . . . Perhaps it wasn't about slavery. Though not articulated at the time, it was about the nation's vision of what the future should be. It was about the wealth and power of the once formidable South being slowly eclipsed by the brash and virile North. It was about the end of the role that cotton was playing as the chief ingredient in the commercial process and the beginning of the railroad as the new engine of industrial progress. It was about 18 free states and only 15 slave states. It was about a way of life that depended on the soil for its wealth being out of tune with a world that was dancing to an upcoming marriage of industry with new forms of transportation. And, oh yes, it was about slavery. Slavery was the whip used to beat the South into submission. And the South playing its part, assigned by the great choreographer of history, eagerly teased the North on.

The fourth political model lasted from 1828 to 1860. The Jacksonians, in returning to the ideas of Thomas Jefferson and his colleagues, extended and fortified the nation's impulse toward democracy. They fought against privilege and befriended the common man. Their agenda included an "extend the frontier policy," removing the Indians and making more land available to the ordinary citizen, getting rid of the national bank, gradually lowering protective tariffs on imports, and cutting government expenditures. Polk, Pierce, and Buchanan all adhered to the Jacksonian policies. Minority presidents Tyler, Taylor, and Fillmore provided only temporary interruptions in the direction the country was traveling.

The Jackson paradigm was much longer than the prior three. But during its entire 32-year span the minority party, the Whigs, were in control of the White House for just 8 years. And in only 4 did they also have a majority in at least one house of Congress to help with agenda setting.

TABLE 5

Second Political Paradigm (1801–1815), 14 Years

Election of:	Majority Paradigm Party Republicans		Minority Paradigm Party Federalists	
Paradigm	Electoral Votes		Electoral Votes	
1800 Begins	Thomas Jefferson*	73	John Adams	65
1804 Preliminary	Thomas Jefferson	162	Charles Pinckney	14
1808 Confirmed	James Madison	122	Charles Pinckney	47
1812	James Madison	128	DeWitt Clinton	89
1815 Ends	Madison reinvents self and party (New Nationalism)			
*Bold = winner.				

	Republicans		Federalists	
Congress	House	Senate	House	Senate
7th 1801–1803	**69***	**18**	36	14
8th 1803–1805	**102**	**25**	39	9
9th 1805–1807	**116**	**27**	25	7
10th 1807–1809	**118**	**28**	24	6
11th 1809–1811	**94**	**28**	48	6
12th 1811–1813	**108**	**30**	36	6
13th 1813–1815	**112**	**27**	68	9

*__Bold__ = in control of House or Senate.

Source: Composition of 7th–13th Congress: *Encyclopedia of American History*

Years in the White House with control of at least one house of Congress:
   Democratic-Republicans: 14
   Federalists: 0

Economic Policies
- National bank charter lapsed
- No internal improvements
- Federal taxes eliminated
- Large portion of debt paid off

Other Important Events
- Size of army and navy cut
- Embargo Act directed at France and England
- Replaced by Non-Intercourse Act and Macon's Bill Number 2
- War of 1812
- Americans barred from participation in slave trade

Agrarian Policies
- Louisiana Purchase
- Western Florida taken from Spain
- Indian removal program suggested
- Price of a homestead reduced
- Tecumseh defeated in battle of Tippecanoe

TABLE 6

Third Political Paradigm (1815–1829), 13 years

Election of:	Majority Paradigm Party Republicans		Minority Paradigm Party Federalists/National Republicans	
Paradigm	**Electoral votes**		**Electoral votes**	
1815 Begins /Mid-term	**James Madison***			
1816 Preliminary	**James Monroe**	183	Rufus King	34
1820 Confirmed	**James Monroe**	231	unopposed	1
Paradigm	**% of Popular Vote**		**% of Popular Vote**	
1824	Andrew Jackson	41	**J. Q. Adams***	31
1828 Ends				

***Bold** = winner.

	Republicans		Federalists/National Republicans	
Congress	**House**	**Senate**	**House**	**Senate**
14th 1815–1817	**117***	**25**	65	11
15th 1817–1819	**141**	**34**	42	10
16th 1819–1821	**156**	**35**	27	7
17th 1821–1823	**158**	**44**	25	4
18th 1823–1825	**187**	**44**	26	4
19th 1825–1827	97	20	**105**	**26**
20th 1827–1829	**119**	**28**	94	20

***Bold** = in control.

Source: Composition of 14th–20th Congress: *Encyclopedia of American History*

Years in the White House with control of at least one house of Congress:

   Democratic-Republicans: 10
   Federalists / National Republicans: 2

Economic Policies
• Second national bank chartered
• Steep increases in tariff: in 1816 and 1828; tariff of "Abominations"
• Taxes collected

Other Important Events
• Size of standing army and navy increased
• Missouri Compromise
• Monroe doctrine
• Panic of 1819 followed by depression of early 1820s

Agrarian Policies
• Florida acquired from Spain
• Indians pushed westward
• Purchase price of land cut

TABLE 7

Fourth Political Paradigm (1829–1861), 32 years

Election of:	Majority Paradigm Party		Minority Paradigm Party	
	Democrats		National Republicans/Whigs/Republicans	
Paradigm	% of Popular Vote		% of Popular Vote	
1828 Begins	**Andrew Jackson***	56	John Q. Adams/NR	44
1832 Preliminary	**Andrew Jackson**	54	Henry Clay/NR	37
1836 Confirmed	**Martin Van Buren**	51	William H. Harrison/W	37
1840 Lose election	Martin Van Buren	47	**William H. Harrison/W**	
			John Tyler—VP	53
1844 Restored	**James Polk**	49	Henry Clay/W	48
1848 Lose election	Lewis Cass	43	**Zachary Taylor/W**	
			Millard Fillmore—VP	47
1852 Restored	**Franklin Pierce**	51	Winfield Scott/W	44
1856	**James Buchanan**	45	John Frémont/R	33
1860 Ends				

*Bold = winner.

	Democrats			NR/W/R/()other	
Congress	House	Senate		House	Senate
21st	1829–1831	**139***	**26**	74	22
22d	1831–1833	**141**	**25**	58(14)	21(2)
23d	1833–1835	**147**	20†	53(60)	20(8)
24th	1835–1837	**145**	**27**	98	25
25th	1837–1839	108†	**30**	107(24)	18(4)
26th	1839–1841	**124**	**28**	118	22
27th	1841–1843	102	22	**133(6)**	**28(2)**
28th	1843–1845	**142**	25	79(1)	**28(1)**
29th	1845–1847	**143**	**31**	77(6)	25
30th	1847–1849	108	**36**	**115(4)**	21(1)
31st	1849–1851	112†	**35**	109(9)	25(2)
32d	1851–1853	**140**	**35**	88(5)	24(3)
33d	1853–1855	**159**	**38**	71(4)	22(2)
34th	1855–1857	83†	**40**	108(43)	15(5)
35th	1857–1859	118†	**36**	92(26)	20(8)
36th	1859–1861	92†	**36**	114(31)	26(4)

*Bold = in control of House or Senate: more than all other parties combined. Senate tie goes to president's party.

†No party controls.

Years in the White House with control of at least one house of Congress:
Democrats: 24
Whigs/Republicans: 4

Source: Composition of 21st–36th Congress: *Encyclopedia of American History*

Economic Policies
- National bank scuttled
- Tariff lowered: Walker tariff reduction
- Independent Treasury
- National debt paid off
- Jackson vetoed Maysville Road Bill: no internal improvements

Other Important Events
- Depression of 1837
- Nullification crises
- Wilmot Proviso
- Gold discovered in California
- Compromise of 1850
- Kansas-Nebraska Act
- Bleeding Kansas
- Dred Scott decision

Agrarian Policies
- Liberal land policies/Preemption Act (1841)
- Indian removal
- Acquired Texas, California, Oregon, and New Mexico

Minority Party
- Raised tariff
- Repealed Independent Treasury
- Attempted to introduce internal improvements

IV

The Great Transition

On the morning of April 12, 1861, Southern artillery at Charleston, South Carolina, opened fire on Fort Sumter and the War Between the States began. A loose agrarian confederacy of about 6 million people with an additional 3½ million slaves challenged a Federal Union with a population of more than 20 million. On the surface it seemed foolhardy. The states of the Union commanded an immense superiority in men, money, railroads, and industrial potential. Ninety-two percent of the nation's manufacturing, 97 percent of firearms production, and 70 percent of the country's thirty thousand miles of railroads were situated in the North. The Union navy was incomparably superior and fully capable of bottling up the South's harbors, which would drastically reduce imports from Europe. Who could doubt that the forces representing the coming industrialism would beat out the dying vestiges of an agrarian society?

But . . . the South was not that foolish. To win, the Union had to conduct an aggressive war that few Northerners wanted to wage. On the other hand, the Confederacy merely had to deny the Union victories until a war-weary people of the North tired of the struggle and let the Southern states go their own way. Southerners also felt they had an ace in the hole: "King Cotton." They were the world's largest exporter of cotton. Surely Great Britain and France would not let the North prevent Southern cotton supplies from flowing across the Atlantic. Finally, the rebels, in their heart of hearts, believed that any man from the land of Dixie could lick five Yankees. In early 1861 a Union victory was certainly not a foregone conclusion.

The South was able to hang on for four long years and make heroic but futile charges against the superior manpower and firepower of the North. And for one brief moment in July of 1863 the dream of Southern independence seemed within reach. General Robert E. Lee and his men in gray crossed the Mason-Dixon Line and invaded the North. They were maneuvering into position to attack Washington, Baltimore, or Philadelphia. Alexander Stephens, vice-president of the Confederacy, was proceeding toward Washington, under a flag of truce, to open peace negotiations on the basis of Southern independence.

The two armies met at Gettysburg, Pennsylvania, and for one day Lee's soldiers clearly had the upper hand. On the third day Lee sent General George Pickett with 15,000 men directly against the heavily fortified center of the Union line. Under a barrage of Union artillery and rifle fire brave Southern soldiers dropped like flies. At day's end more than 6,000 sons of the South lay strewn on the battlefield. As a demoralized Confederate army retreated from the field of combat, a saddened General Robert E. Lee looked back and said, "It's been a sad day for us . . . I never saw troops behave more magnificently than Pickett's division . . . had they been supported . . . the Confederates could have held that position and the day would have been ours." Then after a pause, in a loud voice, "Too bad! Too bad! Oh, too bad!" Finally, in April 1865, after more than 600,000 men had given their lives, the guns of the Civil War fell silent.

Less than one week later, on April 14, Abraham Lincoln was dead, shot in a theater by a Southern sympathizer. While the nation was in mourning, a special train carrying the black-draped casket of the nation's martyr made its slow, circuitous journey through the principal cities of the North on its way to Springfield, Illinois. More than a million men and women lined the way to take a final look at the face in the casket.

Who was Abraham Lincoln: a bumbling second-rate politician, as most had thought a mere nine months earlier, or the great savior of the nation? Had his goal been to save the Union or end the institution of slavery? Had he set a direction for governing that would survive him and provide for a fifth political paradigm, or had he merely led a nation at war?

About Lincoln: Two important things! First, he was completely and thoroughly the politician, and a very ambitious one at that. According to William Herndon, Lincoln's law partner, "he was always calculating and planning ahead. His ambition was a little engine that knew no rest." He was constantly reading, arguing, and debating the political issues of his day. All his adult life Lincoln was busy as either a state assemblyman, congressman, behind-the-scenes political operator, or office seeker, except for a five-year period, when his political prospects were discouraging. Second, up until the mid-1850s he had been a loyal card-carrying. Whig who firmly believed in the party's agenda. In 1856, after the breakup of the Whigs, Lincoln, along with the bulk of the Northern wing of his party, transferred his allegiance to the new Republican Party.

The war, to Lincoln, was not fought to end slavery, nor to guarantee equal rights to all men, but to restore the Union. At the beginning of his first term, Lincoln defined the struggle between the states as one to preserve the Union . . . and from that conception he never wavered, although he would make tactical concessions to those who thought abolishing slavery was the most important reason for the struggle.

In an effort to conciliate the South before the first guns opened fire, he concurred with a congressional proposal for a constitutional amendment guaranteeing that the federal government would never interfere with slavery where it already existed. As the war dragged on and people in the North were becoming discouraged, as Britain and France flirted with recognizing the South, as radical sentiment grew stronger and a majority in his own party were beating the drums for abolition, Lincoln reversed course and reluctantly issued the famous Emancipation Proclamation. This freed the slaves . . . however, only in the states that were in rebellion against the Union. The slaves in the loyal Border States were expressly omitted. As the London "Spectator" gibed, "A human being cannot own another, UNLESS he is loyal to the United States." This was not a particularly zealous antislaver.

Although preoccupied with the war, Lincoln and his administration still found time to pursue the correct Whig pro–economic growth policies. In 1862 his party passed the strongly protective Morrill Tariff, which was scaled up so that by 1864 duties averaged 47 percent, the highest, so far, in the nation's history. There were subsidies to build telegraph and cable lines, and enormous tracts of public land were given to the railroads to support their construction of a transcontinental railroad. In the following year Congress set up a national banking system, which supported the country's first uniform national currency and eliminated the worst excesses of the ramshackle state banking system inherited from the Jacksonians. Banks were able to issue paper money, greenbacks. And, during the war they did—lots of them. The result was a huge wartime inflation. There were also steep tax increases, including an income tax, to help fund the war effort. To round out Lincoln's program, the Republicans also approved a Homestead Act in 1862, intended to encourage settlement of the West by providing free land to settlers.

During the whole of Lincoln's term, he was immensely unpopular. To the people of his day he appeared ineffectual. He seemed hopelessly incompetent as an administrator. Corruption ran rife within his administration. Most of the leading newspapers were violently anti-Lincoln from his election in 1860 until the morning of April 15, 1865. His own party members thought him too slow, too cautious, and too indecisive. His policies appeared confused. In fact, as he himself said, "My policy is to have no policy." Had he not been reelected, he probably would have been written off as one of the great failures of the American political system—the man who presided over a graft-ridden administration and who conducted an incompetent and ineffectual attempt to subjugate the Southern states. And throughout much of 1864 it looked like Lincoln would not be reelected.

In early 1864 Ulysses S. Grant was given command of the eastern campaign and began a march on Richmond, the South's capital. In a series of futile assaults against Lee's lines, he lost sixty thousand men in six weeks' time without being able to open a road to Richmond. Grant's soldiers, recognizing the slaughter they were being led to, took to writing their names and addresses on slips of paper and pinning them on their uniforms before going into battle, so their corpses could be better identified. Meanwhile, after having reached the outskirts of Atlanta, General Sherman's campaign had bogged down. As casualty lists lengthened and victories became infrequent, morale in the North plummeted and Lincoln's chances for reelection looked dismal. Nearly every important member of the Republican Party doubted the advisability of a second term for Lincoln. Even after he was nominated, some leading members of his party, thinking Lincoln a sure loser, maneuvered to call a new Republican convention, in the summer of 1864, to reconsider his candidacy. Lincoln, himself, confessed privately that he would probably be defeated.

However, in the fall of 1864 Northern military successes changed the political equation. Sherman took Atlanta and set out on a march through the heart of the South, destroying everything in his path. Naturally, Lincoln's political situation improved. In the fall of that year the ex-Whig politician from Illinois became the first president since Andrew Jackson to win reelection, and his majority of 55 percent was substantial indeed and suggested an emerging Lincoln paradigm was taking root. Five months later, in April 1865, Lee surrendered. And days later Abraham Lincoln, the president who had won the War Between the States, was dead.

Men swept up in grief took another look at Lincoln, and the vacillating ex-Whig, not up to handling the top job in the country, suddenly became a great statesman who had saved the nation. He had kept his faith in the course he set when all about him were losing courage. He had exercised great power and unlike most leaders had not become intoxicated with it. His lack of action, his shifts in direction, his being on both sides of all questions . . . why, they were merely political diversions to keep Northern support for the war intact. All along he had been moving with muffled oars toward his distant objective of preserving the Union. He was able to communicate his vision, "that Americans were a chosen people, selected to conduct an experiment in self-government, and the Civil War was a test case in the viability of that undertaking," to the people of the North. This inspired them to endure the enormous human and economic cost of the war and fight on. In the end the nation, which Lincoln described as "the last, best hope of earth," had not split apart; the United States stood, not as a loose confederation of sovereign states but tall and strong as one indivisible nation. And that was enough to ensure his greatness. He was, said *Punch*, the British journal, "a true-born king of men."

After the war the most pressing issue was how to mend the breach between the states. The question was, who should control the reins of the South's restored state governments, uneducated black voters or former traitors? A president who has won reelection with a majority of the popular vote has a mandate from the people, and normally a successor will follow his policies. However, Lincoln's views on reconstruction were constantly changing and he was killed before he set forth a final and comprehensive plan for bringing the rebellious states back into the fold. His lenient program of amnesty and reconstruction, without addressing the issue of Negro suffrage, in occupied Louisiana and Arkansas during the war, along with his spoken words "with malice toward none and charity for all . . . to bind the nation's wounds," certainly suggested a conciliatory policy. Furthermore, Lincoln refused to sign a much harsher congressional reconstruction bill, claiming he hadn't had enough time to study so important a measure before Congress adjourned.

On the flip side, after examining the bill Lincoln proclaimed it "as one very proper plan for the loyal people of any state choosing to adopt it." Nor could the members of his party disregard the fact that Lincoln, a very practical politician, was coming around to the viewpoint that the political survival of the Republican Party would depend on the black vote. The calculus of politics indicated that once the Southern states came back in the fold there would be about a million new white voters and hardly any were likely to vote Republican. In 1860 Lincoln had failed to get a single vote in 10 of the Confederate states. Without Negro suffrage the new Southern votes could easily overwhelm the 400,000 majority the Republicans had achieved in 1864. As on most things during Lincoln's presidency, there was grist for each side.

Andrew Johnson, Lincoln's vice-president, was an outsider to the Republican Party. Johnson had been a Democrat and the one remaining Southern senator. He was put on the ticket during the dark moments in the spring of 1864 when the idea of presenting a fusion ticket in order to stave off an electoral defeat seemed compelling. Taking his cue from what he thought was Lincoln's intention, he adopted a conciliatory policy toward the South. He proposed a general amnesty without confiscation of property or Negro suffrage. Southern states quickly took Johnson up on his generous offer and called state conventions. The resulting state constitutions limited suffrage to whites. State legislatures proceeded to pass "black codes," aimed at curtailing the rights and activities of the newly freed slaves. A number of ex–Confederate leaders were elected to Congress in the fall of 1865. To people in the North it looked as if the Democratic Party, whose miscalculations had led to the Civil War, would attain a majority in both houses of Congress and regain control of the political process. The North and the Republican Party would be cheated of the full fruits of their victory.

History does not provide many examples of a victorious nation turning over control of the government to the leaders of a defeated rebellion. A group of Republicans in Congress, called Radicals, could not stomach the idea of ex-rebels returning to power in the South and proposed a militant plan to punish the South and make sure the former slaves attained political suffrage. They also claimed this was the path Lincoln would have chosen had he lived. Surely, they rationalized, he would have wanted to fulfill a moral obligation to the freedman. But more so was their aim to create a flourishing Republican Party in the South to help maintain their grip on government.

To further challenge Johnson, they passed the Fourteenth Amendment, guaranteeing equal rights for the Negro. Johnson opposed the amendment and the entire radical reconstruction program and took the issue to the country during the 1866 midterm elections. The Radical Republicans won an overwhelming majority and used their weight to push through their reconstruction program. Quickly they passed a series of Acts that placed the South under military rule, based readmission on guarantees that "loyal" men would displace the Confederate elite in positions of power, and provided for black citizenship.

Not only were the blacks to be given their freedom, but also civil and political equality. Never before had so large a body of people, ungroomed for the responsibilities of citizenship, attained civil and political rights in such a short period of time. It implied a radical revolution of the whole social system of the South, threatening to upend and force reorganization of millions of lives. The old leaders, having lost their political rights, were on their way down, while the black former slaves were on their way up. Freedom went to the heads of some blacks. They thought that the coming of the "Jubilee" was at hand and with it the promise to put the bottom rung of society on top. Southern leaders trembled with fear that the white South would be put under the heel of a black South. Johnson as a Southerner was sympathetic to the plight of the ex-Confederates and sought to thwart the will of Congress by administering the Reconstruction Acts in an obstructive fashion, dismissing radical sympathizers and countermanding the orders of generals in charge of the Southern districts. This provoked the most serious clash in the history of relations between the executive and legislative branches of the federal government. In late 1867 Congress maneuvered Johnson into violating the Tenure of Office Act, which had denied the president the right to remove a public official appointed by Congress, and impeached him. After a three-month trial in the Senate he was acquitted by the margin of one vote.

The post–Civil War period, the latter part of the nineteenth century, was less about politics and more about a great change that was going on in the American economy. It was about an unprecedented transition from an agricultural to an industrial society. The Civil War had overturned the last barriers to rapid industrialization. With the Southern planters, the vanguard of an agrarian society, removed from political power, no one was able to hold the impulse to industrialization, which had been gathering force for decades, in check. As the government tended more and more to reflect the wishes of the industrial class, the floodgates to rapid business growth opened. And pouring through came a group of bold, adventurous, and acquisitive men. Andrew Carnegie, John D. Rockefeller, J. P. Morgan, Edward Harriman, Thomas Edison, along with a couple of thousand other lesser "captains of industry," seized upon a series of inventions and innovations and used them as vehicles to fame and fortune. Railroads were flung across mountain barriers, telegraph lines were strung across the country, cables were stretched from continent to continent, and factories sprang up overnight. A national transportation network encouraged businessmen to seek countrywide markets for their products, and soon the nation's shelves were stocked with an incredible variety of goods. Year after year America's appetite for the products turned out by her industrial machine grew until it appeared insatiable. As men and women from every hamlet and farm poured into the centers of industry, cities mushroomed. By the early 1870s **it was apparent that wealth-seeking behavior was becoming the dominant aspect of American life.**

In 1882 Thomas Edison flicked a switch and the nation came alive in light . . . and this changed the habits of centuries. Electricity could now light a lamp, illuminate a skyscraper, pull a streetcar, run a sewing machine, or power a mammoth assembly line. During the brief 35 years after the Civil War, gross national product grew fivefold, the standard of living more than doubled, and railroad mileage in the United States expanded from 35,000 to over 190,000, surpassing mileage in all of Europe. By 1900 America had become the leading industrial nation in the world and the signs of prosperity were everywhere. Forty percent of its citizens lived in cities. Carnegie Steel was the largest industrial company in the world, employing twenty thousand workers and producing more steel than all of Great Britain.

Yet during this time, which was called the Gilded Age, there was a dark side. There were no restraints on industrialism. The railroads were gaining tremendous power, and their pricing structure could discriminate between communities and businesses. The trusts (mighty corporate monopolies) also were becoming too powerful and using their bigness to fix prices, rig markets, and hoodwink consumers. The titans of industry considered buying government favors as part of the cost of doing business. Tariffs and subsidies were used to protect their industries and their wealth. Very little was done in response to these predatory practices, and what little was done was ineffectual. The idealism of the prewar years had burnt out in the flames of war and reconstruction.

Post–Civil War politicians appeared particularly unable to handle the problems resulting from the transition to an industrial society. The presidents of this era are usually dismissed as a group of political pygmies. They are called the spoilsmen, that is, men who were more interested in perpetuating the spoils of power than enacting real honest to goodness legislation to help the men and women in the country. During the whole of the period 1865–1901 not one political hero emerges on the scene to help the country cope with the new economic realities. Not one Jefferson! Nor a Jackson! Where had all our heroes gone?

There were good reasons politicians of this period appeared impotent. Following the Civil War neither party felt confident enough to step out front and take on the big issues. The Democrats had been discredited as the party whose foolish policies had gotten us into a bitter and destructive Civil War. They needed to rebuild political legitimacy and were not about to take bold new stands.

As for the Republicans, they were a new, young party, still wet behind the ears, and had not yet solidified their political grip on the country. They lacked a dependable base of loyal followers; in fact, they were not sure of who their constituency was. Lincoln had welded together a diverse group of followers who were deeply divided on most questions. He had spoken with sincerity for Jeffersonian principles and had drawn in a large number of antislavers attracted to the human rights issue, men with an exalted sense of idealism and high purpose. But he also supported Hamiltonian measures to promote economic growth, and this attracted a big following in the expanding new industrial class. The post–Civil War Republican Party was both the party of idealistic reformers and the party sympathetic to "big" business.

But most important, their leader was dead, killed before he had issued marching orders to his followers, and before a successor was anointed. Voters had had eight years to view the policies of Washington, Jefferson, and Jackson and gave approval in two successive elections. And each time there was an heir, who already knew in which direction to lead, and voters knew what to expect.

After the Civil War there was no such legacy! The Republicans had not yet presented a clear-cut policy that had won back-to-back voter approval; nor was there a legitimate successor waiting in the wings to faithfully follow through on the paradigm-setting policies. In trying to be on both sides of the important issues, Lincoln had left the Republican Party confused and without direction. He had said Republicans "are for man and the dollar, but in case of conflict **man** comes before the dollar." But Lincoln also strongly believed that the test of the nation's democracy was its ability to provide opportunities for social ascent to those born in its lower ranks. And he thought Industrial Capitalism the best vehicle. It was, he said, "the just, and generous, and prosperous system, which opens the way to all—gives hope to all." In a world undergoing tumultuous change, Republican presidents would have to find their own way without guidance from Lincoln, and this would be no easy matter. Too bad . . . too bad . . . oh, too bad!

Complicating matters was the fact that the rapid industrial takeoff was a recent phenomenon, untested by time, and people of that day were by no means certain that it would take on a self-renewing life of its own. Naturally they were cautious and resistant to new ideas that might tamper with what they thought the formula for economic success. Just what was that success formula? To the people of the late nineteenth century there were three main pillars holding up their economic structure: the high protective tariff, hard money, and the "iron law of wages."

Almost everyone recognized that some tariff barriers were needed to protect American industries from cheap foreign imports. These barriers enabled American manufacturers to compete successfully with their European competitors and to pile up fabulous profits. This, of course, made it easier to recruit new entrepreneurs, which was very important in a developing economy. Speaking in the 1880s, James Blaine, probably the most popular figure in post–Civil War politics, said "all the wonders of the previous twenty years were the work of high tariff schedules." In accordance with traditional Whig doctrine, Lincoln had raised the tariff schedules to their highest levels in American history. No Republican president would deviate from that high tariff policy during the late nineteenth century, except temporarily to gain an electoral advantage.

The second important pillar was hard money. That meant a currency that did not expand too rapidly. Most economists of the period shared the belief that the gold standard was the only basis for a sound currency and stable prices. When there is general confidence that a dollar today will be worth a dollar tomorrow people will be more inclined to save and businessmen will be more apt to build a factory.

On the other side of the money question were the people who thought the nation's supply of gold didn't provide a sufficiently large or flexible basis for the money needs of a growing economy. They wanted to expand the supply of money, so as to ensure a rising price level, which they believed would increase business activity and ensure prosperity. Early in the period they simply sought to issue more paper money, that is, greenbacks. By the late 1870s the issue was seen as more complicated and the money inflationists focused on the free and unlimited coinage of silver dollars, which would expand the amount of money in circulation. The chief problem with "free silver" was that the rest of the industrial world had abandoned it as a monetary metal. If the United States was alone in adopting it, much of the world's supply would probably find its way to our shores, and this could be very, very inflationary. Yet "free silver" would be one of the most important issues in politics for the following 20 years. As time went on and the price level continued sinking, more and more people would be drawn to the arguments of the inflationists.

The third pillar was a general acceptance of the "iron law of wages," which meant workers sold their labor just like any other commodity; supply and demand, not the welfare of the workers, would dictate wages. Labor organizations that allowed workers to bargain for their wages as a group were not to be allowed. Naturally, this gave the bosses the upper hand and essentially guaranteed "cheap labor." Most politicians, Democrats and Republicans alike, believed that cheap labor was an important component of capitalism, similar to the way twenty-first-century Americans view cheap oil as necessary to ensure the smooth working of our industrial engine. Cheap labor allowed businessman to keep their costs down, which in turn made profits easier to come by, enticing more players into the game of business.

Of course, this meant that the working class was assigned to the bottom stratum of the nation's social structure. But this dovetailed nicely with a great reorganization of society, based on the principle of economic growth, that was taking place in late-nineteenth-century America. Social structures, in general, are built around the talents and skills necessary for the growth or survival of a society. Traditionally those who have such talents or skills, or who society thought had them, get the lion's share of the wealth and power. As society's energies focused on economic development those who had made significant contributions to the nation's industrial economy were becoming a new aristocracy. The talent of being a business innovator was replacing talents that in former times had been in the political, military, or religious spheres.

If you didn't have the skills, or motivation, or discipline, or confidence, or were unfamiliar with American ways, you belonged in a lower layer. Remarkably, this change in the social power structure was peaceful. This was because people, in general, believed the game to be fair. They saw economic life as a race that was won by the ablest runner. Besides, the immense business and economic opportunities were creating an expanding middle class, which was sprouting in size beyond anything the world had ever seen before. If you didn't make it into a top spot, the chance of eventually making it into the middle layer was fairly good. This opportunity for advancement gave the workers hope and wedded them to the system. Late-nineteenth-century America was regressing back toward a class system, not unlike those in times past, wherein the chief determinant of an individual's status was the class he belonged to.

Yet hanging over American society like a dark cloud was apprehension that the laboring class might not go quietly to the bottom layer. Many upper- and middle-class Americans were aware of the mass uprisings by the dispossessed in Europe. Trade unions and socialists had played an important role in the mass revolt of 1848 and again in 1871, in Paris, when workers took to the barricades and challenged the possessing classes. Urging them on was the socialist agitator Karl Marx, who after conducting an exhaustive analysis of capitalism reported that the workers were being exploited, that is, capitalists were underpaying them. Those revolts were put down, but only after some of the bloodiest urban fighting in history. It was not surprising labor unrest was able to strike at the heart of American society.

When the Republicans met in 1868 to select their leader, they recognized the stakes were large. To become the dominant party they would have to find a way to transform Lincoln's popularity into a legacy. The Republicans chose Ulysses S. Grant, head of the victorious Union army and Lincoln's favorite general, to lead them. He won by over 300,000 votes, and a heavy black Republican vote in the South may well have been the decisive factor. It confirmed a Lincoln paradigm had been established.

Grant continued the policy of radical reconstruction. He was truly outraged by the terrorism in the South, as secret societies, such as the Ku Klux Klan (KKK), intimidated and terrorized black voters to ensure white supremacy. He warned Southern whites that the national government would not tolerate overt violence and he pushed Congress to enact a series of Enforcement Acts, which he used to crush the Klan. He also used the federal troops to purge Southern legislatures of undependable members and overturned the duly elected Democratic governments in five Southern states, thereby keeping those states in the radical ranks.

Grant followed the traditional Republican pro-business growth policies from Lincoln's administration. He defended high tariffs, abolished most wartime taxes, including the income tax, and under his direction the Republican Party passed a rash of legislation designed to give encouragement and direction to the nation's economic development.

By 1872 there was news of emerging scandals in Washington, D.C. Although Grant was not personally involved in any of the scandals, many of his aides and comrades were. The most prominent scandal involved Credit Mobilier, a construction company, with a fancy French name, that served as a fraudulent device to channel money from the massive federal land grants received by the Union Pacific Railroad. To make sure no questions were asked, the directors of Credit Mobilier had distributed stock to influential politicians all over Washington, including Vice President Schuyler Colfax. Then there was Orville Babcock, the president's private secretary, who had conspired with distillers to defraud the government of millions of dollars in liquor taxes. Not to forget Secretary of War William Belknap, who took bribes from the sale of Indian trading posts.

A breakaway Republican group of high-minded reformers, disgusted with the corruption and wanting reform, teamed up with the Democrats to oppose Grant for a second term. They were committed to "honest government," tariff reduction, civil service reform, an end to government subsidies for the railroads, and sectional reconciliation. But the general moved swiftly to head them off. Expressing dissatisfaction with the spoils system, he pressured Congress into creating a Civil Service Reform Commission and made one of his chief critics, William Curtis, its chairman. Next Grant had Congress rush through a bill reducing the tariff by about 10 percent. As a result of his deflating these two key liberal issues, a sizable number of the reformers remained in Grant's camp and he won a sweeping victory, capturing 55 percent of the popular vote. After the election Congress repealed the tariff reduction and the reform commission was scuttled. So much for reform!

Early on, Grant committed to the payment of all government obligations in gold. But during his second term he fully took on the money question. There was much concern about the huge supply of greenbacks printed during the war, which were still sloshing through the economy. While it had helped facilitate the boom Americans were experiencing, there was worry that it might precipitate galloping inflation much like that the country had encountered during the war.

In 1873 Congress ended silver coinage and to make the point that he was firmly on the side of sound money Grant vetoed the Inflation Bill of 1874, which would have modestly increased the amount of paper money in circulation. In 1875 he backed the Specie Resumption Act, which committed the banks to paying off the greenbacks in gold. It meant a return to the gold standard. However, showing a willingness to compromise, the Civil War general allowed the effective date to be pushed back to January 1879.

Naturally these measures contracted the supply of money and cast a deflationary pall over the economy. In fact, the period from the mid-1870s to the mid-1890s was to be a time of severe downward price pressure. The wholesale price index, which stood at 174 in 1866, fell to 82 in 1890—a chilling decline of more than 50 percent. But to be fair, because the movement to a sound money basis had been worldwide, all the industrializing countries of the world experienced deep deflation during the last quarter of the nineteenth century. The United States needed a "hard money" policy if it hoped to play an important part in international trade. During this time the government also had immense surpluses in revenue, reaching an annual average of $100 million in the 1880s, and this, no doubt, also contributed to the downward pressure on the price index.

Soon after Grant's reelection another depression began, the first since the nation had become industrialized, and it undermined public confidence in the Republican Party. During the general's second term his administration was plagued by a series of major investigations and the stench of corruption reached into the White House. As it became clear that close friends and personal staff were involved, the president did everything he could to block further investigation.

By election time 1876 the country was in its third year of intractable depression. Business activity had declined by about a quarter, and many industrial plants were shut down. Over half the railroads were in default on their bonds, and tramps began to swarm the countryside. It also had become evident that Grant had gone too far in his clumsy attempts to intervene and protect his friends, even in the corrupt America of the 1870s. The Grant administration was thoroughly discredited and in a shambles.

Nonetheless, during his eight years at the helm Grant was committed to the business revolution that was taking place and staunchly upheld the three pillars of economic success. Nor was he too embarrassed to use the power of government, ruthlessly if necessary, to ensure that the Republican Party stayed on top.

The Grant administration has been tainted by the smell of corruption. Yet it was this president who cleared up the confusion following Lincoln's death. Grant ignored the reformers and gave the new Republican Party unambiguous marching orders, in the direction of economic growth, and the business class would be its ally.

Grant, the Union's most successful Civil War general, was able to break through the stalemate that had occurred on the battlefield. He had recognized the old military strategies weren't working and devised new strategies, which saved the day for the North. This same ability to recognize what is working and what isn't led the general to take on the reformers. He sensed the danger of attempting to tinker with an economy that his contemporaries did not fully understand but still was making America rich and powerful beyond people's wildest dreams. So instead of joining the reformers, this general led another charge, this time to make sure his party became wedded to Industrial Capitalism. According to his friend and fellow Civil War general William Tecumseh Sherman, "Grant's character was a mystery even to himself—a combination of strength and weakness not paralleled by any of whom I have read in Ancient or Modern history."

In 1876 the Grand Old Party rejected Grant's bid for a third term and instead nominated Rutherford Hayes, who had been untarnished by the scandals, to lead them. However, a majority of the people, 51 percent, voted for the Democrat, Samuel Tilden, and it appeared the Republican Party had to give up the keys to the White House. But not so fast! The Republicans were able to use their military muscle in the South to throw out thousands of Democratic votes and contest the results of the election in three key Southern states. A special election commission of seven Democrats and eight Republicans was appointed to settle the dispute, and naturally they decided in Hayes's favor. But it was still necessary to win congressional approval, and the Democrats controlled the House of Representatives. A compromise was reached. Hayes agreed to remove all federal troops from the South, allowing a reemergence of white supremacy and abandoning the freed blacks to their own efforts. In return the Republicans were able to hang on to the presidency for a fifth consecutive term.

Hayes entered the White House and tried to steer a course of "honest" government. However, he was dogged by a bad economy and opposition to reform within his own party. Not only Democrats but even many Republicans referred to him as "His

Fraudulency." In spite of this he was successful in placing some well-known reformers in high office and in ousting some of the corrupt politicians, including the future president Chester Arthur, who had been head of the corrupt New York custom-house. On the other hand, Hayes, like any other politician of his day, was not above dispensing patronage to the men who had put him in office.

It was clear that the American people had enough of punishing the South, and reconstruction was abandoned. Hayes continued an economic policy that emphasized high tariffs and hard money. He vetoed a measure to monetize a small amount of silver, but the bill passed anyway. During 1877, the worst year of the long depression, labor unrest reached a peak. In the summer of that year a railway strike that began in West Virginia brought violence that spread from state to state all the way to Illinois. In Pittsburgh a mob of strikers and sympathizers chased a group of state militia into the railroad roundhouse. The next morning the militia fought their way out and retreated from the city, leaving the mob in control. Pittsburgh was terrorized for three days; fatalities ran into the scores, and a wall of flames, three miles wide, destroyed every railroad car in the vicinity and almost leveled the city. At the request of several governors, Hayes sent in federal troops to restore order, and the strike collapsed. This action marked the first time in American history that the army was used on an extensive scale to crush a labor disturbance. The politicians of the late nineteenth century were truly frightened of labor unrest. According to W. M. Grosvenor, a prominent financial editor, who spoke for much of the business community, "the light of the flames at Pittsburgh" portended "a terrible trial for free institutions in the country. . . . The communist is here."

Hayes was not a candidate for reelection in 1880. The Republicans chose James Garfield, who benefited from an upturn in the economy and eked out a win over Democrat Winfield Hancock by less than one-tenth of 1 percent of the total vote. A few months later Garfield was killed by an assassin, and Vice-president Chester Arthur moved into the White House.

"My God! Chet Arthur," cried the liberals, the reformers, and the Democrats. Arthur had been chief of the corrupt New York custom-house until Hayes dismissed him two years earlier and was a crony of Roscoe Conkling, the head of the conservative, "Stalwart," wing of the Republican Party, which played the spoils system the hardest. Once in the White House, Arthur severed his connections with Conkling and his crowd, prosecuted the "Star Route" frauds in the post office, which had cost the government millions of dollars, and vetoed an unprecedented $18 million river and harbor bill. Although the Star Route prosecution failed and Congress passed the pork-barrel river and harbor measure over his veto, he won the appreciation of the reformers. Furthermore, he disappointed his former "Stalwart" cronies by coming out squarely for civil service reform. His administration passed the Pendleton Act to curb the corruption-breeding patronage in the federal bureaucracy. It required competitive examinations of applicants for many federal positions. Although the act initially affected only about fourteen thousand of some one hundred thousand government offices, it laid the basis for the later expansion of the civil service.

Like his predecessors, Arthur was friendly toward business and followed the traditional Republican economic program. In addition, he gave approval for the construction of a modern American navy. However, sensing that a Democrat might win the next election, he pushed Congress to enact the first general tariff reduction since the Civil War. Although he claimed it reduced duties by an average of 5 percent, a modest amount, it was so complex and contradictory that no one really knew what its true impact was. The party regulars did not take kindly to Arthur's newfound reformist tendencies and rejected his bid to head the ticket during the next election. Nonetheless, when his term was up the liberals and reformers in both parties would say, "Chet Arthur had done well . . . by not doing bad."

A Democratic Interlude

In 1884 the Republican Party turned to its most colorful and popular politician, James Blaine, the senator from Maine. The Democrats put up Grover Cleveland, the reform governor of New York, who won in a close election. Finally, after 24 long years in the wilderness, the Democrats had returned to the White House. Cleveland made a bold attempt to remake the Democrats as the party of commerce. He introduced a purer version of laissez-faire economics than the Republicans. He vetoed every bill that smacked of corruption, showing the courage to defy the groups that were using the government for selfish purposes. He called a halt to the raids on the Treasury by war veterans for pensions and disability pay, curtailed federal subsidies, and proposed a drastic cut in the tariff, the first since the sky-high duties of the 1860s. The tariff issue was to become the major campaign issue during the following election. His administration also passed the Interstate Commerce Act in an attempt to regulate the railroads in the public interest. It forbade rate discrimination, rebates, and other abuses. Although the Act was popularly regarded as a victory for the public, it lacked teeth and could not be effectively enforced in the courts.

A Republican Party Restoration

Harrison, with about one hundred thousand fewer votes than Grover Cleveland, won a majority in the Electoral College and restored the GOP to the White House in 1888. Harrison, who was the grandson of "Old Tippecanoe," the ninth president of the United States, tried to be an activist president. He attempted to answer the rising public clamor to do something about the trusts, and his administration passed the Sherman Anti-Trust Act. It was a confused effort to regulate the trusts, trying to harness big business without harming it, but like the earlier Interstate Commerce Act proved unenforceable.

His administration also passed the McKinley Tariff, which increased the rate schedule to a level higher than ever before. He granted pensions to all Union army veterans (the Dependent Pensions Act), stepped up spending on public improvements, and began a lavish dispersal of public monies to private groups. All told, government expenditures totaled nearly $1 billion. The rationale was that this huge outlay would help eliminate the big government surplus and stop the deflation. But the public wasn't buying. In the 1890 mid-term congressional elections the Democrats won a huge majority.

To win approval for the tariff hike the administration had compromised on the silver question. Congress passed the Sherman Silver Purchase Act, which committed the government to purchasing 4.5 million ounces of silver each month, virtually the entire output of the U.S. mines at the time, and to pay for it with silver certificates that could be redeemed for either gold or silver. But still it was not enough to raise the price level.

Another Democratic Party Interlude

In the election of 1892 Harrison met up with Cleveland once again. This time the Democrat won easily with a 380,000-vote plurality, the largest in 20 years. The Democrats carried both houses of Congress, and for the first time since the Civil War they controlled both the presidency and Congress. During that election a new third party emerged. The Populist Party captured nearly 9 percent of the popular vote and threatened to upset the balance between the two established political parties.

In the midst of widespread agrarian discontent a movement for reform arose in the farms of the Midwest. It centered on issues such as cheap money, the power of monopoly, and Wall Street conspiracies, all of which underscored the isolation and marginality of the little man in a rapidly industrializing society. The number one priority of these "Populists" was to pressure the government to adopt an inflationary monetary policy based on the free coinage of silver. They thought it would raise wages and crop prices and challenge the power of the gold overlords of the Northeast.

Cleveland returned to the White House on the eve of a financial crisis. The worst fears of the sound money crowd had been realized. Merchants were refusing to accept silver certificates, and holders were cashing them in for gold, eating into the reserves of the yellow metal. Gold reserves, which had totaled about $190 million in 1890, had fallen to the psychologically important $100 million level. Public confidence in the government's ability to fulfill its financial obligations was eroding. This precipitated panic on Wall Street, which shattered business confidence and sent the nation's economy reeling downward into another depression. Gold kept flowing out of the U.S. Treasury, threatening to disappear altogether. In desperation, Cleveland asked J. P. Morgan, the head of New York's most powerful banking house, to organize a sale of government bonds for gold. The Cleveland-Morgan deal finally reversed the flow of gold. But the terms had allowed the bankers to reap a huge profit and the Populists and agrarian Democrats seized upon it as proof positive that their suspicions of a Wall Street conspiracy, to rig the economy against them, was indeed correct.

Cleveland blamed the Sherman Silver Purchase Act and the McKinley Tariff—the mistakes of 1890—for the panic and made a frantic effort to get the country back on a sound money footing. He called Congress into special session and persuaded its members to repeal the Silver Act. Then he turned his attention to the tariff. But he was less successful in convincing Congress to lower duties. The final reduction was so modest that Cleveland refused to sign it, though he didn't veto it, either, and it became law.

However, neither measure was able to halt the swift downward spiral of business. By the end of the year more than 15,000 business firms had collapsed, five hundred banks had closed their doors, a quarter of the nation's railroad companies were under the control of bankruptcy courts, and one out of five workers were without jobs. Bands of the unemployed were wandering over the countryside, the fires from their hobo camps flickering a message of despair to frightened townsfolk.

During the following year there were over 1,300 industrial strikes and to many Americans it seemed as if the opening shots in a class war had been fired. The most publicized strike took place at the Pullman Palace Car Company. Cleveland threw his considerable weight on the side of management and against the forces of organized labor. Disregarding the vehement protests of Governor Altgeld of Illinois, Cleveland sent federal troops to Chicago, declaring he would use every dollar in the Treasury and every soldier in the army to deliver a single postcard. Most people applauded. But the disruptions continued.

Jacob Coxey, a businessman from a small town in Ohio, appointed himself general and led an army of citizen-followers to Washington, D.C., to petition for work. Rumors swept the city that other citizen armies were being formed, the vanguard of a revolution, to march on the nation's capital. An anxious Cleveland administration had Coxey's followers dispersed and jailed their leader on a technicality.

The year 1894 was the darkest that Americans had known in thirty years and finally changed the way people looked at things. What had seemed irritating now became pressing. Increasingly people saw American society as unfair. While the government promoted and subsidized the efforts of the economically ambitious, the demands of labor and farmers went unmet. A new plutocracy of predatory capitalists, no less powerful than the planter aristocracy of the Old South, was growing rich beyond anyone's imagination. Yet they maintained a callous indifference to the welfare and safety of workers. There was no such thing as public relief, and the unemployed worker was cast adrift. The cities were becoming a polluted sprawl of human misery as masses of the poor crowded into tenements. Farmers were caught in a downward spiral of prices and credit. Monopolies, "these unnatural and unnecessary monsters," roamed the American terrain, stifling competition, shortchanging the consumer, corrupting the political process, and giving selfish men the power to direct and dispose of the wealth of an entire society. A sense of anger spread throughout the land, and in the mid-term elections the people sent a message. One hundred and sixteen Democrats lost their House seats, the greatest defeat in congressional history.

The time was ripe for someone from the world of politics to move off dead center and address the new economic realities. At the Democratic convention of 1896 a young, obscure congressman from the state of Nebraska strode up to the podium and began: "The humblest citizen in all the land, when clad in the armor of a righteous cause, is stronger than all the forces of error. I come to speak to you in defense of a cause as holy as the cause of liberty—the cause of humanity."

With those words the conventioneers rose to their feet as one, shouting and thumping on the backs of chairs. The audience was captivated and the speaker led them as though they were a trained choir, rising to cheer each point and then sitting back to listen for more.

"Easterners," he said, "liked to praise businessmen but forget that plain people—laborers, miners, and farmers—were businessmen, too . . . we have petitioned, and our petitions have been scorned; we have entreated, and our entreaties have been disregarded; we have begged and they have mocked when our calamity came. We beg no longer; we entreat no more; we petition no more. *We defy them! . . .*"

Finally the famous closing: "Having behind us the producing masses of this nation and the world . . . we will answer their demand for a gold standard by saying to them: You shall not press down upon the brow of labor this crown of thorns; you shall not Crucify Mankind upon a Cross of Gold."

Pandemonium broke out.

The following day the convention nominated William Jennings Bryan, the speaker from Nebraska, to head the Democratic ticket. He preempted the Populist program, proposing the soft money policy of free silver and measures to rein in the freewheeling, "anything goes" capitalism, which favored the rich and powerful. Bryan brought the Democratic Party back to its Jeffersonian roots, but with a subtle change from Jefferson's vision. Gone was the emphasis on limited government. Rather, Bryan would use the force of government to limit the scope and power of the industrial society and provide economic security to the "victims of the marketplace," the new bottom layer of society. The Democrats, once more, were the champions of the "little guy." The proud party of Jefferson and Jackson no longer had to be a poor imitation of the Republicans but could again become an authentic opposition party.

More important, Bryan broke the political stalemate and allowed the Republicans to take advantage of the opening created by the Democrats and become the "sole" party of economic growth and material progress, in the tradition of Alexander Hamilton. They could shed the last of their Jeffersonian ornaments and the **Great Game of Politics** could be resumed. Once again there were two competing visions of the republic. But by the mid-1890s the Federalist-Whig-Republican vision of promoting business activity was also taking on a new cast.

While Hamilton had advocated a mercantilist path, high tariffs, and subsidies to aid economic growth, the eighteenth-century economist Adam Smith advocated another route: laissez-faire, hands off the economy. According to Smith, if men were allowed to compete freely, their selfish attempts to get the most for themselves would result in greater economic production. The government's job was to stand back, not meddle, and let the unchanging laws of supply and demand do their magic and the economy would perform miracles. And during the previous third of a century it had done just that. By the turn of the twentieth century the Republican ideology had become a Hamilton/Smith vision.

This period in the late nineteenth century is usually referred to as high tide for laissez-faire economics. Yet, in reality, mercantilist policies of a protective tariff and government aid to the railroads played a large role. But keep in mind that the definition of laissez-faire as a totally free and unhampered marketplace, without any government meddling, is an ideal. In reality, mankind does not achieve ideals. Mid-nineteenth-century England probably came closest to meeting the definition of a true laissez-faire economy. And late-nineteenth-century America, when the laws of economics ruled and manufacturers faced few legal and social barriers, where the government frequently subsidized but seldom regulated, was probably the closest our country ever came to that ideal. More than any place, before or after, men (OK, white men) were free to seek gain. This combination of protection and free enterprise was a unique American version of laissez-faire.

Ostensibly the election of 1896 was about the gold standard, which economic traditionalists saw as the underpinning to economic prosperity. Bryan marched to battle under the banner of free silver, while to William McKinley, who headed the Republican ticket, it was imperative to rely solely on gold as the nation's monetary standard. But beneath the surface the election was a referendum on whether the capitalistic development of the past 30 years had lost its appeal.

Bryan challenged the direction in which the country had been traveling since the Civil War. He gathered a band of losers in the race of economic life, those for whom the market had meant pain, loss, and a crushing dependency, and proposed a new direction, government intervention in the economy.

McKinley's job was easier. He only had to tailor the appeal of economic nationalism and the advancing urban-industrial society to the winners and wanna-be winners at the marketplace. Both winners and losers now had a home in a political party. Winners to the right, losers to the left.

Another Republican Party Restoration

Despite the shortcomings of laissez-faire capitalism, 51 percent of the voters, the best Republican showing in more than 20 years, rallied to McKinley's banner. It was decided: continue marching forward to the tune of laissez-faire capitalism. The Republicans quickly passed the Dingley Tariff, which raised average tariff duties to record high levels. By 1900 prosperity had returned and Congress passed the Gold Standard Act, which declared gold the standard of currency and ended the silver controversy.

During the last quarter of the nineteenth century there was an imperialistic scramble by the major European powers, Britain, France, Germany, and then Russia, to carve out generous colonies for themselves in Asia and Africa. By the mid-1890s the fever of imperialism reached our shores. There was fear the United States was being left behind in the race for territory and markets. When Spain sent 50,000 soldiers to Cuba to quell an uprising, opportunity presented itself. Cubans were herded into makeshift camps, where they died by the thousands. With American newspapers providing a steady stream of atrocity stories, popular pressure for intervention reached a deafening pitch. How could the United States retain its self-respect if it allowed Spain free rein to act with such brutal abandon in our backyard? Finally, when an explosion in Havana Harbor destroyed an American battleship, the *Maine*, McKinley yielded to the pressure and went to war with Spain. It was a brief war, as the United States made short work of Spain's broken-down navy and demoralized army. Teddy Roosevelt, who was assistant secretary of the navy, resigned and recruited his own brigade, the "Rough Riders," to fight in Cuba. He appointed himself colonel and led a famous daredevil charge, on horseback, up San Juan Hill. According to observer Richard Harding Davis, "No man who saw Roosevelt take that ride expected he would finish it alive." He did and returned home as another "larger than life" American hero. According to Secretary of State John Hay, it was a "Splendid Little War," from which the United States emerged a Pacific power as well as dominant in the Caribbean.

However, imperialism didn't catch on here as it had in Europe. The United States was clearly on a different track from the Old World. It did not need to find more resources or additional markets. America was still a growing country with large reserves of natural resources; it already had the largest free-trading area in the world. Besides, a policy of imperialism negated the nation's republican principles. America allowed Cuba to go its own way, although maintaining the right to intervene at its discretion, but held on to Puerto Rico, Guam, and the Philippines.

McKinley ran again in 1900, and Teddy Roosevelt, who after the Spanish-American War had become the moderately progressive governor of New York, was put in the second spot. McKinley captured 52 percent of the popular vote and defeated Bryan for a second time. He became the first sitting president in more than a quarter of a century to win reelection with a popular majority. Yet the policies he offered, hard money, high tariffs, and little action against the trusts, were staunchly pro-business and not very different from those of the past 30 years. Shortly after his reelection he was killed by an anarchist, and Teddy Roosevelt stepped in.

This put an end to the "Lincoln" paradigm. It was the fifth American political paradigm and spanned a 40-year period that included the Civil War, Reconstruction, and the growth of industrialism, along with two deep and protracted depressions. It was the period in which the infant Republican Party of Lincoln grew to maturity and became the party of Grant and would think nothing of using whatever means it could to remain in power. During the whole 40-year span, the Democrats were in control of both the White House and at least one house of Congress for only 6 years.

The Democrats, bankrupt of their own ideas, merely tried to

copy the Republicans, adopting similar laissez-faire economic policies. Many years later Woodrow Wilson denied Cleveland had been a Democrat at all. "Cleveland was . . . (really) . . . a conservative Republican," he wrote. Both parties believed in limited government and giving business a free hand to grow. Neither was much disposed to halt the merger movement, nor to side with labor. Tariffs remained high, money sound, and reform minimal, notwithstanding two clumsy attempts at regulation, the Interstate Commerce Act and the Sherman Anti-Trust Act. The main difference between the parties was that during each election campaign the GOP would wave the bloody shirt to remind the voters of the sacrifices in men and money that were made to save the Union. Perhaps the presidents of this period did not show much vision. But they did have the good sense to stand in the background and not try to wrestle with the force of industrialism, which they did not fully understand but which seemed to be changing man's fortune for the better. And this was no mean achievement.

During the post–Civil War period the social revolution of the early nineteenth century, which had gone a long way to level the social structure, was modified to conform to an industrial society. Wealth became the primary means of distinguishing one person from another. The captains of industry, the Rockefellers, the Mellons, the Du Ponts, and other great industrialists, received a larger slice of the wealth and power and went straight to the top of the social ladder. A couple of rungs below came a burgeoning middle class that was growing more affluent year by year. And riding in the rear was the working class.

Moreover, a new code of social conduct was in the ascendancy as people took strong pride in virtue and self-control. A strict Victorian morality, which put restraints on casual sex, alcohol, and gambling, replaced the moral confusion and loose social relationships of the early nineteenth century. The master–slave relationship was permanently changed as political rights for the blacks were put on the books to become the foundation in their subsequent struggles against inequality.

By the turn of the century, it was clear Bryan had been Crucified on a Cross of Silver; and the Populists, who in their hearts wanted to restore the lost world of an agrarian society, lost out at the national level. Yet, at the grass roots level, there was a similar distrust of entrenched power. Another group of reformers with a different interpretation of the American dream was emerging, and they were triumphing in the nation's cities. Although riding on the same wave of popular discontent as populism, this progressive strain of the reform movement was not a rejection of modernity. And in the following two decades it was to gain control of the political process and ameliorate the impact of industrialization and improve the quality of public and private life.

TABLE 8

Fifth Political Paradigm (1861–1901), 40 Years

Election of:		Majority Paradigm Party		Minority Paradigm Party	
		Republicans		Democrats	
Paradigm		% of popular vote		% of popular vote	
1860	Begins	Abraham Lincoln*	40	S. Douglas	29
1864	Preliminary	Abraham Lincoln	55	G. McClellan	45
1865		Andrew Johnson			
1868	Confirmed	Ulysses Grant	53	H. Seymour	47
1872		Ulysses Grant	56	H. Greeley	44
1876		Rutherford Hayes	48	S. Tilden	51
1880		James Garfield	48.3	W. Hancock	48.2
1881		Chester Arthur			
1884	Lose election	James Blaine	48.2	G. Cleveland	48.5
1888	Restored	Benjamin Harrison	48	G. Cleveland	49
1892	Lose election	Benjamin Harrison	43	G. Cleveland	46
1896	Restored	William McKinley	51	W. Bryan	47
1900		William McKinley	52	W. Bryan	46
1901	Ends	McKinley killed = paradigm ends			

*Bold = winner.

	Congress	Republicans House	Republicans Senate	Democrats House	Democrats Senate
37th	1861–1863	**106***	**31**	42(28)	11(7)
38th	1863–1865	**103**	**39**	80	12
39th	1865–1867	**145**	**42**	46	10
40th	1867–1869	**143**	**42**	49	11
41st	1869–1871	**170**	**61**	73	11
42d	1871–1873	**139**	**57**	104	17
43d	1873–1875	**203**	**54**	88	19
44th	1875–1877	107	**46**	**181(3)**	29
45th	1877–1879	137	**39**	**156**	36
46th	1879–1881	128	33	**150(14)**	**43**
47th	1881–1883	**152**	37†	130(11)	37(2)
48th	1883–1885	119	**40**	**200(6)**	36
49th	1885–1887	140	**41**	**182(2)**	34
50th	1887–1889	151	**39**	**170(4)**	37
51st	1889–1891	**173**	**47**	156(1)	37
52d	1891–1893	88	**47**	**231(14)**	39(2)
53d	1893–1895	126	38	**220(10)**	**44(3)**
54th	1895–1897	**246**	44†	104(7)	39(5)
55th	1897–1899	**206**	**46**	134(16)	34(10)
56th	1899–1901	**185**	**53**	163(9)	26(11)

*__Bold__ = in control of House or Senate: more than all other parties combined. Senate tie goes to the president's party.

†No party controls.

Source: Composition of 37th–56th Congress: Information Please®, copyright © 2003 Pearson Education. (www.infoplease.com)

Note: All figures reflect immediate result of election.

Years in the White House with control of at least one house of Congress:
    Republicans: 30
    Democrats: 6

Economic Policies
- Tariff increased to new record high levels: Morrill, McKinley, and Dingley tariffs
- Railroads subsidized
- Specie Resumption Act provided for return of gold standard
- Banking Act
- Wartime taxes eliminated
- Sherman Silver Purchase Act
- Sherman Anti-Trust Act, 1890
- Government budget surplus

Other Important Events
- Civil War
- Emancipation Proclamation

- Postwar reconstruction
- Thirteenth and Fourteenth Amendments
- Tenure of Office Act reduced Johnson's power / impeachment
- Depressions of 1873/1893
- Civil service reform
- Pension giveaway to war veterans
- Spanish-American War

Minority Party
- Passes Interstate Commerce Act, 1886
- Tries to lower tariff
- Holds the line against huge government spending
- Repeals Sherman Silver Purchase Act

V

The Progressives

By the turn of the century simmering angers in the nation's cities and states had boiled over into a spontaneous demand for reform. Urban progressives wanted to bring democratic society under their control and humanize it. They thought that by turning the routine tasks of administration over to a professional civil service, men chosen for their expertise and devoted to the public good, the most glaring ills of society could be cured. These progressives proposed solutions and reforms to a wide range of activities. In the cities they tackled problems such as streetcar fares, dangerous railroad crossings, and poor sanitation facilities. On the national level their chief concerns were corporate regulation, banking reform, and improvement of working conditions.

By 1900 progressive insurgents had taken seats in both the House and the Senate, but by no means did they approach a majority. Congress remained stubbornly conservative under the Republican leadership of Nelson Aldrich in the Senate and Joseph Cannon in the House. The progressives needed a leader if they were to take their program to the national level. When the youthful, dynamic Teddy Roosevelt took the helm of government in 1901 the country got its champion of reform. On one hand, Colonel Teddy Roosevelt was a compulsive man of action who often shot from the hip. He frequently talked nonsense. His recommended method for handling mobs was "taking ten or a dozen of their leaders out, standing . . . them against a wall, and shooting them dead." His motto was: "Get action; do things; be sane."

On the other hand, Teddy Roosevelt, TR to the American public, was a highly partisan student of American history. He had a grandiose sense of American destiny and wanted to lead the people to national greatness. An admirer of Alexander Hamilton, TR shared his fear of the mob, his "love of order," and was drawn to the old Federalist concept of using the power of government to set priorities and provide direction. TR was especially concerned about the rise of radicalism and the growing popularity of the socialist movement. The best antidote, he thought, was social reforms made by the right. By lessening the harshness of the industrial environment, the Republican Party would become the champions of a fairer and more stable corporate capitalism, and voters for years to come would not forget the party that brought them order and prosperity.

On taking the oath of office Roosevelt declared his intentions "to continue, absolutely unbroken, the policy of President McKinley." This meant high tariffs, the gold standard, and a not-too-vigorous prosecution of the trusts. But within the year the "Rough Rider" abandoned the laissez-faire approach to economic matters and was fearlessly promoting a bold program of reform that was to profoundly change the direction of the nation.

To achieve his goals the colonel had to steer both party and country between the reactionary policies of Senate leader Nelson Aldrich and the radicalism of the progressive insurgents. TR bargained with the Republican old guard, agreeing to keep his hands off the tariff question in exchange for freedom to pursue his interventionist concerns elsewhere. First he centered on the trusts. He wanted to put teeth into the Sherman Anti-Trust Act so as to restore competitive conditions to markets that were in danger of becoming "monopolized" by giant firms. In early 1902 the hero of San Juan Hill shocked Wall Street by giving the signal to move against Northern Securities, J. P. Morgan's railroad combine, which controlled a massive railroad network in the Northwest. When, two years later, the Supreme Court ordered the company dissolved, Roosevelt's credentials with the progressives were established and his legacy as a trustbuster made. Other antitrust suits soon followed.

Roosevelt, however, had no intention of destroying the trusts. He merely wanted to halt the evil they created, not the prosperity they brought. His solution was to regulate and control them. In the face of considerable Senate opposition he was able to establish the Bureau of Corporations to police business practices and report its findings to the public. The Elkins Act, which increased the powers of the Interstate Commerce Commission (ICC), soon followed. The Hepburn Act, which granted the ICC power to set rates railroads charged to shippers, would follow during a second term. It forced the railroads to surrender one of the capitalist's cherished privileges—the right to set prices.

When a coal strike threatened to leave American homes and factories short of coal as winter was approaching, Roosevelt intervened, pressuring the coal companies to compromise with the workers. This was the first time an American president had shown sympathy to the concerns of labor. All he wanted, he said, was "to see to it that every man has a **'square deal,'** no more and no less." Nor was that all. At his urging Congress enacted a workmen's compensation law for all government employees and a child labor law for the District of Columbia.

Roosevelt's love of nature and knowledge of the West gave him a sentimental yet highly intelligent interest in the issue of conservation. He was concerned about the greedy and wasteful destruction of natural resources and thought "protection of the environment" second only to trust-busting as "the most vital internal question of the United States." Millions of acres of federally owned land, mostly in the West, were withdrawn from commercial exploitation and turned into national forests or public monuments. Roosevelt broadened the concept of conservation further to include power sites, coal lands and oil reserves and placed them in the public domain. When the colonel retired from the presidency in early 1909, land in government preserves totaled almost 195 million acres, a whopping increase from the 45 million acres the government owned in 1901.

By 1904 Roosevelt had shown the American people that strong government action could reduce the terrible uncertainty and risks of a wide-open society. So when he ran for another term on the promise of a "square deal" for labor, capital, and the public, it was no surprise that Roosevelt won with the largest popular majority up to that time, surpassing Jackson's 1828 margin. The voters had given their preliminary stamp of approval to a new progressive paradigm. On election night an overjoyed Roosevelt pledged that "under no circumstances will I be a candidate for or accept another nomination."

A group of "reform" journalists, "muckrakers," Roosevelt called them, had launched an attack on the underside of American life—exposés on sweatshops, the white slave traffic, insurance company scandals, city bosses, and a multitude of others—in the early 1900s. Revelations about the sickening conditions in the meatpacking industry and fraudulent advertising in the patent medicine business shocked and frightened the American public. To protect the consumer Roosevelt led the forces for a Meat Inspection Act, which increased appropriations for inspectors to go into the packinghouses to prevent bad meat from coming to the market. A Pure Food and Drug Law prohibited the manufacture and sale of misbranded or adulterated foods and drugs. The colonel signed both acts on the same day, significantly enhancing the regulatory power of the federal government.

The "Rough Rider" modernized the army and doubled the strength of the navy to ensure the United States was the dominant power in our hemisphere. He sought to promote regional stability and exclude foreign influence. His chief concern was that European governments, who were extending credit to the poor and unstable countries of Latin America, would intervene if our neighbors were unable to repay their loans. With that in mind, he announced the Roosevelt Corollary to the Monroe Doctrine, which warned Latin American nations to keep their affairs in order or else face American intervention.

Roosevelt was attracted to the idea of a canal across the Isthmus of Panama, which would facilitate interocean transportation and enhance the prestige of the United States. He covertly supported a Panamanian revolt against Colombia and in return was rewarded with the rights to a 10-mile swath of Panama. The colonel denied any impropriety and took great pride in the canal, calling it "by far the most important action in foreign affairs."

By the time he left government Teddy Roosevelt was clearly the most popular and dynamic public figure of his time. He had taken the progressive movement to the national level, challenged the dogma of his own party, laid the foundation for administrative government, and raised the office of the presidency to its twentieth-century position of dominance. Although frequently criticized by progressives in his own party for getting only half a loaf, he was, in the face of a very conservative old guard Senate, able to get reform laws on the books that established precedents and in years to come would be expanded. Astonishingly, he was able to carry off what no other president—but for Madison—had been able to do successfully, that is, reverse course and take his party and its natural constituency with him toward the other side of the political spectrum.

In 1908 he hand-picked his secretary of war and trusted lieutenant, William Taft, to be his successor and "carry on the work substantially as I have carried it on." Taft refused campaign contributions from any corporation that might face antitrust prosecution. Nonetheless, he was still able to win 52 percent of the popular vote and easily defeat William Jennings Bryan, who was running for yet a third time. It was settled; the Teddy Roosevelt mini-revolution had become the sixth American paradigm.

William Howard Taft could not manage his party as Roosevelt had. Taft lacked the political adroitness to steer between the old guard conservative forces in his party and the progressive firebrands. Try as he did to follow in TR's footsteps, things would not go smoothly for him. He took up tariff revision, which had been the hot potato issue of the early twentieth century. Even TR had backed away from dealing with it. Taft, however, had promised meaningful downward tariff revision, and the House complied with a moderate cut. But when the high-tariff forces of Aldrich and the old guard in the Senate loaded the bill with duties considerably higher than the original measure, Taft refused to intervene, even rhetorically. Although rates in the finished bill were still slightly below the Dingley Tariff levels, the measure was quite unpopular. In a supreme act of political maladroitness, Taft then proclaimed the Payne-Aldrich Act the "best tariff bill the Republican Party has ever passed."

Next came the Pinchot-Ballinger affair. Gifford Pinchot, chief of Forest Services and dubbed "Sir Galahad of the Woods" by admiring progressives, was the most popular conservationist from Roosevelt's administration. When he accused Taft's new secretary of the interior, Richard Ballinger, of unsavory conduct, Taft was caught in the crossfire between conservatives and progressives. After a congressional commission absolved Ballinger of any wrongdoing, Taft proclaimed his support for the secretary. Pinchot, not about to back off, attacked the president publicly. Naturally the president fired the insubordinate Pinchot. The incident earned Taft the enduring enmity of the reformers and compelled him to lean on the conservatives even more.

Taft continued to apply the Roosevelt Corollary to Caribbean affairs but added his own personal touch known as "dollar diplomacy." He thought that substituting economic ties for military alliances, or "dollars for bullets," would bring lasting peace to the region.

Although Taft initiated more antitrust indictments than TR did, he was walking through a door that Roosevelt had already opened, and TR's successor did not open many new doors to reform, which was disheartening to the progressives. Teddy Roosevelt, who in private life was turning more radical, was watching from the sidelines and becoming increasingly disenchanted with his former protégé. TR thought Taft unfit to lead the country and in 1912 decided to challenge him for leadership in the Republican Party. When Taft, who controlled the party's apparatus, won another Republican nomination, the colonel and his progressive friends walked out of the convention and mounted a third party challenge. Later that summer ten thousand of the Roosevelt faithful gathered in Chicago, to hear their leader pronounce himself fit as a "Bull Moose," to sing with him the "Battle Hymn of the Republic," and determined to stand with him at Armageddon.

Meanwhile the Democrats, sensing that the Republican split meant victory was within their grasp, nominated the progressive governor of New Jersey, Woodrow Wilson, to head their ticket. With Roosevelt, the former foe of radicalism, now running to the far left and Taft on the right, Wilson's 42 percent of the popular vote was enough to win the presidency for the Democrats.

Woodrow Wilson offered a more liberal variant of progressivism than his two predecessors. He thought the nation was drifting toward oligarchy. As he saw it, the bureaucratic government of the Roosevelt-Taft administrations, with its reliance on the "opinion of experts," was thwarting the "will of the people," which had been the cornerstone of a democratic society.

Wilson's aim was to break up the clusters of privilege, reestablish democracy, and restore competition. His program, the "New Freedom," would dismantle the vast federal bureaucratic power that had grown during the Roosevelt-Taft years and pursue reform in a "small" government setting. It would liberate the energies of the people and renew the nation from the bottom up. Wilson maintained: "The history of liberty is the history of the limitation of government power."

With the House and Senate now both comfortably in Democratic hands the stage was set for one of the most comprehensive legislative programs enacted up to that time. Wilson began his legislative assault by calling Congress into special session to make good on his promise to lower the tariff. He used patronage adroitly to turn aside the attacks of the protectionists and achieved the first significant reduction of rates since the Civil War. The Underwood Tariff lowered duties about 15 percent. As compensation for reduced government revenues a small graduated income tax was added.

The new president then threw his energies into bringing order into America's complex many-tiered paper-money system. The outcome was the Federal Reserve Act, which created a new national currency—Federal Reserve notes—and a Federal Reserve Board, which was responsible for controlling the nation's credit along with managing crises.

Next Wilson turned his attention to filling in the holes in the Sherman Act, so as to check business concentration. He guided Congress to pass the Clayton Anti-Trust Act, which created the Federal Trade Commission to police business. Although the courts stripped it of its power to define unfair practices, it reassured the public that there was now a sheriff watching out for their interests. And it helped bring the era of the robber barons to an end.

The president's promises to liberate the energies of the American people whetted the appetites of groups that formerly had been excluded. They descended upon Washington, seeking to push the progressive agenda even further. But Wilson could say no. He refused to endorse women's suffrage, he sidetracked a child labor bill on the grounds it was unconstitutional, he refused to lift the burden of antitrust suits from the backs of labor, and he

backed immigration restriction. Furthermore, he tacitly supported the efforts of a couple of cabinet secretaries to segregate
blacks in the rest rooms, cafeterias, and offices of their departments. When liberals objected he quietly backed away from the
policy, though still insisting segregation benefited the Negro.

In early 1916 with a new election looming, with many progressives voicing disappointment with Wilson's limited reforms, with
Teddy Roosevelt's progressive Bull Moosers returning to the
Republican fold, it looked like Wilson would be in for a tough
reelection fight. With that in mind, Wilson switched his focus and
began a second, more national-minded phase of the "New Freedom." A river of new reform laws followed. He gave farmers
cheap agricultural credits. Labor got a workmen's compensation
act, a national child labor act, and Wilson's endorsement of an
eight-hour day for all of the nation's workers. And finally, he
threw his weight behind the constitutional amendment for female
suffrage. This remarkable stream of reform legislation was to be
the high-water mark for the progressives.

However, the meaning of all these reforms was unmistakable:
an increase rather than a decrease in governmental agencies; a
greater rather than a lesser reliance on experts and bureaucratic
procedures; more, not less, government. Wilson's dream of reversing the movement to government bureaucracy, which Teddy Roosevelt had begun, and returning to a world of less government had
ended in perplexity and defeat. His administration had, in fact,
completed Roosevelt's bureaucratic revolution.

In foreign policy Wilson repudiated the "dollar diplomacy" of
the Taft administration and embarked on a highly idealistic policy
of moral diplomacy, designed to bring right to the world, preserve
peace, and extend the blessings of democracy to other peoples.
On Independence Day 1914, he told his audience, "America . . .
puts human rights and 'national integrity' above all other rights
and her flag is not only that of America but of humanity." Meanwhile, earlier in that year Wilson had ordered the occupation of

Veracruz to vindicate American honor after a fracas had led to the arrest of American sailors.

A brutal coup in Mexico by General Huerta outraged the president, so much so that he refused to recognize the new Mexican government. When a boatload of American sailors was arrested and unlawfully detained in Tampico, Mexico, Wilson immediately demanded an apology along with a twenty-one gun salute. Huerta predictably refused and Wilson ordered the occupation of Veracruz. As the two nations hovered on the edge of war, a timely offer by the so-called ABC Powers (Argentina, Brazil, and Chile) to mediate the dispute allowed Wilson to withdraw American forces and save face.

Again in 1916, after the Mexican revolutionary "bandit" leader "Pancho" Villa raided a tiny New Mexico village, killing 16 Americans and burning the town, Wilson ordered General John Pershing on a punitive expedition to seize Villa in Mexico. Pershing chased the bandit some three hundred miles into Mexico without managing to catch him. When the Mexican government, now under the control of the liberal Carranza, demanded the withdrawal of American troops Wilson complied. After nearly three years of tampering in Mexico's affairs Wilson had nothing to show for the effort.

In 1914 war broke out in Europe, with Great Britain and the Allied Powers on one side and Germany and the Central Powers on the other. The toll of destruction during the opening phases of the conflict strained human comprehension. In the first battle of the Marne the Allies and the Central Powers together sustained more than a million casualties. Wilson immediately proclaimed neutrality. But he soon recognized the United States was wedded to England and France by dint of shared histories and traditions of "individualism" and "democracy." As those customs had not taken root in Germany and its sidekicks, the possibility of an arrogant, militaristic, nondemocratic German hegemony in Europe and in control of the Atlantic sea-lanes appeared threatening.

In 1915 the Wilson administration proclaimed trade with the Allies "legal and welcome," beginning a tilt toward England and France. In the meantime, Germany was using its new sea weapon, the submarine, to undermine Britain's naval superiority. After a number of Americans, traveling through the war zone on British passenger ships, had been killed in submarine attacks, Wilson issued a stern warning that the United States would break relations if the Germans persisted in their submarine warfare. Not wanting to provoke the world's most powerful neutral nation into the war, Germany yielded, agreeing to conduct its submarine war according to American rules.

In the meantime, the mini-revolution launched by the progressives was having a profound effect on the character of American society. The brutally competitive business world of the late nineteenth century, along with the vicious swings from prosperity to depression, was tamed, and in its place was a more orderly and cooperative society with its citizens devoted to high public purpose. The business plutocrats, who had been the rock stars of the earlier period, were on the outs, while scores of educated young men and women, who could use their knowledge for the benefit of society, were gaining admiration. A new "professional class," of doctors, lawyers, teachers, social reformers, and scientists, devoted to the public good and completely unconnected to the business or agrarian sectors of the economy, was attaining status, power, and a larger portion of the American wealth pie. The income tax would be raised and an excess profits tax added during WWI. Soon three-quarters of federal revenue would be coming from these sources, shifting the burden of supporting the government from the less well off, who, due to the previously high tariff, had paid dearly for consumer goods, to the wealthy, who felt the new tax bite the most. Furthermore, the working class was finally able to get its foot on the economic ladder.

In 1916 Woodrow Wilson ran for reelection on the slogan "He kept us out of war." The GOP nominated Charles Hughes, a moderate progressive, and Wilson beat him in a cliffhanger with 49 percent of the popular vote. The more ardent of the progressives read the election results as a mandate to undertake a moral cleansing of American society, to purify democracy. A time of crusades began: against alcohol, prostitution, immigrant radicals, and for "Prohibition," which banned the production and sale of liquor and became law as twilight was descending upon the Wilson administration.

Meanwhile, after nearly three years of fighting, Germany was frustrated with her inability to bring the war to a favorable conclusion. Hoping to deliver a quick knockout blow to Britain and France, before America could put troops in the field, she resumed submarine attacks in March of 1917. During that month alone four unarmed American merchantmen were sunk and days later the United States entered the war.

As America prepared for war, a Committee on Public Information was set up to inaugurate a propaganda campaign of unprecedented proportions. Rigid censorship combined with political repression reached into the American press, schools and universities, the churches, and even the new movie industry. The result was a fevered public uprising against nonconformity of all kinds and the ruthless suppression of American liberties, which the Wilson administration was either unable or unwilling to check. The head of the Socialist Party, Eugene Debs, 62 years of age and in failing health, was jailed for violation of the Espionage Act because of a speech he gave denouncing capitalism and the war. A mob in Centralia, Washington, dragged a left-wing union (IWW) agitator from jail and castrated him before hanging him. In April 1918 a Missouri mob seized a young man whose sole crime was being born in Germany. They bound him with an American flag, paraded him through town, and then lynched him. A jury acquitted the mob's members.

War provided the government with a need for centralization and controls. Wilson created a War Industries Board to mobilize industry, a Food Administration, with Herbert Hoover at its head, and other administrative boards to manage railroads, fuel, and labor. They were given near dictatorial powers. The result was a Byzantine maze of rules and regulations, which restricted competition, thus limiting the productive might of the nation. The costs of complying with the new regulations and reforms made it difficult for new businesses to gain entry into many industries, while many smaller competitors were driven out. When wartime government spending took off for the sky, industrial output had trouble keeping pace and this inflicted a raging inflation on the nation that the government seemed powerless to quell. From 1916 through early 1920 the price level more than doubled.

In the meantime, the United States mounted a mobilization effort that bordered on the miraculous. American entry into the war provided a "bridge of ships" that brought badly needed troops and supplies to the nearly exhausted Allies. By late summer of 1918 more than a half-million American troops had landed in Europe and General Pershing, in charge of American forces in the field, opened a counteroffensive that pushed the German army relentlessly back toward its own frontier. In early November, Austria-Hungary collapsed on the home front. Six days later the Kaiser abdicated the German throne, and it took only 48 hours until a coalition of socialists and liberals accepted the Fourteen Points, for a liberal peace, that Wilson had proposed earlier that year. The Great War was over . . . or so it seemed.

Wilson hoped to extend the idealism of Jefferson and the French rationalists onto the world stage. He figured that by establishing a moral and just peace, "a peace without victory," World War I would become the "war that ended all wars." He threw everything, all his ideals and his legacy, into the peace he hoped to achieve. The heart of his program was to set up a League of Nations as a worldwide legal community. The nations of the world would then be able to replace a balance of power approach to foreign affairs with a new form of collective security. However, the Allies were not enamored. They had suffered grievously during the war and wanted a punitive peace, one that would assign war guilt to Germany, strip it of all possessions, and exact enormous reparations, while providing the necessary safeguards against future aggression.

Meanwhile, the Republicans had regained control of Congress in the mid-term elections and were not about to let Wilson have his way without some modifications. They were worried about the open-ended nature of the commitment to the League of Nations and proposed additional amendments. But Wilson was on a moral crusade and refused to compromise. No half-loaves for this politician. He decided to take his case to the people and began what was to be a futile 8,000-mile tour of the nation to educate the public on the importance of the League to their future security and welfare. As he was wont to do, Wilson accused his opponents of malice, while avowing the purity of his own motives. In September of 1919, while on tour, he suffered a stroke, from which he never recovered. During the final year of his term Wilson's administration was rudderless, with his wife acting as advisor and gatekeeper. And during that time nothing was done on the peace treaty. It would not be until July 1921 that Congress passed a joint resolution officially ending the war.

Wilson's pandering to various groups had awakened an appetite for more democracy and ignited social tensions between capital and labor, black and white, immigrant and old stock American. Following World War I there was a whiff of excessive democracy, not unlike what the nation had experienced in the 1850s. It was a period of lawlessness with a devastating series of strikes, riots, and bombings. In the summer of 1919 a race riot erupted in Chicago and 38 people were killed and another 500 injured. Similar, although smaller-scale, riots soon followed in more than 20 other cities. Labor unrest spread throughout the nation, prompting a series of spectacular strikes. In Boston the police force struck for the right to unionize, and the city experienced a wave of looting and theft. Calvin Coolidge, the governor of Massachusetts, intervened and declared, "There is no right to strike against the public safety by anybody, at any place or at any time." His deft handling of that dangerous police strike, when public order was under threat virtually all over the world, became the model for government executives everywhere to follow.

Meanwhile, a Marxist revolution in Russia had alarmed many Americans. A series of bombings during 1919 set off a panic that the Bolsheviks had reached our shores. There was a public outcry that something be done. Attorney General Mitchell Palmer sent federal agents on a series of raids. The agents broke into homes, meeting halls, and union halls without search warrants. Several thousand suspected anarchists and communists were held for deportation without hearings or trials. In December of that year 149 aliens, nearly all of whom were innocent of the charges against them, were sent to Russia aboard a ship that the press dubbed the "Soviet Ark." Prominent citizens, such as the evangelist Billy Sunday, voiced their approval and urged even more drastic steps. Sunday wanted to take "these ornery, wild-eyed Socialists" and "stand them up before a firing squad." Finally this hysteria became too much and other public leaders voiced disapproval. Among those urging restraint was Warren Harding, senator from Ohio, who expressed the opinion that "too much has been said about bolshevism in America." Palmer, nevertheless, predicted that there would be massive bombings on May Day 1920. The entire New York police department, eleven thousand strong, was placed on duty and prepared for imminent disaster. When May Day came and went without incidents, the public began to lose interest and the Red Scare died out.

By election time 1920, the postwar inflation had given way to the most serious economic recession since the 1890s. A divided and dispirited Democratic convention nominated James Cox, governor of Ohio, to head their ticket, and they chose the popular assistant secretary of the navy, Franklin Roosevelt, cousin to

Teddy, for the second spot. The Republicans put up Warren Harding, who campaigned on the promise of a "return to normalcy."

Just what was normalcy? Historians like to make light of this slogan. But the public knew what Harding meant: An end to zealous reform-minded presidents like Woodrow Wilson and Teddy Roosevelt; an end to rationing, controls, and planning; and a return to the traditional, late-nineteenth-century GOP policies. The vice-presidency was given to Calvin Coolidge, hero of the Boston police strike. When the voters, and there were a lot of them and they were very unhappy, went to the polls in November of 1920, they registered their disapproval of the past four years by giving Warren Harding the largest percentage of the popular vote, over 60 percent, to that time.

The period from 1901 to 1920 was the progressive paradigm, wherein the nation began to control, tame, and bend capitalism to its will. The progressives believed that by putting men of goodwill into positions of leadership they could clean up the social environment of American cities, purge the world of sin, and rescue the nation from the excesses of corporate power. A strong national government was created, which curbed the trusts, regulated business, humanized working conditions, made business more consumer-friendly, lowered the tariff, instituted a sound banking system, and reformed the political process by giving women the vote and allowing for direct voting for senators. Teddy Roosevelt, William Taft, and Woodrow Wilson all followed in the progressive mode, broadening the use of executive power and initiating similar type reforms. In the fall of 1916 it was Wilson, the Democrat, who defined the period when he claimed, ". . . we are all progressives."

This period was the first attempt to have the federal government intervene in the economy, and it marked the beginning of the modern age.

TABLE 9
Sixth Political Paradigm (1901–1921). 20 Years

Election of:	Majority Paradigm Party Republicans		Minority Paradigm Party Democrats		Third Party Progressive
Paradigm	**% of popular Vote**		**% of popular Vote**		
1901 Begins	**Teddy Roosevelt***†				
1904 Preliminary	**Teddy Roosevelt**	56	Charles Parker	38	
1908 Confirmed	**William Taft**	52	William Bryan	43	
1912 Lose election	William Taft	23	**Woodrow Wilson**	42	Teddy Roosevelt 27%
1916	Charles Hughes	46	**Woodrow Wilson**	49	
1920 Ends					

***Bold** = winner.

† Replaces McKinley, who is killed.

Source: Composition of 57th–66th Congress: Information Please®, copyright© 2003 Pearson Education. (www.infoplease.com)

Note: All figures reflect immediate result of election.

	Republicans		Democrats/()Other	
Congress	**House**	**Senate**	**House**	**Senate**
57th 1901–1903	**198***	**56**	153(5)	29(3)
58th 1903–1905	**207**	**58**	178	32
59th 1905–1907	**250**	**58**	136	32
60th 1907–1909	**222**	**61**	164	29
61st 1909–1911	**219**	**59**	172	32
62d 1911–1913	162	49	**228**(1)	42
63d 1913–1915	127	44	**290**(18)	**51**(1)
64th 1915–1917	193	39	**231**(8)	**56**(1)
65th 1917–1919	216	42	**210**(9)†	**53**(1)
66th 1919–1921	**237**	48	191(7)	47(1)‡

***Bold** = in control of House or Senate: more than all other parties combined.

†Able to organize the House with help of other parties.

‡No party controls.

Years in the White House with control of at least one house of Congress:

Republicans: 11½
Democrats: 6

Economic Policies
- Trust breaking / antitrust legislation
- Government intervention to help miners
- Lower tariff / Underwood Tariff

- Federal Reserve Act / sound money
- A spate of reform legislation including:
  more humane labor practices;
  consumer protections;
  powers of ICC strengthened
- Income tax

Other Important Events
- Conservation
- Sovereignty over Panama Canal gained
- Roosevelt Corollary to Monroe Doctrine
- World War I
- Treaty of Versailles / League of Nations defeated
- Eighteenth Amendment: Prohibition
- Nineteenth Amendment: Woman suffrage
- Post–WW I social disorder / strikes, bombings, and Red Scare

—⊶∞⊷—

VI

The Roaring Twenties: A New Era

W arren Harding, an affable, well-liked senator and former newspaper publisher from Ohio, rode into the presidency on a wave of popular enthusiasm. He appointed men of genuine talent and vision to the important economic and financial posts. Herbert Hoover, as secretary of commerce, Andrew Mellon as secretary of the Treasury, and Henry Wallace, as secretary of agriculture, all sat at Harding's elbow advising him on economic matters.

Harding, with an eye to the public's rejection of the Wilson years, thought the nation in greater danger from "mistaken government activity" than from "lack of legislation." He aimed to limit the federal government's role to assisting and encouraging business, primarily by providing high tariffs, halting further regulatory legislation, helping in the search for markets and raw materials, and cutting tax rates from the embarrassingly high levels they reached during the progressive years.

Harding took over the reins of government while the nation was in the throes of a very serious business slump. To restore business confidence and bolster the economy his administration enacted the Fordney-McCumber Tariff, which raised rates substantially from the Underwood Tariff schedules of the Wilson period. The wealthy got a modest tax cut, but future cuts, Harding promised, would benefit all, not just the rich. To bring the spending of the monster state back under control, Harding created a new Bureau of the Budget to scrutinize and control expenditures. The Bureau took the axe to federal spending, reducing expenditures by 40 percent. Government spending, which ran at $18 billion during World War I, was further reduced to just over $3 billion by 1925, and this created a huge budget surplus. Consequently, government debt, which had reached $25 billion following World War I, was on its way down to a slim $16 billion by 1930. Within six months of the time the new business-friendly administration arrived in Washington the economy was in full recovery and clearing a path toward the prosperity that would subsequently define the decade.

Harding also sought to end the social turmoil of the postwar period and heal a torn nation. He opened the barred gates of the White House, began to hold news conferences with members of the press, and in an act of reconciliation released Eugene Debs and 23 other political prisoners from jail.

When Harding began his presidency forces were already in place that were trying to enforce the values and ways of life of an older, more uniform culture. In the early 1920s the Ku Klux Klan, which had risen from its late-nineteenth-century ashes a few years earlier, was spreading its tentacles throughout the nation's small towns. It resorted to intimidation and violence, midnight whippings and cross burnings, to enforce its middle-class cultural and moral vision of America. Harding did not challenge its growing power; nor did Coolidge; nor, for that matter, did any prominent Democrat. At the time there was also a pervasive feeling that immigrants, with their alien living habits, their political radicalism, and a willingness to accept low-paying jobs, were corrupting American society. When Congress passed the first bill in nearly 40 years restricting immigration on the basis of nationality and race, Harding signed it.

After the devastation of World War I, the Republicans did not want to commit the nation to any agreements that might draw it into another war. They limited involvement in world affairs to moral injunctions—paper agreements promising "moral cooperation"—against aggression and war. A conference in Washington, during the winter of 1921–22, limited the amount of warships the United States, Great Britain, Japan, France, and Italy could maintain. Another provision of that same conference committed those same nations to the principle of equal opportunity, an "open door," inside an independent China.

By early 1923 word was leaking out of scandals in the Harding administration. Several of Harding's cronies, men he had appointed to office, were involved. The most notorious involved government oil reserves at Teapot Dome in Wyoming and Elk Hills in California. Two oilmen, Harry Sinclair and Edward Doheny, bribed Secretary of the Interior Albert Fall, with almost half a million dollars, to obtain the leases to those properties. In August 1923 a despondent President Harding, demoralized by the betrayals of his friends and fearing he was about to be tarnished by scandal, died of a heart attack. In an extraordinary demonstration of public affection enormous crowds, numbering in the millions, knelt in prayer, sang hymns, and wept as they waited, often throughout the night, for the funeral train bringing Harding's body back to Ohio.

Vice-President Calvin Coolidge inherited the White House, and in his early months in office the corruption that had spread through Harding's administration oozed to the surface and became public knowledge. However, Coolidge, whose integrity was unimpeachable and stoic steadiness soothing, won over the American public. Coolidge forced resignations, appointed special prosecutors, insisted that justice be done, and when indictments resulted in jail sentences for Albert Fall and others, breached no interference and issued no pardons. Coolidge's handling of the scandals was done with such honesty and integrity that by the time the 1924 election season began, the offenses had disappeared from the public's radar.

As a politician, Calvin Coolidge employed the strategy of silence. He said little but calculated carefully. When badgered by reporters for saying little during the 1924 campaign, "Silent" Cal's retort was, "I don't recall any candidate for president that ever injured himself very much by not talking." When visitors arrived at the White House with some proposal, he often sat mute. He later wrote: "Nine tenths of a president's callers at the White House want something they ought not to have. If you keep dead still they will run down in three or four minutes." Like Queen Elizabeth I of England he was a supreme exponent of masterly inactivity. His philosophy was: "If you see ten troubles coming down the road, you can be sure that nine will run into the ditch before they reach you."

Coolidge, like Harding, had low regard for government intervention in economic matters. "Government and business," he said, "should remain independent and separate." Naturally, he continued Harding's policies of shrinking the role of the federal government in the business life of the country. As an arch foe of government spending, Coolidge used his veto power freely to shoot down any congressional measure that he thought too costly. In labor–management conflicts he steered his administration to the side of management. According to Coolidge, "the chief business of the American people is business."

By election time 1924 a rising curve of prosperity and business optimism was working in Coolidge's favor. Silent Cal, running with the slogan "Keep Cool with Coolidge," received 54 percent of the popular vote, swamping John Davis, a Wall Street lawyer, who headed the Democrat ticket, and "Fighting" Bob La Follette, who led a breakaway movement of the remains of the old progressive wing of the Republican Party. The American public had given their preliminary endorsement to a Harding-Coolidge paradigm.

By mid-decade a new calm had settled over the nation. The battle against radicals, unions, and immigrants had largely been won. The Klan was fading. Membership had fallen way off, and the organization would soon be tottering on the verge of extinction. The number of strikes declined dramatically and a nationwide spirit of cooperation filled the air.

In 1926, with the budget surplus whittling away the government debt, Congress enacted a stiff income tax cut and the result was "velvet for the taxpayer." Another tax cut followed in 1928. By the end of the decade the government was collecting one-third less in taxes than it had in 1921. Much of those savings found its way onto Wall Street to help fuel the great bull market, which was gathering steam.

By the mid-1920s it was becoming apparent that the modern economy was performing miracles. While prices remained stable, Gross National Product (GNP), a measure of the economy's overall strength, climbed a substantial 5 percent, year after year, and would continue to do so until 1929. The automobile, which had come to play a leading role in everyday American life, stood at the center of the boom. In 1920 there were 10 million cars in the nation; by the end of the decade there would be 26 million on American roads.

A new entrepreneurial spirit was spreading across the land, and it was receptive to adopting and implementing the new technology of its day. Electricity provided cheap electrical power so that more and more middle-class families could obtain washing machines, refrigerators, vacuum cleaners, toasters, and radios, making the American dream of the good life a reality to many. The growing affluence gave more Americans the wherewithal to put a greater emphasis on leisure and play. A vision of limitless prosperity took hold, and contemporaries hailed the dawn of a golden age. It was, as the business leaders and commentators labeled it, a **"New Era."**

Prosperity ratified the policies of the "New Era" and confirmed to the Republicans that their devotion to high tariffs and limited government had been well placed. Grandiose claims were made promising a chicken in every pot, two cars in every garage, and that anyone with self-discipline and common sense could become a millionaire. And during the 1920s almost no one rose to challenge these visions. Former critics of American society became its ardent champions. John Spargo, once a leader of the Socialist Party, said socialism was "reactionary" and American capitalism offered "the greatest hope for mankind."

As growing numbers of people reached middle-class status and were more able to partake in pleasure-seeking activities, the Victorian moral code, which had been firmly in place since the end of the previous century, began to tarnish and a new set of morals and manners made an introductory appearance. Women flattened their breasts, bobbed their hair, donned loose-fitting clothes with short skirts, and handed back the keys as keepers of society's morals. They could be seen on the golf course or in a speakeasy, without a chaperone, smoking a cigarette or drinking alcohol. And in the nation's cities many were also participating in a mini–sexual revolution, kissing and petting on a first or second date.

To be sure, there was a flaw in this pretty picture of American prosperity. In this mad rush for riches a large number of Americans were being left behind. There was much distress on the nation's farms. The end of the European war led to a sharp decline in agricultural prices and a farm depression, which lasted throughout most of the 1920s. In order to provide some relief to farmers, Congress twice passed a measure designed to raise domestic crop prices by having the government sell the surplus overseas at low world prices. Twice Coolidge vetoed the legislation on grounds that it involved unwarranted government interference in the economy.

Also, many of the workers in America's factories found it difficult to keep up. While Secretary of Commerce Herbert Hoover proudly proclaimed that the average industrial wage had reached $1,200 a year in 1927, he did not mention that it took almost $2,000 a year for a family of five to live in a secure lifestyle. And even during the best years of the New Era about two-thirds of the nation's families had incomes that fell below that level. But keep in mind American workers had become the highest paid in history; most were able to purchase some of the new goods that were being turned out on assembly lines and ratchet up their standard of living. Millions, in fact, moved up the ladder and were able to taste the fruits of a middle-class standard of life.

Nonetheless, a growing inequality in wealth was becoming more noticeable as time went on. Wealthy and upper-class Americans were becoming richer, while the middle and working classes were having difficulty keeping up. Consumption, as a result, would not be able to match the vast growth in the productive capacity of American industry. But for a long time most people didn't seem to mind. Wall Street had captured the public's imagination. Stock prices had been in an unprecedented rise since the summer of 1921. But this was only prelude for what was to come. In 1927 prices on the New York Stock Exchange were up 33 percent. And in 1928 prices tacked on another 50 percent to heights that bore little relation to the earning power of the nation's corporations. Anyone fortunate enough to have purchased $25,000 worth of General Motors, the genuine growth stock of the decade, in 1921 was to become a millionaire by 1929. The public's interest in the stock market had become so great that newspapers began carrying the stock averages on their front pages.

By the summer of 1929 the stock market had come to dominate a new American business culture built around risk taking and materialistic values. The average American had faith in the future and believed in free markets. The successful businessman was the popular idol, and none more so than Henry Ford, who became the American folk hero of the 1920s. He had turned mechanical genius and dogged persistence into a fabulous fortune and international fame. Yet he gave the appearance of a man who had remained true to the simple virtues of an earlier time.

By late 1927 Silent Cal had become one of the most popular of American presidents. To most observers, it seemed the public wanted to give him another term. But at that very time Silent Cal summoned reporters to his office and offered each a slip of paper that read: "I do not choose to run for president in 1928." He allowed no questions, gave no comments.

Herbert Hoover, secretary of commerce and the most important political spokesman for the New Era, stepped forward and offered his services, promising to keep the country moving in the same direction set by Harding and Coolidge. Hoover personified executive competence. He had a passion for order and a breathtaking capacity for work. Insiders of the Coolidge administration often said Hoover was "secretary of commerce and undersecretary of everything else." Prior to his service in the Harding-Coolidge administrations he served under Wilson as food administrator during World War I. Wilson dragged him along to the Paris Peace Conference, as one of his advisors. He handled himself so well that John Maynard Keynes, the eminent British economist who was also a member to the Conference, concluded that Hoover was the "only man who emerged from the ordeal of Paris with an enhanced reputation." In fact, during 1919 Democratic Party bosses thought him a potential candidate for president. "There could not be a finer one," chimed in a rising young star from New York named Franklin Roosevelt. Hoover, however, rejected the call of the Democrats.

Voters, convinced that the nation was riding an escalator of unlimited progress, gave Herbert Hoover and the Republican Party a huge vote of confidence. He beat the Democrat, Al Smith, with the second largest majority up to that time. The voters had spoken, confirming the New Era as another American paradigm.

After the election the stock market hardly skipped a beat as it continued to climb week after week until, by September 1929, it stood a dizzying 300 percent above its level of only five years earlier. The risk-free environment of the 1920s had produced globs of free-flowing capital and consequently more specula-

tion, especially in the stock market. It was a genuine *"bubble."*
However, hardly anyone noticed that in scenarios such as those
panics are bigger and the chances of innocent bystanders getting hurt multiply.

In September 1929 spasms of doubt shook the stock market.
Then in late October the stock exchange was a mad scene of frantic sellers, elusive buyers, and exhausted clerks. By the end of
October all the paper profits of 1929 had disappeared. Early in
November the gains of 1928 were gone too, and by the summer of
1931 the hopes of 1927, 1926, and 1925 also dissolved. The collapse of the great bull market undermined the confidence of the
American public, and this had severe effects throughout the economy. Banks, some of them deeply implicated in the speculation,
sharply retrenched. The economy sputtered, turned down, and
kept going down, down, down. Soon the downward spiral was
pulling both the strong and the weak into a national depression.
Consumers cut their spending, pulling the rug out from under
thousands of small businesses that been just making it in good
times. During the following three years the economy was relentlessly squeezed to one-half its former size.

Hoover's response was clear and firm. From 1929 to 1932 the
president acted positively, and often vigorously, but within the
principles of the New Era. Hoping to stimulate business activity,
he signed the Smoot-Hawley Tariff Act, which sharply raised tariffs. Hadn't the economy responded positively to the Dingley Tariff
increase in the late 1890s and then again to the Fordney-
McCumber Tariff in the early 1920s? Like most Republicans,
Hoover was a firm believer that high tariffs played an important
confidence-building role in the economy.

When Secretary of Treasury Andrew Mellon said the country
needed to "liquidate labor, liquidate stocks, liquidate farmers,"
Hoover liquidated Mellon, by easing him out of the cabinet. When
Democratic leaders in Congress demanded that all federal

employment and salaries be cut by 10 percent, Hoover called the idea "heartless" and "medieval." Instead he cut his own salary and developed the first presidential plan ever to fight a depression.

Hoover was doing all he could to promote recovery, more than any president had in times past. He used the president's office as a clearing-house and coordinator for private relief. He invited business leaders to the White House and pressured them to promise to spread the work, rather than just fire a percentage of their employees. From 1929 to 1932 donations for relief increased about eightfold, a remarkable accomplishment by any previous standard. He set up a new Farm Board with $500 million to stabilize agricultural prices. In 1931, with the crises spreading throughout the developed world, he called for a moratorium on all war debts and reparations. In 1932 he established the Reconstruction Finance Corporation, which provided an astonishing $1.5 billion to a few key corporations. At Hoover's request Congress cut taxes in an attempt to restore public confidence. However, all this was not enough to stem the swelling tide. And Hoover's repeated attempts to restore confidence by publicly asserting that prosperity was just around the corner eventually bred cynicism and distrust.

If recovery had followed, Hoover would have been a hero, tough enough in crises to protect the American way. But nothing Hoover did worked. Consumers and investors refused to spend. The economy did not recover, and by early 1932 his policies were in a shambles. Employers, in a desperate effort to survive, discarded their programs for spreading the work; the Federal Farm Board ran out of credit and crop prices continued to tumble; and state and local governments ran out of funds to provide relief. When reduced revenues threw the federal budget out of balance, Hoover called for tax increases and Congress responded by enacting the largest peacetime tax increase to that date.

By 1932 almost 15 million workers, more than a quarter of the nation's labor force, were without jobs. Desperate, dispirited unemployed people stood in breadlines or congregated in shanty-towns called Hoovervilles. Almost every bank in the country had either closed its doors or severely restricted its operations; farmers burned their corn and left their cotton unpicked, as it no longer paid them to market their crops; the international gold standard was gone; and world trade was at a standstill. The U.S. financial system essentially stopped functioning; financial transactions came to a halt; the market for real estate and other assets dried up. And 89 percent of the dollar value of the stock market had vanished. The entire nation teetered on the edge of total collapse.

In that summer of 1932 a group of some twenty-two thousand World War I veterans descended on Washington to lobby for an immediate payment of a bonus due in 1945. After the Senate rejected the bill, some of the veterans stayed in Washington, living in ramshackle huts along the Potomac. Hoover ordered General Douglas MacArthur to clear the "bonus army" out of the capital, and the soldiers burned the veterans' shacks and blinded them with tear gas. Hoover's public image plummeted even more. By election time, millions were disenchanted with Hoover and blaming him in a harsh, personal way for the nation's troubles.

Amidst deepening national pessimism, the Democrats met in Chicago and nominated the popular governor from New York, Franklin Delano Roosevelt. FDR broke tradition and dramatically boarded a plane the next day to become the first nominee to accept in person. He told the cheering delegates, "I pledge to you—I pledge myself to a New Deal for the American people." During the campaign he attacked Hoover from the left, from the right, and from the mushy center. That fall a tidal wave of popular sentiment to repudiate Hoover and the Republicans swept FDR to victory. Thus ended the seventh political paradigm.

*   *   *

The Harding-Coolidge political model was an attempt to turn away from the government intervention of the progressive years and return to the freer economy of an earlier time. Their administrations had set out to slay inflation, to lower barriers to business entry, to unleash an entrepreneurial spirit in America, and to enhance the productive power of the economy. And they did! For eight marvelous years the nation's economy and stock market performed spectacularly. The post–World War I disruptions were ended. There was peace, prosperity, and social harmony throughout the land, and during that time the foundation was laid for the great mid-century prosperity that was to follow.

But the good times did not last. The economy fell off a cliff and a disillusioned American public was ready to back another round of government intervention in the economy.

TABLE 10

Seventh Political Paradigm (1921–1933), 12 Years

Election of:	Majority Paradigm Party Republicans		Minority Paradigm Party Democrats	
Paradigm	% of popular Vote		% of popular Vote	
1920 Begins	**Warren Harding***	60	James Cox	34
1923	Calvin Coolidge†			
1924 Preliminary	**Calvin Coolidge**	54	John Davis	29
1928 Confirmed	**Herbert Hoover**	58	Alfred Smith	41
1932 Ends				

*Bold = winner.

†Replaces Harding, who dies in office.

Congress	Republicans		Democrats/()Other	
	House	Senate	House	Senate
67th 1921–1923	303*	59	131(1)	37
68th 1923–1925	225	51	205(5)	43(2)
69th 1925–1927	247	54	183(4)	40(1)
70th 1927–1929	237	48	195(3)	47(1)

71st	1929–1931	**267**	**56**	167(1)	39(1)
72d	1931–1933	218	**48**	216(1)†	47(1)

Source: Composition of 67th–72th Congress: Information Please®, copyright © 2003 Pearson Education. (www.infoplease.com)

Note: All figures reflect immediate result of election.

*Bold = in control of House or Senate: more than all other parties combined. In Senate a tie goes to the president's party.

†Democrats organized the House due to Republican deaths.

Years in the White House with control of at least one house of Congress:

> Republicans: 10
> Democrats: 0

Economic Policies
- Budget Bureau set up / government spending cut
- Tariffs raised/ Fordney-McCumber and Smoot-Hawley
- Budget balanced and government reduced
- Taxes cut
- Business regulations loosened

Other Key Events
- Immigration restricted
- Ku Klux Klan
- Harding scandals
- Great bull market
- Stock market crash
- Great Depression

VII

The New Deal—Great Society

Early 1933 was, perhaps, the darkest year in the nation's history since the Civil War. In March of that year, just days before Franklin Roosevelt was due to take office, a nationwide banking panic threatened to collapse the whole economic system. Immediately after his inauguration FDR declared a "Bank Holiday" to check the panic, while the Treasury Department worked on an Emergency Banking Act. The law passed, virtually sight unseen, in a special session of Congress. When the banks reopened two weeks later people were waiting in line to redeposit money removed just a short while earlier. It was as if a magic wand had been placed over the entire banking system.

Franklin Delano Roosevelt had grown up in a world with all the advantages of wealth—a pony at age four, private tutors, and then Groton and Harvard. After serving as assistant secretary of the navy in Woodrow Wilson's administration, Roosevelt was tapped to be the Democratic vice-presidential candidate during the Republican landslide of 1920. Shortly thereafter personal disaster struck. In the summer of 1921 he fell victim to a devastating polio epidemic. Although he would never walk again unaided, he refused to give in. He reentered politics and was elected governor of New York in 1928. Roosevelt was a quick learner and, unlike Hoover, willing to experiment with a variety of schemes to achieve his goal. He was a master of popular phrasing—the famous line during his inaugural address "the only thing we have to fear is fear itself" still rings—and he artfully used the new mass medium, the radio, for twice-yearly "fireside chats," which left a great many people with the feeling he intuitively understood and sympathized with them.

FDR entered office with a firm attachment to the New Era and was to remain loyal to its principles until 1935. He assumed that private companies, with encouragement from Washington, would be able to regain their strength and lead business in a march back to prosperity.

Roosevelt began his presidency by calling Congress into special session and he plied it with proposals. During a whirlwind "Hundred Days" he guided through 15 major laws, the greatest burst of legislative activity in American history. Two measures, the National Industrial Recovery Act (NIRA) and the Agricultural Adjustment Act, formed the heart of the early New Deal. Both provided for industry itself to regulate its own members. The NIRA allowed the various industries to prepare a code of self-governance, which usually included some agreement on prices, wages, and acceptable limits to competition. The National Recovery Administration (NRA) was established to supervise the process. The Agricultural Adjustment Administration (AAA) did for farmers what the NIRA did for industry, and in much the same way. However, during its early months in operation, at a time with so much hunger in the nation, the AAA, hoping to raise the prices of farm crops, created a public relations fiasco by paying farmers to plow under their crops and slaughter their livestock.

The same principles were operating with the rest of the New Deal. The government created an agency to deal with the pressing problem of public relief. But again it was restrained in the use of government power. However, to the starving, all that mattered was that a little help had finally arrived. The nation felt a sense of relief that somebody was there in Washington attempting to do something about the dire situation in the country.

In Roosevelt's mind, finance and Wall Street were guilty of causing the depression. In his inaugural address Roosevelt stated bitterly, "The money changers have fled from their high seats in the temple of our civilization." Subsequent congressional investigations revealed that much speculation on the New York Stock Exchange had been conducted to fleece the public. To police the nation's stock exchanges the government created the Securities and Exchange Commission. It also set up the Federal Deposit Insurance Corporation to protect the public's savings when a bank failed.

Yet the most daring and controversial venture of the early New Deal was the Tennessee Valley Authority (TVA), which had sweeping authority over a domain that wound through seven southern states. It created a network of dams and canals to protect against floods and enabled millions of homes to hook up to government power lines and operate refrigerators and electric lights and gain access to the outside world through the radio.

By late 1934 confidence in the New Deal was ebbing. The depression had refused to lift. Unemployment, though it had declined since the darkest months of early 1933, was still about as bad as it had been the day Roosevelt was elected. The NRA was in a shambles. The idea of trying to overcome the depression by relying on voluntary cooperation between competing businesses and labor leaders had collapsed in the face of individual self-interest and greed. A series of strikes and labor walkouts were brutally suppressed and ushered in a spirit of class conflict. It was apparent that the New Deal was not working, and millions of angry, suffering people were beginning to look elsewhere for cures.

To many Americans the radical schemes of the flamboyant Louisiana senator Huey Long to "Share Our Wealth," which meant taking from the rich and giving to the poor; of the Catholic priest Charles Coughlin to inflate our money; and of Dr. Francis Townsend of Long Beach, California, to pension the unemployed senior citizens struck a responsive chord. These men appeared to be attracting a substantial following. Although no one knew the strength of these movements, the New Dealers, with these threats in mind, dropped their conservative stance and shifted to the left.

In January 1935 Roosevelt and his crowd called for three new groundbreaking acts. First they laid the foundation for a huge work relief program, the Works Progress Administration (WPA). During the next few years it employed on average about 2 million Americans in a variety of projects ranging from road maintenance to theatrical productions. Next was the crown jewel of the New Deal, the Social Security Act of 1935, which provided pensions for the elderly, insurance for the unemployed, and direct assistance to the disabled, the elderly poor, and single mothers. For the first time the government acknowledged its responsibility to provide for the welfare of those unable to care for themselves in an industrial society. It became the cornerstone of the American welfare state and the New Deal's most enduring monument. Third was the National Labor Relations Act (the Wagner Act), which committed the New Deal to supporting unions that were independent of management. It created a National Labor Relations Board (NLRB) to ensure the employees free choice of a bargaining agent and to compel employers to comply with the new rules. It was the most important piece of pro-union legislation in U.S. history and led to the revitalization of the American labor movement, which acted to balance corporate power. Between 1933 and 1941 union membership would more than triple, from well under 3 million to more than 8 million.

The legislation of 1935 signaled the New Deal had shifted from relief and recovery to reform and set up a system that Congress could build on in the future to reach more generous levels. While it did not cure the depression and the actual help it provided was modest, it did give hope to the bottom of society and enabled millions to avoid starvation and stay out of humiliating breadlines. The thrust of the "new" New Deal became clear: protect the "little guy."

In 1936 Roosevelt went before the electorate once again. Although the depression had not lifted, unemployment was down to 15 percent and there were definite signs of recovery. The election was to be the test of the New Deal's radical departure from past economic policy. Those with a stake in the fading New Era system—bankers, lawyers, corporate managers, and doctors—were horrified at the new direction society was taking. Their inability to explain what had gone wrong with the economy or predict what the government would do next deepened their frustration. By 1934 their doubts about the New Deal had turned into charges of incompetence and a year later into outward hatred. They formed organizations such as the American Liberty League, which spent millions to discredit the New Deal and FDR himself. Was it syphilis rather than polio he had? They were encouraged when the *Literary Digest*, after conducting a nation wide telephone survey, predicted victory for Alf Landon, the Republican presidential candidate. But to their surprise Roosevelt won a second term in the largest landslide in American history, up to that time. Not until after the election did the pundits realize the *Literary Digest* had not accounted for the fact that most people couldn't afford telephones.

FDR's stunning political victory was a preliminary endorsement of a New Deal paradigm. It meant that from now on responsibility for the national economy was placed squarely in the lap of the government. Victory also brought with it a new political alignment. Millions of Catholics, Jews, Italians, Irish, blacks, and laborers from the nation's industrial centers became tied to the New Deal and joined with an already solid "white" South in a fresh Democratic political coalition that was to dominate American politics for the next four decades. The Roosevelt administration put the local big-city politicians, the "bosses," in charge of distributing the public funds in their own areas and by their own standards. This gave them a greater ability to dispense favors and enabled them to expand and fortify their own political machines. Most big-city bosses became the Roosevelt administration's most dedicated supporters.

During the tense climate of 1935 and 1936 the Supreme Court challenged the government's primary source of power over the economy: its authority to regulate interstate commerce. The Court had ruled that many areas of business activity did not qualify as interstate commerce, and this threatened to severely limit the federal government's ability to regulate the economy.

Following the election, Roosevelt stated the New Deal could not function with a "horse and buggy" conception of interstate commerce and launched a frontal attack on the Court. In early 1937 he submitted a judiciary reorganization bill to Congress. In it he requested the right to enlarge the Court from 9 to up to 15 members, unless justices over 70 years of age resigned. Congress resisted, and when Roosevelt refused to compromise it appeared as if a classic fight between the executive and legislative bodies was about to take place. However, the justices blinked, and in the next important case the Court sided with the administration and soon after a series of retirements enabled the president to appoint a majority who were committed to the New Deal. The Court then issued a series of rulings approving such controversial New Deal measures as the Wagner Act and Social Security.

Shortly after the election Roosevelt, thinking he could move in the direction of a more balanced budget, cut federal spending and the slow but steady improvement in the economy gave way to another bout of deep recession. Industrial production fell by a third, the stock market plunged, and unemployment shot up by nearly 4 million. The Roosevelt administration quickly shifted gears and renewed the spending programs.

During 1937 union-organizing drives were ending in bloody battles between management and labor. Employers were gassing and beating workers and even resorting to murder to intimidate them so they would not unionize. In a show of support for labor the Roosevelt administration pushed through the Fair Labor Standards Act of 1938, which established a minimum wage level and an official rate of time and a half for overtime work and abolished child labor. This measure further stimulated the growth of labor unions and made clear the national government was determined to protect the welfare of its poorer citizens. But it was to be the only important new expansion in the New Deal during Roosevelt's second term.

FDR's clumsy attack on the Court, along with the severe recession of 1937, tarnished his reputation as a leader. In the mid-term elections of 1938 the Republicans staged a strong comeback. While the Democrats still retained a 93-member majority in the House, all 93 were southern Democrats, most of whom usually voted with Republican conservatives to block new social and economic reform measures. By the end of 1938 the New Deal was essentially over. Attempts to institute national health insurance met with stubborn resistance and Congress did not extend the New Deal into any new areas.

Meanwhile on the world stage, three powerful and discontented nations were on the march. Adolf Hitler denounced the Treaty of Versailles, took Germany out of the League of Nations, and reoccupied the Rhineland. Italy, under the rule of Benito Mussolini, invaded the independent African nation of Ethiopia. The emperor, Haile Selassie, called on the League of Nations for support, but the League's halfhearted measures utterly failed to halt the Italian conquest. Collective security failed its first important test. On the other side of the globe, Japan left the League and, in clear violation of the Open Door Treaty of 1922, seized Manchuria, the rich province in northern China. All the while the United States stood mute, doing nothing to stop the growing tide of aggression. FDR refused to assume a leadership role and unite the other nations against this Axis threat.

In September of 1939 German troops attacked Poland. France and England, who had mutual defense pacts with the Poles, joined in and the Great War was back on. Roosevelt clearly sympathized with England and France, America's old allies from World War I. When Britain was under siege, in the "Battle of Britain," in late 1940, Roosevelt risked violation of traditional neutrality and announced an exchange of 50 old American destroyers for the lease of eight British bases in the British West Indies. It was a formal declaration of America's commitment to the British cause.

In this tense atmosphere Roosevelt allowed the Democratic convention of 1940 to nominate him for an unprecedented third term. As the American people were not about to abandon a government committed to helping the needy and supporting the economy, Roosevelt handily won a third term against the Republican Wendell Wilkie. The voters had given a back-to-back endorsement of the New Deal, and there was now no doubt FDR was another pattern-setting president.

Roosevelt began his third term declaring the United States the "arsenal of democracy" and asked for authority to lend and lease goods and weapons to friendly countries fighting against aggressors. In March of 1941 Congress approved, giving Britain almost unlimited access to American production and credits and thereby wiping out all traces of American neutrality.

Meanwhile, in an effort to gain control of Southeast Asia's rich natural resources, Japan was extending its reach into French Indochina. The United States, anxious about Japan's growing territorial appetite, demanded a withdrawal from the mainland of China and, as leverage, imposed an increasingly tight embargo on trade with Japan. This policy had a sharp effect on the Japanese economy, and conciliatory forces in the Japanese government sought some way of mollifying the United States short of complete capitulation. But the United States was unrelenting. It would not negotiate before Japan declared its acceptance of an open door

throughout its area of expansion. Tensions between the two countries escalated. Without warning, on December 7, 1941, Japanese
planes struck the U.S. naval base at Pearl Harbor, Hawaii, crip-
pling America's Pacific fleet. The United States declared war on
Japan the following day. Within days Germany declared war on
America and the United States was fully involved in World War II.

Unlike its allies, America, from the beginning, was engaged in
two different wars. In the Pacific theater, the United States fought
almost alone. But America's priority was the European theater,
where it was part of a joint effort. In the early months both arenas
of the war offered a dismal picture of retreat and jeopardy. By
May of 1942 American forces in the Philippines had surrendered
to the Japanese and Japan's navy was firmly in control of the
Western Pacific. Germany's successes were even more ominous.
Its fleet of submarines, which had been held in check before
December 1941, unleashed a devastating attack on the Atlantic
supply lines. Meanwhile, Nazi mechanized divisions were driving
across North Africa into Egypt, threatening the Suez Canal. But
most important, a renewed offensive in Russia spread German
troops from the outskirts of Leningrad in the north to the gates of
Stalingrad in the south. In late fall of 1942 a Soviet collapse
loomed as a distinct possibility.

Yet, with an incredible swiftness, the United States mobilized
its military and industrial strength. American armies were soon
fighting on two fronts, the U.S. Navy gained control of the world's
oceans, and the country's factories revved up their mammoth
engines for the production of war goods. In 1942 America's production of tanks, planes, and supplies equaled the combined total
of the Axis powers; in 1944 it doubled the enemy's total. As the
crushing wave of American war materials reached the war zone
the balance in both theaters slowly changed in the Allies' favor. In
the summer of 1943 Russian armies took the offensive and slowly
began a drive westward toward Germany. Then, on June 6, 1944,
American and British troops executed a brilliant landing at Nor-

mandy, establishing a second front in France. By September the Russian army was pressing toward Poland, while American and British troops had reached German soil.

Meanwhile, the balance of sea power in the Pacific shifted in favor of the United States. In a campaign of island hopping, American troops slowly made their way closer and closer to Japan proper. In October 1944, in the battle of Leyte Gulf off the Philippines, Japanese naval power was destroyed. In early 1945, after a month of heavy fighting leaving more than 20,000 Americans dead and wounded, the United States won the island of Iwo Jima and was able to bomb the Japanese mainland at will.

World War II solved the problem of depression. In 1940 there were over 8 million unemployed; by war's end there was a shortage of skilled labor. Besides putting the formerly unemployed back to work, an additional 7 million workers, half of whom were women, were added to the labor force. There was an extraordinary expansion of government power during the war. The federal bureaucracy swelled to four times its 1939 size. To help fund the war effort, the revolutionary Revenue Act of 1942 established a steeply graduated income tax and for the first time covered most middle- and lower-income groups. As it outstripped all other taxes in revenue-generating potential, it was to become the heart of America's modern tax structure. The Servicemen's Readjustment Act promised unemployment compensation, medical care, mortgage funds, and educational subsidies for the returning veterans.

Wanting to preserve continuity of leadership during wartime, Roosevelt decided to run for yet a fourth term in 1944. Recognizing the fragility of FDR's health, Democratic leaders bargained to replace Henry Wallace Jr., the "controversial" vice-president, with Harry Truman. Things were going smoothly on both war fronts, at home the economy was humming, and FDR won an unprecedented fourth term. Then, on April 12, 1945, only a couple of months after his fourth inauguration and with victory on both fronts within eyesight, the president died of a cerebral hemorrhage.

The nation's grief was overwhelming. Franklin Roosevelt had been the nation's knight in shining armor who had come to rescue the poor, the weak, and the victimized. His administration had created the underpinnings of the welfare state, which would shape American politics for years to come. And obviously the people approved. He had been reelected three times by wide majorities.

Vice-President Harry Truman was suddenly thrust into the top spot. He portrayed himself, perhaps unwisely, as a simple man "overwhelmed" by the prospects of filling a giant's shoes. Truman had been considered a machine politician. Prior to his Senate tenure he was a Missouri judge, who owed his election to "boss" Tom Pendergast, the head of the Kansas City political machine. Although fair and honest personally, Truman had walked a fine line between honest service to his constituents and partisan loyalty to a corrupt machine.

Less than one month after Roosevelt's death, Germany collapsed and a tottering Japan was utterly exposed. By summertime a superbomb America had been working on in secrecy was ready for use. An array of civilian and military advisors counseled Truman to use the new weapon against Japan, and the inexperienced president agreed. On August 6 a single atomic bomb demolished the city of Hiroshima, killing about 140,000 people, and three days later a second bomb razed Nagasaki, killing 70,000 more. Five days later Japan agreed to surrender and World War II was over.

Truman had to switch gears to peacetime politics and initially he floundered. He could not withstand the pressures for a rapid demobilization of the armed forces and a quick dismantling of most wartime regulations. In June of that year he allowed an abrupt end to price controls, and the result was a burst of inflation. Farm prices rose nearly 30 percent by the end of the year. Labor, feeling shortchanged in the wartime prosperity, was quick to brandish its powerful new weapon, the right to strike. In early 1946, 3 percent of the labor force was on strike. When the country's railway workers went out on strike en masse, threatening a nationwide shutdown, Truman demanded they return to work voluntarily or else be drafted into the army and forced back to their jobs. They returned to work, but at a steep political cost. Not only had he offended large parts of the labor movement, a "key" component of the Democratic Party constituency, but Truman also appeared incapable of governing a nation wracked by consumer shortages, labor strife, soaring inflation, and an approaching cold war. In the mid-term congressional elections of 1946 the Republicans scored an impressive victory and took control of Congress for the first time since the Hoover administration.

In that same year, Congress passed the Full Employment Act, which created the Counsel of Economic Advisors to assist the president and asserted the principle that the government was responsible for maintaining a healthy economy. By war's end the ideas of the prominent British economist John Maynard Keynes were becoming fashionable in the United States. During the late 1930s Keynes had come up with a solution for the depression. He thought everyone was looking at the slump through the framework of a classical economy, wherein problems originated on the supply side. However, he insisted, this time the problem was on the demand side. Fear had set off a general strike against spending, and unless people could be induced to step up their purchases, the economy would remain unable to start up its engines of growth. His solution was to have the government move into the breach and borrow and spend when the public was disinclined to. Government intervention would ensure enough jobs and a buoyant economy.

Actually, the New Deal Democrats had already stumbled onto the Keynesian prescription. The new New Deal legislation had put hundreds of millions of dollars, perhaps billions, directly into the pockets of millions of senior citizens, WPA workers, and people who had lost a job. The difference was that Keynes advocated government fiscal policy, borrowing, spending, and tax cutting to bring about a robust recovery. Soon Keynes's followers would use the Keynesian macro-mechanisms of easy credit, lower taxes, and an increase in the government's deficit to fine-tune the economy. It would inaugurate a quarter-century of rising living standards, and during that time tens of millions of impoverished Americans would move up into the middle class.

Keynesian ideas dovetailed nicely with the Democrats' penchant to buttress the position of the lower classes. According to theory, enhancing the purchasing power of those groups would ensure a higher level of aggregate demand and provide booster rockets for the economy. The Democrats now had their own economic vision. The party of Jefferson and Keynes could now claim to be the party of economic legitimacy.

During the remainder of his first term Truman became engaged in a running battle with a Republican Congress to prevent a rollback of the New Deal. The new Congress was able to pass the Taft-Hartley Act, which curtailed some of the harsher antibusiness provisions of the Wagner Act, despite the president's veto. If a strike threatened to damage the economy, the president was given the authority to impose an 80-day "cooling off" period.

FDR's blueprints for a postwar foreign policy placed a great deal of reliance on the United Nations, which was another attempt at collective security, to guarantee America's security. Roosevelt took a soft line with Stalin, the Russian premier, looking the other way while the Soviets made plans for the domination of Poland and the Balkans, in hopes the wartime cooperation with Stalin would carry through into the postwar years and enable the United Nations to work. But Roosevelt's faith in Soviet goodwill would soon prove misplaced.

Following World War II, mutual distrust rendered the Soviets and the United States unable to agree on how to govern Europe. So Truman and Stalin began to divide it. The Soviet Union swallowed up the Eastern European nations and undertook an independent administration of the eastern zone of Germany in an attempt to create its own sphere of influence. But when Stalin seemed intent on fomenting a communist revolution in Greece, Truman veered from Roosevelt's policy of cooperation and adopted a hard line toward the Soviets.

Truman embraced the policy of "containment" authored by George Kennan, a career officer in the State Department, which committed the United States to the defense of nearly the entire free world against communist aggression and subversion. "Containment" was to become an article of faith during the remainder of the FDR paradigm.

Three important initiatives underpinned containment. First came the Truman Doctrine. Though aimed to shore up the Greeks, it was an open-ended offer of assistance to nations anywhere in the world who were resisting subjugation by armed minorities or outside pressures. But it was essentially an informal declaration of "cold war" against the Soviet Union. The "Marshall Plan" came next. Instead of demanding payments of its war debts as it had done after World War I, the United States underwrote the economies of Western Europe. This program would eventually funnel $12 billion in American aid to its Western allies, including West Germany, enabling their war-torn economies to achieve a minor miracle in recovery, and it brought the United States an extraordinary amount of goodwill in Europe. Third was the North Atlantic Treaty Organization (NATO), which involved a mutual assistance pact between the United States and 11 European nations that basically placed the North Atlantic nations under the shelter of American power.

The Soviets responded by blocking allied access to Berlin, which was buried deep within the Soviet sector of Germany, putting the two countries on a collision course. The United States decided against mounting a direct challenge to the Russians and instead began an airlift of essential supplies to the citizens in the isolated zones. After a year the Soviets were convinced to end the blockade.

As the parties lined up for the 1948 election the unpopular Truman looked like a sure loser. Without much enthusiasm and with little hope the Democratic national convention dutifully nominated Truman for another term. Sensing victory, the Republicans nominated Thomas Dewey, governor of New York, who four years earlier had run a tighter race against the indestructible Franklin Roosevelt than any of his Republican predecessors. And almost everyone expected Dewey to win.

Truman responded vigorously. He painted the Republican congressional insurgency as an attempt to dismantle the New Deal and presented himself, Franklin Roosevelt's successor, as its lonely defender. He labeled the Republican legislature a "do nothing" Congress and promised the people a "Fair Deal." And the people responded. When the ballots were counted, Truman had pulled off one of the most stunning political upsets in American history.

Truman's second term was filled with problems. In late 1948 Mao Tse-tung's Communists poured out of Manchuria and, in less than a year's time, swept through China, driving Chiang Kai-shek's tattered Nationalist remnants to the island of Taiwan. As China was thought to be the key to all of Asia, the Truman administration had to explain why they did not (or could not) save China. Then in the same year the Soviets detonated an atomic bomb, signed a mutual defense pact with China, and suddenly it seemed as if America was terribly vulnerable.

In February 1950 Senator Joseph McCarthy took advantage of the public's anxiety and claimed we were losing the cold war because the Truman administration was infiltrated with "traitors" who wanted the communists to win. To prove his point he claimed he had a list of authentic communists employed in the State Department. During the next four years McCarthy made anticommunism his personal crusade, frightening government officials with charges of communist infiltration in their departments, staging melodramatic investigations of suspected enemy agents, and exercising a powerful influence over government appointments. He gathered enormous support. According to a national poll in early 1954, three out of five Americans with an opinion about McCarthy favored his activities.

In June 1950 troops from North Korea, a puppet state of the Soviet Union, attacked South Korea, which was under the protection of the United States. Truman's policy of "containment" was put to its first important test. If he ignored this blatant act of aggression it could invite belligerency elsewhere. Furthermore, it would reaffirm McCarthy's charges that the president was soft on communism. Truman invoked the United Nations to declare a police action, with the United States providing the bulk of the troops, to roll back the North Korean invasion. By early 1951 the "quasi-war" had settled into a grudging, bloody struggle along the original boundary.

Despite having a Democratic Congress, during his second term, Truman couldn't get his Fair Deal program through Congress. Southerners still held the balance of power and were able to help Republicans block proposals for national health insurance and federal aid to education. Truman, however, was able to extend some of the New Deal's key programs. Social Security was broadened and the minimum wage was raised. The president also confronted the issue of racial segregation, long ignored by the Roosevelt White House. He desegregated the armed forces and appointed the first black judge to the federal bench.

By 1952 Truman's prestige as a leader was in the dumps. Evidence of corruption among the president's associates sullied his reputation, and the Korean War had brought with it renewed inflation. Add to this the public's growing frustration over his inability to bring the "police action" in Korea to a conclusion and it was clear Truman's presidency was in a shambles. According to polls only one in four approved of the president—one of the lowest approval ratings ever recorded for an American president. Truman chose not to run for another term.

The Democrats selected Adlai Stevenson, governor of Illinois, to head their ticket. The Republicans nominated the popular World War II general Dwight "Ike" Eisenhower for the top spot and Richard Nixon, senator from California, for the number two position. Eisenhower was unpretentious and easygoing. In contrast, Nixon had a history of red-baiting and a reputation for insincerity. During the campaign when faced with charges of unethical use of campaign contributions he had to go on television to defend himself, which he did quite successfully. In November 55 percent of the voters cast their lot with the Eisenhower-Nixon ticket and put an end to 20 years of Democratic rule.

Republican Interregnum

Initially the Republicans had high hopes of rolling back the New Deal. Eisenhower set out to balance the federal budget and minimize government influence in economic matters. But the attempt to revive the past faltered during the recession of 1953–1954. Reluctantly, but realistically, Ike abandoned the goal of a balanced budget. Within the year the Eisenhower administration had committed itself to protecting the economy with fiscal countermeasures, and when the recession lifted the president gave due credit to "the automatic workings of the fiscal system." This ended the debate on dismantling the Democrats' approach to the economy. Both parties now stood ready to support a slumping economy by adjusting taxes and federal spending, and this consensus bred a new confidence in the economy.

During the 1950s the nation witnessed a period of vigorous economic growth. A pent up demand for consumer goods, along with heavy government spending, during the cold war provided a strong stimulus to propel the economy upward. Affluence replaced the poverty and hunger of the Great Depression for most Americans. The middle class grew bigger and more prosperous than ever before. By the mid-1950s the average American family had twice the real income that a similar family had in the boom years of the 1920s. A mounting number of Americans could now afford homes, suburbia mushroomed, and an increasing number of the nation's youth were choosing college.

When Eisenhower took office he insinuated that atomic weapons might be used in Korea and broke the stalemate. The general was determined not to lose any more people or territory to communism but wanted to do it on the cheap. In 1954 his secretary of state, John Foster Dulles, announced a policy of massive retaliation. It was an implied threat that, rather than becoming involved in limited wars, such as Korea, the United States would consider the possibility of using nuclear weapons to halt any communist aggression that threatened the vital interests of America, anywhere in the world. By relying on its superior nuclear striking power to keep the communists at bay, the Republicans were able to cut defense expenditures by about a quarter. And that helped to keep overall government spending in check.

Meanwhile Senator McCarthy had pushed on with his anticommunist crusade and took his attack to the upper echelons of the army. The American people, watching the proceedings on television, were shocked by the skimpiness of the evidence and the senator's crude, bullying behavior. It became apparent that the senator was overstepping his boundaries, and public opinion turned against McCarthy, providing cover for the Senate to strip him of authority. A chastened Senator Joe McCarthy soon faded into obscurity.

By election time 1956 the nation was bathing in prosperity. Eisenhower had taken a strong stance on inflation and the rate had fallen precipitously, the Korean War had ended, the Red Scare had subsided, and there was peace. Ike easily defeated Adlai Stevenson, once again. It was the first time a president from the minority party, running for reelection, had won a majority of the popular vote. However, this was also the first time, since 1848, that a winning presidential candidate lost both houses of Congress to the opposing party.

The World War II general resisted demands for more extensive government involvement in American life. He fought to control government spending and encourage as much private initiative as possible. Example: Eisenhower guided passage of the Highway Act of 1956, which appropriated funds to build a 41,000-mile interstate highway system that would connect the nation's major cities. However, he insisted on obtaining the funding from taxes on fuel, tires, new cars, and trucks and not using general revenue funds.

But, most important, Ike also maintained the nation's commitment to the basic social programs of the New Deal. He signed bills extending Social Security benefits, agreed to a further increase in the minimum wage, liberalized unemployment insurance and workmen's compensation, and backed the creation of a Department of Health, Education, and Welfare.

By 1960 the national mood was less troubled than when the decade began. Yet brewing on the national plate was concern over Russian advances in technology and growing military might. In 1957 the Soviet Union shocked Americans with the successful launching of a *Sputnik* spacecraft into orbit. The Soviet premier, Nikita Khrushchev, taking advantage of the furor, boasted to the American people, "We will bury you . . . Your grandchildren will live under communism." This set off a spasm of insecurity and doubt in the country, and many Americans began to question whether we were still the leading nation of the world. Adding to the country's anxiety, in the prior year Fidel Castro had led a band of revolutionaries to overthrow the Cuban government and install a communist satellite at our "very doorstep."

Democratic Restoration

In 1960 Vice-President Nixon carried the Republican standard. He conducted his campaign as an heir apparent would, promising to continue the policies of Eisenhower's popular rule. Meanwhile,

John Fitzgerald Kennedy, the youthful senator from Massachusetts, captured the nomination of the party of FDR. Kennedy selected Lyndon Johnson, the Senate majority leader, who was from Texas, for the second spot to shore up the ticket in the South, which no longer could be taken for granted to vote Democratic.

Kennedy skillfully exploited the national mood of frustration that had followed *Sputnik* and attacked the Republicans from the "right," which is typically GOP territory. He faulted Eisenhower for holding down defense spending, for allowing a missile gap with Russia to occur on his watch (it hadn't), and for letting communism gain a foothold in Cuba, which was just 90 miles from Florida. Kennedy promised not to relinquish a single piece of territory to the communists and recaptured the Oval Office for the Democrats in the closest election since 1888. John Kennedy, at 43 years of age, was the youngest elected president in America's history. His stirring rhetoric and skillful use of symbolism would rekindle the nation's "devotion to the public good" ethic. "Ask not what your country can do for you; ask what you can do for your country" from his inaugural speech, and the establishment of the Peace Corps, wherein American volunteers would take their skills to the poor nations of the world, were an inspiration to the nation's youth. Many would become deeply involved in social issues, such as civil rights, which were in the process of moving to center stage in the liberal tent.

Kennedy's "New Frontier" program aimed to carry forward the traditional long-overdue Democratic reforms in education, health care, and civil rights. But they were blocked by the conservative coalition of Republicans and southern Democrats. JFK had to settle for a modest increase in the minimum wage, expanded Social Security benefits, and the passage of a bill for manpower training. But he did act boldly in initiating the first deliberate use of fiscal policy to sustain—up until that time it had only been used to stimulate recovery from a slump—an economic expansion.

In the early 1960s there was a great deal of unrest in the black community. They had won an important victory in the mid-fifties when the Warren Supreme Court desegregated the public schools. Although the Eisenhower administration had quietly and unobtrusively worked to desegregate federal facilities, progress was excruciatingly slow and the blacks were anxious and expected more. JFK had raised hopes during the campaign, when he promised to launch an attack on segregation in the Deep South. However, as the "white" South was an important part of the Democratic coalition, the Kennedy administration was slow to follow through on their promises. Soon, however, black leaders, such as Martin Luther King, Jr., took the offensive and began to challenge the white southern power structure by staging marches and demonstrations aimed at integrating public facilities and promoting blacks' right to the vote. This forced the hand of the Kennedy administration. It ended its long hesitation on civil rights and sounded the call for action. But Congress was not ready to go along.

In the fall of 1962 Khrushchev thought he could improve the Soviets' strategic position vis-à-vis the United States by deploying missiles in Cuba. Russia was in the processes of moving missiles to Cuba when the Kennedy administration got wind of it. Kennedy responded with a naval blockade, quarantining Cuba from receiving new missiles, and demanded the removal of those already there. The world held its breath for six days until 16 Soviet supply ships turned from their Cuban-bound course and went home. Russia dismantled their bases, America promised to honor Cuba's sovereignty, and in the United States JFK emerged a hero. The American people who had felt on the defensive since *Sputnik* were suddenly bursting with national pride.

Convinced that the Vietnamese struggle was primarily a fight to halt the spread of communism in Asia, Kennedy increased the amount of American aid and upped the number of American advisors in the field from a few hundred in 1961 to over 16,000 in 1963.

And when he tacitly approved a coup that led to the overthrow and death of Ngo Dinh Diem, head of the South Vietnam government, it raised the stakes even more.

In November 1963, while on a trip to Dallas, Texas, Kennedy was assassinated and Vice-President Lyndon Baines Johnson (LBJ) became president. LBJ had a reputation as a wheeler-dealer. Although a politician all his life, he had amassed a personal fortune. Johnson took Kennedy's policies, along with some of his own, and began pushing them through Congress. He declared "War on Poverty" and convinced Congress to spend billions of dollars to reach out and help the various groups that had been left behind. The Civil Rights Act of 1964 provided a framework for racial reform and began a program to include blacks in the American mainstream. Nor did he forget the economy: LBJ guided a modest tax cut through Congress, reducing personal income taxes by $10 billion.

In 1964 LBJ ran for election in his own right. Proposing a program labeled the "Great Society," which would take the New Deal to a new level, he steamrolled over conservative Republican Barry Goldwater, who advocated dismantling the welfare state and returning to unregulated free enterprise. Johnson received the largest popular majority in the nation's history and was able to carry scores of liberal Democratic congressmen to victory with him and break the conservative grip on Congress. An explosion of groundbreaking and far-reaching laws that would make fundamental changes in American life followed.

Before the new "do everything" Congress ended its first session in the fall of 1965 it had passed the entire Democratic reform agenda. Medicare and Medicaid, a food stamp program, federal aid to education, federal rent supplements for the poor, a Head Start program for disadvantaged preschool children, vocational training for high school dropouts, and, above all, the Civil Rights Acts of 1964 and 1965 had moved the nation beyond the New Deal. The aged and the poor were now guaranteed access to medical care; communities saw an infusion of federal funds to improve local education; African Americans could now begin to attend integrated schools, enjoy public facilities, and gain political power by exercising their right to vote. As Johnson's Great Society committed his administration to a vigorous management of matters that were once controlled by localities, the federal government gained more control than ever before over American economic and social life.

The Supreme Court, under Chief Justice Earl Warren, sought greater social justice by protecting the rights of the underprivileged and minorities and permitting free expression to flourish. He led the Court in decisions to extend constitutional guarantees, for the rights of the accused, banning school prayer, and permitting the publication of obscenity.

LBJ, like prior Democratic presidents, was committed to the policy of containment. Beginning in the summer of 1965, Johnson enlarged the American contingent in Vietnam until it exceeded half a million men in 1968. His strategy was to increase the level of punishment until the price of continuing the war became too high and the enemy quit. However, it didn't work out that way. The North Vietnamese did not fold. In fact, in 1968 they mounted a surprising show of strength, the "Tet Offensive," that carried into the primary cities of South Vietnam, which had been thought beyond the reach of the guerilla army. A growing number of Americans lost heart, and Johnson threw in the towel. He stopped escalating the war, announced a serious willingness to negotiate, and said he would not seek reelection.

Meanwhile, years of government intrusion in the economy had crimped its productive ability, much as during the progressive era. Johnson's "guns and butter" program generated a great deal of purchasing power which practically guaranteed inflation. While this was certainly a sign of economic disarray, many commentators believe that a nation's inflation rate is also a barometer of its social health. As inflation took off for the sky, so too did racial and social strife. There was a wave of violent crime, drug usage, divorce, illegitimacy, and other social problems producing what sociologist Frances Fukuyama called "The Great Disruption." And with it, Johnson's and the liberals' great dream of social justice ended.

An excess of individualism plagued the American nation. In many ways, it was 1848 all over again. The rapid social change, the increasing individual choices concerning jobs, where to live, and marriage partners, had produced a breakdown in the traditional rules of behavior. Civil rights legislation had raised the expectations of urban blacks for improvement. Indeed, the War on Poverty was to cut the number of indigent Americans almost in half. However, for those left behind in the nation's ghettos, frustration rose. In the summer of 1965 an outburst of rage in Watts, the black section of Los Angeles, culminated in a riot that cost 34 lives and destroyed millions of dollars' worth of property. And it was just the curtain-raiser for what was to follow during the next three summers.

At the same time, the children of the upper middle class led a cultural insurgency, which challenged the white power structure. Some protested the war in Vietnam, burned their draft cards, seized campus buildings, forcing temporary university shutdowns, and joined in exhilarating antiwar rallies chanting, "Hell no, we won't go." They held demonstrations that confronted the president; so much so that he couldn't travel to the nation's major cities. LBJ became a hostage in the White House.

Others challenged the traditional manners and morals of America. They experimented with drugs, sex, and rock music. Their exotic clothes or no clothes, narcotics instead of alcohol, and the right to sex on demand were extensions of personal freedom . . . or so they thought. They flocked to places like Woodstock to participate in love-soaked, dope-hazed happenings. This revolutionary assault led by the children of the affluent sought to change the social structure to a more utopian one they fantasized about. But to ordinary middle- and working-class Americans it seemed as if the nation's youth had gone berserk. Traditional institutions and ideals such as the family, sexual morality, the work ethic, and patriotism were under attack, and middle- and working-class Americans felt threatened.

By 1968 social strife seemed out of control. Early in the year Martin Luther King, Jr., was shot and killed. Within days ghettos from New York to California exploded with riots and violence. Then two months later Bobby Kennedy, John Kennedy's brother, was shot and killed in California, while campaigning for the Democratic presidential nomination. That summer thousands of mostly "upper"-middle-class youngsters rallied at the Democratic convention in Chicago to protest the war and Hubert Humphrey's inevitable nomination. They slept in parks, staged demonstrations, and egged on the police with chants, taunts, and rocks. On the third night, demonstrators tried a march on the convention hall and police dispersed the protestors with tear gas and billy clubs. The delegates, looking out from their hotel windows, gasped with horror as they saw the streets below them running red with the blood of the sons and daughters of their own affluent friends and neighbors.

Another Republican Interlude

Richard Nixon, the loser by a hair in the 1960 election, was able to come back and win the Republican nomination that year. He selected Spiro Agnew, an obscure governor of Maryland, as his running mate and gathered 43 percent of the popular vote, which was enough to beat Hubert Humphrey, in a close contest. Third party candidate George Wallace, governor of Alabama, had mounted an attack on the liberal elite and received almost 14 percent of the ballots. The combined Nixon-Wallace vote was nearly 57 percent, suggesting there was a silent majority out there, who were fed up with psychedelic drugs, rock music, long hair, and sexual permissiveness; who were against school busing and swelling welfare rolls, but for the death penalty and greater protection from crime; and who wanted to put a halt to the growth of federal power. Nixon had been on the right side of those social issues.

Richard Nixon promised to impose law and order on a permissive society. He appointed a more moderate justice, Warren Burger, as Chief Justice of the Supreme Court and gave the police wider latitude in dealing with suspected criminals. Nixon tried to stem the runaway liberal programs that had become a giveaway to every group who claimed a grievance. He dismantled the Office of Economic Opportunity, which had administrated the War on Poverty, and announced a period of "benign neglect" in the government's policies for racial equality. He tried to reduce government spending and make the federal bureaucracy operate more efficiently. In an effort to shift authority away from Washington he initiated a revenue-sharing plan, which transferred responsibility for social programs from Washington to state and local authorities.

However, Nixon, like Eisenhower before him, accepted the main outlines of the welfare state. In 1972 he went along with Wilbur Mills, head of financial matters in the House, to raise Social Security benefits 20 percent and index them to the Consumer Price Index. Nixon supported a significant expansion of the food stamp program and allowed his Labor Department to introduce regulations creating the first "affirmative action" programs.

Nixon also showed a willingness to abandon past convictions and innovate. In August of 1971, with inflation proving stubborn, he acted boldly to spruce up the economy for the coming election year. He announced a 90-day freeze on wages and prices to be followed by federally imposed guidelines. In addition he devalued the dollar, which led to a greatly improved balance of trade. Also, tellingly, he claimed, "We are all Keynesians," acknowledging Republicans also had become believers in the New Deal paradigm.

Richard Nixon realized that one way or another he had to end the Vietnam War. He reduced the number of American troops in Vietnam from over half a million when he took office to under 100,000 in 1972. These withdrawals significantly lessened criticism of the war, giving him more time to reach some kind of an accommodation with North Vietnam. In 1972, with little progress toward reaching a settlement, Nixon expanded the scale of America's air attacks on the North Vietnamese, increasing the punishment considerably above the levels the Johnson administration had inflicted. North Vietnam modified its demands, and the president got his face-saving treaty.

At the same time, Nixon, with his advisor Henry Kissinger, showed exceptional imagination in international diplomacy. They recognized China's break with Russia presented an opportunity to play one off against the other. With Kissinger as the man in motion, Nixon dramatically improved America's relations first with China, then with the Soviet Union. The United States abandoned the cause of the Chinese Nationalists, accepted Red China in the United Nations, and prepared the way for a broader interchange. Then, using the new U.S.-China friendship as leverage, Nixon moved toward détente, a relaxation of tension, with Russia. The United States and the Soviet Union negotiated a sale of American grain to Russia, welcomed each other's citizens more liberally, and reached agreement on regulating their nuclear weapons. The weapons treaty (SALT I) was a symbolic first step toward control of the nuclear arms race and helped ease long-standing fears of a thermonuclear war.

By election time 1972, unemployment was below 5 percent while GNP was expanding at an impressive clip, cold war tensions were much reduced, and Nixon won one of the most impressive political victories of modern times, capturing over 60 percent of the popular vote, the third best showing ever. Shortly after the

election, inflation, which had been slowly gaining ground, accelerated, reaching an annual rate of over 10 percent, GNP dropped by
6 percent, the worst falloff since World War II, and unemployment
rose to over 9 percent, the highest level since the Great Depression, while the stock market fell off a cliff. Nixon, as the manager
of the national economy, took most of the blame for this predica-
ment. But this wave of inflation was worldwide, as basic resources,
from grains and sugar to oil and copper, soared in price. When
inflation was superimposed on an American recession, the standard techniques of economic management no longer worked.
Attacking the recession risked an even wilder inflation, and fighting inflation risked even deeper recession. And to make matters
worse, an energy crisis was soon added to the mix.

In late 1973, during a Middle Eastern war between the Arab
nations and the Israelis, the oil-producing Arab nations, upset
with the U.S. effort to resupply Israel, cut production by about 25
percent, leading to a worldwide shortage of oil. Millions of Americans feared they might not have the oil to heat their homes, and
every morning weary consumers scoured the city for an open service station, then waited in line for hours for a few gallons of
gasoline. Then in a second blow the Organization of Petroleum
Exporting Countries (OPEC), a cartel of the world's oil producers, quadrupled the price of oil. In a few weeks' time gasoline
prices at the pump doubled in the United States, while the cost of
home heating fuel rose even more sharply.

This was one of the most momentous events of the postwar
era. Cheap energy had been the underlying force behind the
amazing growth of the American economy after World War II. The
huge gas-guzzling cars, the flight to the suburbs, the long drives to
work each day, the detached homes heated by fuel oil and natural
gas and cooled by central air-conditioning, represented a dependence on cheap oil that everyone took for granted. The American
people had come to base their way of life on gas prices that averaged about thirty-five cents a gallon. When OPEC raised their

prices Americans were suddenly faced with drastic and unexpected increases in such everyday expenses as driving to work and heating their homes. Add an "oil shock" to world economies, which were in the process of losing their productive might, and the result was an inflation that swept over the United States and flooded the world, overwhelming all national economies.

Meanwhile, a third-rate burglary of the Democratic headquarters at the Watergate Apartments in Washington, D.C., began to lead on a trail back to the White House. A special prosecutor was appointed to investigate whether the president was involved in a cover-up. As more and more evidence surfaced, pointing in the direction of Nixon's involvement, the House of Representatives prepared to vote articles of impeachment. In August of 1974 Richard Nixon recognized the handwriting on the wall and resigned. During the proceedings and aftermath 25 presidential aides, including Attorney General John Mitchell, were sentenced to jail terms.

Watergate and disillusionment with the war in Vietnam discredited strong presidential leadership. Congress passed the War Powers Act in 1973, which required the president to get its approval before sending troops into action beyond America's borders. Capitol Hill had successfully challenged the long-held tradition of allowing the chief executive a relatively free hand in foreign matters, which presidents from George Washington to Lyndon Johnson had relied upon.

Vice President Gerald Ford, former minority leader of the House, took the reins of government. Nixon had selected Ford to succeed Spiro Agnew, who was forced to resign in order to avoid prosecution for accepting bribes during his prior tenure as governor of Maryland. Gerald Ford took office in the dark days of 1974, following the first presidential resignation in American history, with the economy in deep recession and with inflation skyrocketing. Ford's initial style, in contrast to Nixon's, was unaffected, amiable, and open, and this soothed the public.

Shortly after taking office Ford issued a broad pardon to Nixon, so that an ex-president of the United States would not end up joining his aides behind bars. This badly damaged Ford's presidency and dogged him for the rest of his term. In the early months of 1975, the new administration, hemmed in by the Case-Church Amendment to the new War Powers Act, which forbade further U.S. involvement in Southeast Asia, was unable to lift a finger to stem North Vietnam's flagrant treaty violations, and America's old allies in South Vietnam and Cambodia suddenly collapsed. About the same time, the president was able to engineer a modest tax cut, which helped the economy struggle to its feet.

A Second Restoration

By 1976 it was apparent that Ford, still smarting from Nixon's downfall and the aftermath of the worst recession since the Great Depression, was in for a tough reelection fight. The Democrats selected Jimmy Carter, a former one-term governor of Georgia and a born-again Christian, who ran a campaign based on trust. Carter beat out Ford in a close contest, and once again the Democrats were back in the White House. But Carter was unable to restore a sound economy. Although inflation had eased during Ford's reign, it was by no means tamed. Carter banked on an energy program to hold down inflation, while pursuing modest increases in government spending in hopes of getting the economy moving again. In addition the minimum wage was raised by nearly 50 percent. However, he could not get the bulk of his energy program passed, and by 1978 inflation was heating up once again. Revolution broke out in Iran, a leading member of OPEC, and a new round of international oil shortages began. Gasoline prices in the United States climbed to over one dollar a gallon. Carter proposed a second energy program, but it was no more acceptable to Congress than the first. As election time was approaching, inflation was running at an annual rate of more than

14 percent, the greatest in 30 years, while unemployment was also rising.

The Carter administration took a new approach to foreign affairs. The flexible Nixon-Kissinger-Ford policy of détente was out. So too was the traditional Democratic policy of containment. In their places was a new crusade for human rights. Meanwhile, socialism seemed to be on the march again and the Carter administration appeared unconcerned. Nicaragua fell and Carter's response was to extend aid to the new "leftist" government in hopes that it would keep them out of the Cuban-Russian orbit. Then when the Soviets invaded Afghanistan, to preserve a friendly Marxist government, the administration's response was mostly symbolic. They embargoed the export of grain to the Soviets, boycotted the 1980 Moscow Olympics, and scuttled the tentative SALT II agreement. But rather than halt the Afghan invasion, it put the United States and the Soviet Union back on a collision course.

Yet the worst foreign policy crisis of Carter's term was still to come. In early 1980 radical Iranian students seized the American embassy and imprisoned 53 Americans, most of whom were entitled to diplomatic immunity under international law. At first Carter relied on diplomacy and economic sanctions to attempt to free the hostages. But this went nowhere, and after a few months Carter was pressured to do something. A feeble rescue attempt failed when two helicopters collided in the Iranian desert, underscoring America's inability to act as a world power. As the hostage crisis dragged on through the summer and fall of 1980, it revealed the extent to which American power had declined and people began to question whether the United States could protect its people and its interests on the international stage.

By 1980 it was apparent that the New Deal–Great Society welfare state had become bloated. Inflation had taken on a life of its own and was threatening to become a permanent fixture in the

American economy. The nation was humiliated by a third-rate power holding 52 (one had been released) of its citizens in captivity. And the social programs of this period seemed to be losing their magic to do much good. Despite billions of dollars spent and thousands of arcane regulations, crime was increasing, the educational performance of the nation's youth was dropping, and poverty, though much reduced, persisted. But not to worry! Like in times past when paradigm policies had lost their punch and the future looked bleak, a fresh voice, espousing an alternative vision, appeared on the scene. Those whose eyes were turned westward were able to see Ronald Reagan, who had a stubborn disregard for the accepted wisdom, coming over the hill and riding rapidly toward the White House.

The eighth and longest political paradigm was finally over. Franklin Delano Roosevelt had set the country on a new direction, and during the ensuing 48 years nearly every aspect of economic, social, and political developments bore his imprint. The Democrats set out to make the government responsible for protecting the poor, the elderly, and low-income workers and soon even the welfare of the "middle class" became the government's responsibility. The Democrats, believing every problem had a government solution, consistently enlarged the scope of the federal government's responsibilities.

Democrats Truman, Kennedy, Johnson, and Carter were in wholehearted agreement with the Rooseveltian philosophy and attempted to extend it further. They taxed and spent and kept on increasing the amounts until government spending as a share of Gross Domestic Product (GDP), which had been under 2 percent before World War II, was running well over 20 percent, requiring levels of taxation that would have caused riots in the earlier time. Republicans, under Presidents Eisenhower, Nixon, and Ford, went along with the general direction that Roosevelt had set but wanted to restrain the thrust of government's intrusion into the economy or manage it better. They also served to reduce cold war tensions. But during the whole of the FDR political model the Republicans were able to control both the White House and at least one house of Congress for only one two-year period—1953–1955.

TABLE 11

Eighth Political Paradigm (1933–1981), 48 Years

Election of:	Majority Paradigm Party		Minority Paradigm Party	
	Democrats		Republicans	
Paradigm	**% of Popular Vote**		**% of Popular Vote**	
1932 Begins	**Franklin D. Roosevelt***	57	Herbert Hoover	40
1936 Preliminary	**Franklin D. Roosevelt**	61	Alfred Landon	37
1940 Confirmed	**Franklin D. Roosevelt**	55	Wendell Willkie	45
1944	**Franklin D. Roosevelt**	53	Thomas Dewey	46
1945	Harry Truman replaces FDR			
1948	**Harry Truman**	49	Thomas Dewey	45
1952 Lose election	Adlai Stevenson	44	**Dwight Eisenhower**	55
1956 Lose election	Adlai Stevenson	42	**Dwight Eisenhower**	57
1960 Restored	**John Kennedy**	49.7	Richard Nixon	49.5
1963	Lyndon Johnson replaces Kennedy			
1964	**Lyndon Johnson**	61	Barry Goldwater	39
1968 Lose election	Hubert Humphrey	42.7	**Richard Nixon**	43.4
1972 Lose election	George McGovern	38	**Richard Nixon**	61
1974	Gerald Ford replaces Nixon			
1976 Restored	**Jimmy Carter**	50	Gerald Ford	48

*Bold = winner.

	Democrats		Republicans / ( ) other	
Congress	**House**	**Senate**	**House**	**Senate**
73d 1933–1935	**313***	**59**	117(5)	36(1)
74th 1935–1937	**322**	**69**	103(10)	25(2)
75th 1937–1939	**333**	**75**	89(13)	17(4)
76th 1939–1941	**262**	**69**	169(4)	23(4)
77th 1941–1943	**267**	**66**	162(6)	28(2)
78th 1943–1945	**222**	**57**	209(4)	38(1)
79th 1945–1947	**243**	**57**	190(2)	38(1)
80th 1947–1949	188	45	**246**(1)	**51**

*Bold = in control of House or Senate: more than all other parties combined. In Senate a tie goes to the president's party.

	Democrats		Republicans / ( ) other	
Congress	House	Senate	House	Senate
81st 1949–1951	**263**	**54**	171(1)	42
82d 1951–1953	**234**	**48**	199(2)	47(1)
83d 1953–1955	213	46	**221**(1)	**48**(2)
84th 1955–1957	**232**	**48**†	203	47(1)
85th 1957–1959	**234**	**49**	201	47
86th 1959–1961	**283**	**64**	153	34
87th 1961–1963	**262**	**64**	175	36
88th 1963–1965	**258**	**67**	176	33
89th 1965–1967	**295**	**68**	140	32
90th 1967–1969	**248**	**64**	187	36
91st 1969–1971	**243**	**58**	192	42
92d 1971–1973	**255**	**54**	180	44(2)
93d 1973–1975	**242**	**56**	192(1)	42(2)
94th 1975–1977	**291**	**61**	144	37(2)
95th 1977–1979	**292**	**61**	143	38(1)
96th 1979–1981	**277**	**58**	158	41(1)

Source: Composition of 73rd–96th Congress: Information Please ®, copyright© 2003 Pearson Education. (www.infoplease.com)

Note: All figures reflect immediate result of election.

†No party controls.

Years in the White Hose with control of at least one house of Congress:

> Democrats: 30
> Republicans: 2

Economic Policies
- Tariff cut
- Government regulations
- Unbalanced budget
- Increased government spending
- Social safety net

Other Key Events
- Prohibition repealed
- Pearl Harbor attacked and U.S. enters WW II
- Berlin blockade
- Korean War, begun in 1950
- Berlin Wall erected
- Bay of Pigs
- Cuban missile crisis
- Vietnam War escalation in 1965
- Civil rights
- Civil strife (on campus, in inner cities)
- Great inflation

———∞∞∞———

VIII

The Modern Era: The New Economy

In early 1981 an almost seventy-year-old Ronald Reagan became the oldest man ever to serve as president of the United States, yet he seemed vigorous and even youthful to many. When wounded in an assassination attempt two months into his presidency, he joked with doctors on his way into surgery and appeared to bounce back with remarkable speed. He had been a two-term governor of California and before that a B-movie actor, best remembered for his role as the legendary Notre Dame football star George Gipp, the "Gipper." Ronald Reagan, more so than any other modern president, did not involve himself in the day-to-day affairs of running government. His style of leadership was to surround himself with tough, energetic administrators, who shared his political beliefs, and provide general guidance. Reagan got off to an auspicious start when just 35 minutes after he took the oath of office Iran released the American hostages.

The Gipper set the tone of his regime in his inaugural address when he stated, "The government is not the solution to our problems . . . **it is the problem.**" To restore America's industrial might he proposed a bold new program to limit the government's role in the economy, reduce taxes, cut domestic spending, and lessen regulations. Furthermore, he was determined to strengthen America's defenses so as to face down the Soviet Union. He thought that by taking a tough stance, instead of compromising, the United States could win the cold war against communism.

At the core of Reagan's domestic strategy was a new approach to the economy, "supply-side" economics. In sharp contrast to the prevailing Keynesian theory, which relied on government spending to boost consumer demand, supply-siders believed the problem in the 1970s was on the supply side. A half-century of increasing government regulations and taxes had crimped the productive ability of the American economy. The supply-siders thought freeing the economy from the burden of government spending, taxation, and regulations would unleash a surge of new production, which, in turn, would alleviate inflationary pressures and produce an economic boom. This remedy to cure the nation's economic ills was dubbed "Reaganomics" by the press.

First, Reagan and his cohorts attacked federal spending. They decided not to touch the popular entitlement programs of Social Security, Medicare, and other critical social services for the "truly deserving needy." Instead they cut into other social programs, such as food stamps, student loans, mass urban transit, and public-service jobs, slashing $41 billion from the Carter budget. While cutting back on domestic spending, Reagan insisted on a massive increase in military spending—nearly doubling it.

Next Reagan made good on his promise to cut taxes. He backed an across-the-board tax cut of 25 percent over three years. There were other reductions on capital gains, estates, and gifts. Within a matter of months the American political landscape had shifted with a suddenness unmatched since Franklin Roosevelt's accession to power in 1933. As *Time* magazine commented, no president since FDR had "done so much of such magnitude so quickly to change the economic direction of the country."

The Reagan administration relieved troubled automakers of many of the regulations adopted in haste in the 1970s to reduce air pollution and increase passenger safety. His secretary of the interior opened up federal land to coal and timber production and made available more than a billion acres of territory for offshore oil drilling. The deregulation of finance, transportation, and telecommunications worked as if designed intentionally to prepare America for the arrival of the "New Economy."

The most daring of Reagan's early moves was the handling of the air traffic controllers' illegal strike in the summer of 1981. Although government employees were legally prohibited from striking, they had been doing so with increasing frequency and heads of government had not challenged it. So when the Gipper had his transportation secretary, Drew Lewis, fire all 13,000 controllers and decertify the union, the public held its breath and waited for planes to fall from the sky or for the nation's air traffic system to shut down. No such thing happened. There was not a single major accident. New controllers were hired, though at a huge additional cost. But the price had been worth it, as the Reagan administration made its point: the strikers had something to lose, and the larger point was this president meant what he said.

Shortly before Reagan took office, Paul Volcker, chairman of the Federal Reserve, had mounted an aggressive campaign to restrict the growth of the money supply so as to rein in inflation, once and for all. It precipitated a recession, but the Gipper stood by the Fed chief even when unemployment reached a post–World War II high of 10.4 percent. As tax revenues fell below projections and government spending on unemployment insurance and other social services increased, the deficit ballooned to over $100 billion and was on its way to $200 billion, nearly three times the previous record. The pressures on Reagan to ease up on the tax cuts mounted. But the president, an adept student of the "art of avoiding compromise," stood firm, refusing to scale back his income tax reductions and vowing to "stay the course." Yet Reagan proved flexible enough to moderate the defense buildup and accept fewer cuts in social programs than he had proposed.

The mighty brew of sweeping reductions in domestic spending and income taxes, along with the hefty increase in defense spending, soon acted as a potent stimulus to business. By the beginning of 1983 the economy was in full recovery and on its way to what was to be the longest peacetime expansion up to that time. And just as the supply-siders predicted, inflation was tamed. From a level of 14½ percent reached in the final year of Carter's reign, inflation fell to under 2 percent by 1986, lower than any figure in 20 years.

In Reagan's view the Soviets were "the focus of evil in the modern world," which threatened the well-being and security of the United States. The Gipper thought there was little room for reasonable compromise with the Soviets and scuttled the Nixon-Ford-Kissinger policy of détente. He placed 572 Pershing II and cruise missiles in Western Europe within range of Moscow and other Russian population centers, matching the late 1970s Soviet deployment of medium-range missiles aimed at NATO countries. As the nuclear arms began arriving in Europe a deep chill settled upon U.S.-Soviet relations and a new arms race appeared to be under way.

Reagan pressed on and stepped up research and development for Strategic Defense Initiative (SDI), an antimissile system based on the use of lasers and particle beams to destroy incoming missiles in outer space. It was to be the crown jewel of his defense program. Although dubbed "Star Wars" and ridiculed by the media, it may have finally convinced the Kremlin it could not compete in a high-tech arms race. A number of high-level Russian government participants have claimed it helped hasten the end of the cold war. At the Carnegie Endowment for International Peace in Washington in 1992, Vladimir Lukhim, Soviet foreign policy expert and later ambassador to the United States, stated that "it is clear that SDI accelerated our catastrophe by at least five years."

The Reagan administration did not want any more communist

regimes or bases for leftist guerillas in the U.S. backyard. When Marxist revolutionaries attempted to take over the government of Grenada, a small island in the West Indies, Reagan took decisive action. American troops were sent and quickly restored constitutional authority. He provided support to the government of El Salvador, enabling it to beat back a leftist guerilla insurgency. In neighboring Nicaragua left-wing "Sandinista" revolutionaries had already overthrown the pro-American Somoza regime. Reagan cut off aid that the Carter administration had extended to the Sandinistas and backed an antigovernment guerilla movement, the Contras, who aimed to topple the new Nicaraguan government. However, Congress, fearful of another Vietnam, passed the Boland Amendment in 1984, which cut off funding to the Contras and put the administration in a precarious position. To fund the Nicaraguan freedom fighters some Reaganites diverted money from Iranian arms sales to the Contras, violating the Boland Amendment.

Furthermore, Reagan took decisive action against international terrorism, which had become a growing scourge during the 1970s and early 1980s. He singled out Iran, North Korea, Cuba, Nicaragua, and Libya as "members of a confederation of terrorist states." When a terrorist bomb exploded in a Berlin disco frequented by U.S. servicemen, killing a soldier and a Turkish woman and injuring 200 more, Reagan took action. He authorized U.S. bombers to attack the headquarters and barracks of Gadhafi, the Libyan strongman, thought responsible for the disco bombing. Reagan got the message out to Gadhafi and others; if they pursued terrorism, the U.S. military was coming after them personally.

The new president's program of military expansion, his repudiation of détente, his contempt for arms control, and his "Star Wars" antimissile defense system convinced the liberal media that he was a trigger-happy Neanderthal. And they braced for all kinds of doomsday scenarios. In fact, in 1983 ABC dramatized the unthinkable—what would happen after the bomb dropped.

Yet Reagan, despite his tough talk and saber rattling, was cautious about committing troops to foreign adventures. The president had sent American marines to Lebanon as part of a multination force to restore order following a bloody civil war. After a terrorist bombing of the U.S. military barracks left 241 marines dead, Reagan pulled the remainder of the American forces out.

In 1984 the Democrats nominated former vice-president Walter Mondale to challenge Reagan. The nation was enjoying prosperity without inflation and showing a new assertiveness in world affairs. It was, according to Reagan, "Morning in America." Mondale was reduced to harping on the deficit and Reagan's age, while promising the American people "higher" taxes. But no dice; the voters weren't buying. As large numbers of southern whites, northern Catholics, and working-class Democrats streamed into the Republican fold the Gipper won an overwhelming victory, capturing 58 percent of the popular vote and 525 electoral votes, the most ever. Permission was granted to continue on down the path Ronald Reagan had chosen.

During his second term the Gipper cut taxes further and got a major overhaul of the income tax, the Tax Reform Act of 1986, which created a simpler and fairer revenue system. The new rates exempted 6 million people at the lower end from paying taxes, while an alternative minimum tax prevented most of the rich from escaping their share.

Meanwhile, the budget deficit was not closing. It had reached $221 billion in 1986 and appeared to be heading higher. The air was filled with dire warnings. Take your pick! Massive deficits would soon rekindle double-digit inflation, or else cause sky-high interest rates, which would derail economic growth, perhaps for a generation, and bankrupt our children. However, Reagan seemed to be ignoring the potential problem, probably because the large flow of red ink was preventing Democratic legislators from expanding social programs or enacting new ones. Congress, however, grew impatient and took matters into their own hands, passing the Gramm-Rudman-Hollings Balanced Budget Act, which set targets for eliminating the deficit by 1991, through mandated "across-the-board" spending cuts. As spending targets were not met, Congress kept pushing back the date for eliminating the deficit. Nevertheless, the law did help to halt the spiral of red ink so that by 1988 the deficit fell to a more manageable $155 billion. And as a percent of GNP it did even better, falling from almost 6 percent to a bit over 3 percent, a level in line with many other industrial nations.

Reagan was able to reshape the Supreme Court in a more conservative fashion. Outgoing Chief Justice Warren Burger was replaced by the Court's strongest conservative, William Rehnquist. Antonin Scalia, an even more extreme conservative, was added at the same time. Reagan also appointed the first woman, Sandra Day O'Connor, to the Court. This new Court was to curb the expansion of minority rights and privileges generated by the Warren Court.

In 1986 the press got wind of the Iran arms sales and the money diversions to the Contras. Remembering Watergate and the political fallout from the cover-up, the administration broke the bad news itself. The emerging scandal served as a rallying point for those opposed to the Reagan revolution. Just as FDR's enemies went on the attack after his attempt to pack the Supreme Court, Reagan's opposition coalesced around the apparent illegality of the administration's actions in Iran-Contra. There was a protracted congressional hearing during the summer of 1987 to find out the extent of the president's personal involvement. But National Security advisor John Poindexter insisted under oath the president had not been informed, and the only other government official who knew what actually happened, William Casey, director of the CIA, died that summer of a brain tumor. The investigation was not able to tie the president to serious violations of the law.

Nonetheless, the Reagan presidency was weakened. The Democratic Congress became more defiant and overrode his vetoes, rejected his nominees, and killed even humanitarian aid to the Contras. It looked like the end of the Reagan revolution, just as FDR's episode with the Supreme Court a half-century earlier had halted New Deal reform.

But the Gipper was not washed up. Regan had met the new Russian premier, Mikhail Gorbachev, in Reykjavik, Iceland, in 1986. Although the American president continued his tough stance and refused to scale back his SDI plans one iota, the two world leaders reached an understanding to keep talking. Then, in late 1987, they agreed to remove all intermediate-range nuclear forces (INF) from Europe and to permit on-site verification. ABC was correct—the unthinkable *did* happen; Reagan and Gorbachev signed the most significant arms control agreement of the nuclear age. Most impressive of all, the Russians began a withdrawal from Afghanistan. Again Reagan had succeeded where Carter had failed. By the time Reagan left office in January of 1989, he could claim that his policy of building up America's defenses and talking tough to the Russians had paid off handsomely.

In 1988 Reagan passed the mantle to his loyal vice president, George H. Bush, who promised to remain faithful to his predecessor's policies. To underscore that he had become a true believer in Reaganomics, his favorite line during the campaign was "read my lips—no new taxes." Bush easily defeated the Democratic candidate, Michael Dukakis. The voters had spoken. It was a ringing endorsement of a ninth, "Reagan," political paradigm.

By the time Ronald Reagan had ridden off into the sunset, it was apparent that this detached yet eloquent and visionary leader had truly changed the course of American history. During two terms he had provided the first successful cutting of taxes and government domestic spending in 50 years, led a worldwide movement to rely on the marketplace rather than government

bureaucrats to direct a nation's economy, tamed a defiant inflation that destabilized the 1970s, launched an ongoing economic
boom that spawned the greatest period of wealth creation the
world has ever seen, restored traditional American pride and self-
respect, and revitalized the Republican Party. And soon the cold
war would end and his demagogic rhetoric about the Soviets
being an "Evil Empire" would not seem so far-fetched.

To be sure, his tenure was also a time of a growing inequality of
wealth. As in past periods of rapid business growth, such as the
late nineteenth century and the 1920s, the winners in the economic game became fabulously rich. Aided by the tax cuts, especially for the wealthy, the top layer of society prospered while the
middle portion inched ahead and the poor languished.

In early 1989 George H. Bush took over as the nation's leader
and continued to pursue the Reagan theme of limiting federal
interference in the everyday lives of American citizens. Bush
vetoed family-leave legislation, refused to sponsor meaningful
health-care reform, and watered down civil rights proposals from
Congress. But much of his time was taken up with two pressing
domestic problems. Most important was the ballooning federal
deficit. In the fall of 1990, with the deficit running over $200 bil-
lion and a war in the Middle East looming, George Bush finally
agreed to break his "no new taxes" pledge and support a budget
compromise to reduce the deficit by about $500 billion over a five-
year period. The legislation included new taxes on the wealthy,
along with substantial spending cuts, mainly for the military.
However, as it coincided with a lingering recession, the red ink,
instead of declining, swelled to just under $300 billion in 1992.

Bush also led the fight to resolve the savings and loan crises.
As a result of lax regulation and unwise, even possibly fraudulent,
loan policies, the nation's savings and loan industry was in grave
trouble. After record losses of greater than $13 billion in 1988,
more than 250 savings and loan banks had been forced to close
their doors. Bush's legislation created a new federal agency, the

Resolution Trust Corporation, to aid the ailing savings and loans by selling off their properties, mostly at distressed prices, and merging or closing the weaker institutions. But $400 billion more were added to the nation's swelling debt.

George H. Bush was the beneficiary of the collapse of the Soviet Empire. Gorbachev, after taking over as head of the Soviet government in the mid-1980s, instituted policies of "glasnost" (political openness) and "perestroika" (economic restructuring). As the winds of change swept over the Soviet Union, puppet governments in Eastern Europe broke away, and Gorbachev refused to use force to buck up the Soviet-backed regimes. Shortly thereafter the Soviet economy, which was one-sixth the size of America's, cracked under the weight of trying to keep up with a $300 billion U.S. defense budget. In August of 1991 Gorbachev resigned and the Communists made their exit. Boris Yeltsin took over and established democracy, along with a free-market economy. The cold war, which as late as 1985 had seemed a permanent fact of international life, was over, and the world order was radically transformed. No other nation stood tall enough to challenge America as world leader, and the threat of nuclear confrontation had been drastically reduced.

Bush's toughest challenge came in the summer of 1990. Saddam Hussein, ruler of Iraq, stunned the world by invading Kuwait and threatening Saudi Arabia and the Persian Gulf region, which contained the bulk of the world's oil reserves. With the United States importing almost half the oil its people used each day, there was no question that control of the Persian Gulf was vitally important. The president responded firmly. Carefully he persuaded Saudi Arabia to accept a huge American troop buildup and then secured UN support for a U.S.-led liberation of Kuwait. However, with most Democrats opposed to the use of force, he was able to win only a narrow, five-vote approval in the Senate to use American military power to gain his objectives.

In early 1991, in an operation dubbed Desert Storm, the president gave the order to unleash a devastating aerial assault on Iraq and five weeks latter approved a ground assault. In just one hundred hours, the American-led offensive freed Kuwait and sent Saddam Hussein's vaunted Republican Guard fleeing back into Iraq with allied troops in hot pursuit. Fearful of disrupting the allied coalition, and hoping that a chastened Saddam would help balance Iran in the volatile Persian Gulf, Bush decided to let Saddam Hussein survive. Bush called a halt to the American advance and agreed to an armistice with Iraq. The United States had lost just 146 lives while inflicting a stinging defeat on a dangerous bully, and the public was euphoric. George Bush's personal approval rating shot up to nearly 90 percent, higher than even Eisenhower's and Kennedy's had reached.

Yet by the summer of 1992 Bush was in political trouble. The recession that had begun in mid-1990 proved unusually stubborn. Although the economy officially turned up in early 1991, the recovery stalled twice before sustained growth began in late 1992. The sluggishness led to a 1.9 percent decline in the average real income during 1991, the worst showing in over 10 years. By the summer of 1992 corporate downsizing was gaining momentum and nearly 10 million Americans were without a job, 3 million more than when Bush had taken office in 1989. To complicate matters, the budget deficit was still swollen and projections were for a sea of red ink as far as the eye could see. The political impact would be devastating for the Bush administration.

The Democrats chose Bill Clinton, a centrist five-term governor of Arkansas, to lead them. The Clinton team focused voter attention on the lackluster economic performance. Tacked up on the bulletin board at campaign headquarters was the message: "It's the economy, stupid." Clinton promised to stop the growing income inequality and bring back the salad days for the middle class. At the same time, Texas billionaire Ross Perot formed a third party, which aimed its guns at the frightening budget deficit that was blamed on the Reagan-Bush policies. With Perot racking up 19 percent of the vote, Clinton was able to handily beat Bush, even though receiving only 43 percent of the popular vote. George H. Bush's share totaled just 37½ percent, less than any sitting president since Howard Taft in 1912.

A Democratic Interregnum

The Democrats got their turn at governing. Clinton had been dogged by doubts as to his character and trustworthiness. Questions and rumors from his past concerning draft dodging, youthful experiments with marijuana, numerous extramarital affairs, and "Whitewater," a cover-up of his and his wife's role in receiving an improper loan from a savings and loan bank, were bandied about.

In his first days in office Bill Clinton chose to pay back gay and lesbian supporters, who had been a vocal part of his constituency. He issued an executive order to end the ban on homosexuals in the military. This stirred up a ruckus and got the administration off on the wrong foot. After the Joint Chiefs of Staff and many leading Democrats warned the measure would destroy morale and seriously weaken the armed forces, Clinton settled for a Pentagon-suggested compromise of, "Don't ask, don't tell." Homosexuals could continue to serve in the military, as they had in the past, as long as they did not reveal their sexual preference and refrained from homosexual conduct. The inept handling of the "gays in the military" issue, along with several botched cabinet appointments, cost Clinton the usual honeymoon period new presidents enjoy, and he was only barely able to get his first major economic plan through Congress.

Clinton's economic program would stay basically true to Reaganomics. His important economic bill sought to cut the budget deficit in half over four years. The objective was to give the Fed enough breathing room to keep interest rates low and help fulfill his campaign pledge to grow the economy. Half the savings were to come from a moderate income tax increase for the well-to-do, replacing a small portion of the Reagan reduction, along with a slight increase in the gasoline tax. The other half would come from a net decrease in spending. True to the words of his first speech, "there can be no more something for nothing," Clinton outlined deep cuts in federal spending, which were only partially offset by increased government spending for education and job training. But he was able to get an earned income tax credit included, which was to help lift many struggling families out of poverty and keep the true blue liberals, his party base, satisfied.

Shortly thereafter, with strong Republican backing in Congress, Clinton pushed through the North American Free Trade Agreement (NAFTA), which had been initiated by the Bush administration several years earlier. The agreement combined the United States, Canada, and Mexico into a common market without trade barriers. In siding with the pro-NAFTA forces, Clinton was defying traditional Democratic allies, including organized labor and environmentalists, who bitterly opposed the measure. Another agreement to lower international trade barriers, GATT, soon followed.

Health care had been primed to be the centerpiece of the Clinton domestic program. It was clear that the public was concerned about the affordability and availability of health care, and this type social legislation normally played to the Democrats' strong suit: social reform designed to help the people. Clinton put his wife, Hillary Clinton, who in private life had been an accomplished attorney, in charge of a task force to come up with a plan. What Hillary and her team proposed was a sweeping overhaul of the American health system, reminiscent of the old New Deal programs. But people in this political model were not receptive to proposals that smacked of "big" government intrusion, and the plan could not sell on Main Street. More important, it did much to erode Clinton's image as a centrist Democrat.

Failure to deliver on his health-care promise, and a new image as a big-spending liberal, rendered Clinton and his party vulnerable. During the 1994 mid-term elections, Newt Gingrich, GOP House minority leader, fashioned a strategy to capitalize on Clinton's unpopularity and capture Congress. Gingrich asked all Republican candidates to sign a 10-point "Contract with America," which included a middle-class tax cut, a balanced budget amendment to the Constitution, and term limits for members of Congress. The result was a stunning Republican victory, and for the first time since the 1950s the party of Abraham Lincoln and Ronald Reagan controlled both houses of Congress.

However, the Republicans interpreted their win as a mandate to dismantle the welfare state. Unlike Reagan, who had bashed the New Deal while preserving its most popular programs, the congressional firebrands attacked the Democrats' core programs. But they made a gross miscalculation. They shut down the government in an attempt to force Clinton to accept their plan to balance the budget. Clinton, who skillfully adapted to the mood of the American public, agreed to a balanced budget in principle but then, portraying himself as the defender of the downtrodden, refused to accept GOP plans to slash programs like Medicare and Medicaid. The result was a public outcry directed mostly at Gingrich and the GOP. Finally a compromise was reached, which largely spared entitlements such as Medicare. Clinton had won the right to define what the nation's budget priorities would be, turning the Republican shutdown of the government into political victory.

Clinton read the 1994 mid-term election results correctly. He scrambled back to the center and outmaneuvered the Republicans on a variety of fronts. The most notable was to fulfill one of his "moderate Democrat" pledges "to end welfare as we know it." In 1996, just before his reelection campaign, Clinton signed a welfare bill, slightly more acceptable than the two he had vetoed before, which dismantled a fundamental part of the welfare-state structure going back to the New Deal in the 1930s. The new legislation turned the program over to the states, scaled down the federal grants, and required recipients to find work within two years. But to please his constituency he pursued a few modest social programs. He was able to boost the minimum wage and ensure portability of health-care insurance when people changed jobs. He also got a Family Leave Act through Congress, which provided 12 weeks of unpaid leave for childcare or to tend to ill family members.

Unlike previous presidents of the past half-century, Clinton had the luxury of dealing in a world without a strong American foe. He offered U.S. prestige and power to broker peace around the world. In the Middle East he guided the Israelis and the Palestinians through a peace treaty. When the Serbs started pushing the Bosnians around, he used the threat of American military power to force the Serbs to make a deal with Bosnia. But probably his greatest success came from persuading the former republics of the Soviet Union to scrap their deadly nuclear stockpiles.

By election time 1996, Clinton was in a strong position. His gamble on beginning his presidency with deficit reduction had paid off, the economy was sailing along, unemployment was below 5 percent, inflation was tame, the stock market was at record highs and climbing rapidly for the second year in a row, and the budget deficit was halved.

His only problem was the issue of character; a series of scandals, ranging from Whitewater to charges of sexual harassment, still dogged him, and the GOP tried to make it the campaign issue. Nevertheless, he was still able to gather 49 percent of the actual voters and easily defeated his Republican challenger, Bob Dole. Ross Perot ran again as a third party candidate. But with the deficit moving back in the direction of balance, his share of the vote slipped to 9 percent. The Republicans, however, retained control of both houses of Congress, and it was the first time since 1928 they reelected a House majority.

Another major budget deal followed along the same lines as the last one. Again there was a fight over budget priorities. The congressional Republicans got some additional tax cuts, notably a reduction in the capital gains rate. Clinton got to protect some of his cherished social programs, such as Medicare and education. But most important, as this deal was being fashioned news came that the monster budget deficit that had thrown a dark shadow over the economy for over a decade was turning into surplus. The federal government, for the first time since 1969, was on track to operate without a deficit. And for the following four years the federal budget would be in surplus. In the waning days of the Clinton administration the surplus for the next 10 years was projected to be over \$4 trillion, or an average of more than \$400 billion a year. And during the remainder of his term, Clinton skillfully blocked GOP attempts to convert the funds into big tax cuts.

In early 1998 a bombshell exploded. News that the president was having sex in the White House with a 22-year-old intern shocked the nation. At first the president denied that he had a sexual relationship with the intern. But as new evidence surfaced he had to retract, and his evasive and misleading accounts of the affair opened him up to charges of perjury and obstruction of justice. In December 1998 the House of Representatives passed two articles of impeachment against Clinton. However, as the GOP could not convince any Senate Democrats the president's actions warranted removal from office, he was acquitted. Still, impeachment and the spectacle of a Senate trial snapped Clinton's moral and legislative clout and for the remainder of his term the government drifted. Democratic attempts to expand Medicare eligibility and raise tobacco taxes to fund antismoking initiatives flopped. But so too did Republican initiatives.

Early in 1999 the situation in the former Yugoslavia turned ugly again. Serbian troops, under the direction of Slobodan Milosevic, were pursuing a policy of "ethnic cleansing," butchering and torturing men and raping the women, in an attempt to pressure the ethnic Muslim population to leave the Serbian province of Kosovo. Americans and Europeans, watching the slaughter on TV, were horrified and demanded something be done. After much hesitation, Clinton led a NATO group to bomb the Serbians into stopping the massacre. After six weeks of relentless American and NATO bombing, Serbian troops pulled back and UN observers went into Kosovo to supervise the return of the indigenous population.

During his two terms Clinton was able to pull the Democrats to the center. He moved his party away from its traditional reliance on big government and helped erase its tax-and-spend image. He made incremental, but not significant, changes in a wide range of social programs and resisted Republican plans to slash taxes, reshape the federal tax code, and overhaul Social Security with private accounts. However, like Reagan and Bush before him, he was unable to arrest the growing disparity in income and wealth between the rich and poor. In the 1960s the pay of the average corporate CEO was only about 30 times that of production workers. By 2000 it was estimated to be well over 400 times higher and widening. No wonder many middle- and working-class people still had the gnawing fear that they weren't moving ahead as fast as the upper classes. According to Congressional Budget Office data, in the 1990s the wealthiest 5 percent of Americans enjoyed an inflation-adjusted 15 percent boost in their income while the poorest 20 percent of Americans actually suffered a decline.

But most important: Just as Wilson had legitimatized the Teddy Roosevelt paradigm, when he declared, "We are all progressives," just as Nixon legitimatized the New Deal paradigm, with his "We are all Keynesians" statement, Bill Clinton, when facing the first Republican Congress in 40 years, announced, "The era of big government is over," legitimatizing the New Economy paradigm and indirectly acknowledging Ronald Reagan as another pattern-setting president.

A Republican Party Restoration

In November—no! Make that late December 2000—George W. Bush squeaked by Al Gore to become the nation's forty-third president. George W. was the son of George H. Bush, the forty-first president of the United States, and had been governor of Texas. The new president, while often seeming clumsy-tongued, was a meticulous planner and had a highly developed sense of pragmatism.

During his first two years on the job Bush Junior pushed through a $1.3 trillion tax cut, rolled back some of the red tape put on during the Clinton administration, fought to hold the line on domestic spending, presided over a hefty increase in defense spending, with more scheduled to follow, and proposed an expensive missile defense shield that reminded people of "Star Wars."

By summertime 2001 it began to look as if Bush Junior's presidency had stalled. Jim Jeffords, the fiftieth Republican senator and from Vermont, bolted from the GOP, and the president's party lost control of the Senate, leaving only a slim Republican majority in the House and a presidential legislative program in jeopardy.

At about that time people were beginning to realize that the biggest stock market "bubble" in U.S. history had popped. An economy that throughout the 1990s could do no wrong suddenly was unable to do any right. Corporate profits plummeted; by some measures it was the largest decline since the 1930s. A series of corporate and accounting scandals, the biggest of which involved Enron and WorldCom, surfaced, along with revelations of how Wall Street brokerage houses had hoodwinked investors during the great bull market, and free-market capitalism suffered a black eye.

Actually, the stock market had peaked a full 10 months before Bush Junior took the reins of government; the economy officially went into recession barely two months after the president moved into the White House. Since the stock market peak in March 2000, bloodied investors had lost almost $9 trillion—equivalent to about 90 percent of America's GDP—as of October 2002. And the "darlings" of high tech and the Internet, which had captured the public's imagination, crashed. The NASDAQ, which largely comprises those type companies, was down 77 percent in the two and a half years from its high-water mark.

Then there was that matter of the federal budget. After four years of budget surpluses—three of them in triple digits—and estimates of more to come as far as the eye could see, the budget suddenly turned to deficit; $159 billion of red ink in fiscal 2002, amounting to 1.5 per cent of GDP. Actually, this was well below the 5 to 6 percent levels of the late 1980s. Nonetheless, according to Congressional Budget Office (CBO) estimates, red ink was due to flow until 2006.

But all these problems would pale when, on September 11, 2001, a group of suicidal terrorists flew three airplanes into the World Trade Center in New York City and the Pentagon in Washington, D.C. It was the most devastating attack against Americans in America since 1814. The president quickly grasped America was involved in a new sort of war that demanded a fresh and tough response—not just a spectacular display of firepower. People took another look at George W. Bush, the winner of a disrupted election, and they saw a firm, confident leader, who had found his voice; the president's approval ratings shot up.

In the 2002 mid-term elections "Dubya" was able to focus the nation's attention on national security and lead his party to a stunning congressional victory. His party picked up seats in both the Senate and the House, marking only the third time it happened, in a mid-term election, since the Civil War. Furthermore, George W. became the first Republican president since Eisenhower in the early 1950s to have control of both houses of Congress. This, no doubt, strengthened his hand and with it his chances to move his legislative agenda forward. Already, as of December 2002, he has gained a huge new Homeland Security Department, to guard against another September 11 type attack, and he got it on his terms, free of most union rights for its more than 170,000 expected workers.

*   *   *

The ninth American political model was authored by Ronald Reagan, whose programs and governing style sparked an entrepreneurial spirit that revitalized and transformed the American economy. There was an 18-year-long business boom, lasting until century's end, and interrupted by only one brief recession. Most Americans experienced a vast improvement in living standards, unemployment reached a 30-year low, and inflation, the scourge of the 1970s, was tamed. The American economy, once again, became the world's leader, far outdistancing Japan, which in the early 1980s seemed poised to overtake the United States. Surging tax revenues eliminated the budget deficit, just as the supply-siders had predicted. (Of course, it took about a decade longer than the Reaganites prophesied, and there had been some help from the Bush and Clinton tax increases. The current deficit, if it lasts, follows four years of surplus and is a fresh problem.) In addition, a concentrated defense buildup had coincided with the breakup of the Soviet Union and an end to the cold war. As Reagan prophesied in 1981, communism was a "sad, bizarre chapter in human history whose last pages are even now being written."

Bush and Clinton governed in accordance with the blueprints Ronald Reagan had provided, and as for Bush Junior (so far) . . . well, let's call him Reagan Junior. As in the previous three long paradigms, the minority party was unable to control both the White House and at least one house of Congress for very long. To date, in this political model it has done so for only one two-year period—1993–1995.

Furthermore, a shift of emphasis from government to individual responsibility has already had an impact on the nation's social structure. The relentless cultural decline that had seemed a fact of nature ground to a halt and reversed itself, as the values of an earlier time, which emphasized devotion to family, church, nation, and God, are slowly making a comeback. Moreover, teenage pregnancy rates have dropped dramatically. The divorce rate leveled off and, then, beginning in 1990, experienced a slow falloff. The number of two-parent households has begun to show small year-to-year increases, reversing a twenty-year decline. Yet most impressive, in 1998 the FBI reported that serious crime in the United States fell for the seventh straight year, with murder and robbery rates reaching 30-year lows.

TABLE 12

Ninth Political Paradigm (1981–). 24 Years till 2005 "and Still Counting"

Election of:	Majority Paradigm Party Republicans		Minority Paradigm Party Democrats	
Paradigm	% of Popular Vote		% of Popular Vote	
1980 Begins	Ronald Reagan*	51	J. Carter	41
1984 Preliminary	Ronald Reagan	59	W. Mondale	40
1988 Confirmed	George H. Bush	53	M. Dukakis	46
1992 Lose election	George H. Bush	37	W. Clinton	43
1996	Robert Dole	41	W. Clinton	49
2000 Restored	George W. Bush	47	Al Gore	48

*Bold = winner.

	Republicans		Democrats /( ) other	
Congress	House	Senate	House	Senate
97th 1981–1983	192	53*	242(1)	46(1)
98th 1983–1985	166	54	269	46
99th 1985–1987	182	53	253	47
100th 1987–1989	177	45	258	55
101st 1989–1991	175	45	260	55
102d 1991–1993	167	44	267(1)	56
103d 1993–1995	176	43	258(1)	57
104th 1995–1997	230	52	204(1)	48
105th 1997–1999	226	55	207(2)	45
106th 1999–2001	223	55	211(1)	45
107th 2001–2003	221	50	212(2)	50†
108th 2003–2005	228	51	209(1)	48(1)

*Bold= control of House or Senate: more than all other parties combined. In the Senate a tie goes to the president's party.

†After the election, Jeffords quit the Republican Party and voted with Democrats, giving the Democrats the right to organize the Senate.

Source: Composition of 97th–108th Congress: Information Please®, copyright ©2003 Pearsen Education. (www.infoplease.com) Note: All figures reflect immediate result of election.

Years in the White House with control of at least one house of Congress:

Republicans: 10 (to 2005)
Democrats: 2

Economic Agenda

- Taxes cut
- Domestic spending cut
- Deregulation
- Trade agreements: NAFTA and GATT

Other Important Events

- PATCO (airline controllers) strike
- Massive defense spending / "Star Wars"
- Gramm-Rudman-Hollings Balanced Budget Act
- Communism ends in Soviet Union
- Desert Storm
- Savings and Loan crisis
- Welfare program restructured
- Clinton impeachment

IX

Dueling Parties

Since the beginning of the republic the American people have been both participants in and spectators to a duel between competing political parties, each representing a different way of thinking, behaving, and organizing society.

During the past 210 years there have been three major parties of the "right," and the primary goal of all three has been to create an environment conducive to economic growth, so as to increase the material wealth of society. The Federalists were the first party to occupy the right side of the political spectrum. Alexander Hamilton, their chief spokesman, thought the primary concern of the new nation should be **to encourage commercial growth.** He argued for a strong central government, which would join hands with the producers of wealth, the rich, whom he thought best suited to govern and maintain public order. However, this tainted the Federalists with aristocratic pretensions and in the early nineteenth century Jefferson's Democratic-Republican Party drove them from the political playing field.

To fill the vacuum on the right, a faction in the Democratic-Republican Party split apart and was to morph into the Whig Party. Their chief spokesman was Henry Clay, who welcomed the market economy and industrialism and wanted the Whig Party to serve as its advance agent. He formulated the "American System," which echoed Alexander Hamilton's policies. However, the Whigs, unlike the Federalists, thought economic development should not be put into the hands of a commercial elite; rather, it should be left open so that individuals born without silver spoons in their mouths would be provided with opportunities to move up the social and economic ladder. This was the conservatives' idea of social mobility.

However, Whig presidents, during their two brief stints in power, were not sufficiently dedicated to the party's program, and it was never fully instituted. Yet Henry Clay's vision would play a leading role in the agenda of the third party of the "right," the Republicans.

Abraham Lincoln, a Clay admirer, became an ardent believer in orthodox Whig economic policies and early in his presidency signed legislation implementing Clay's program. Yet, at the time of Mr. Lincoln's death, it wasn't entirely clear whether his primary "after the war" priority was to establish the conditions to let industrialism blossom or to lead a crusade for a social and political reform of the nation. There was a struggle between the pro-business wing and the liberal-reform faction for the soul of the new Republican Party.

It fell upon Ulysses S. Grant's shoulders to settle the issue, and with no "ands, ifs, and buts" about it, Grant choose the pro-business direction . . . paving the way for the success of Industrial Capitalism. It was decided! The Republican Party would fall in line behind Hamilton and Clay and become a muscular pro-business party **allied to society's overdogs.** The Republicans would stand guard and make sure industrialization took root and sprouted on American soil. But, as time went on, the Clay-Lincoln idea of opening up avenues of opportunity to ordinary Americans became somewhat less important.

What if? What if the GOP had decided in favor of liberal reform and became the party on the political left? Why, then the way would have been open for the Democrats to become the nation's pro-business party, but because of their ideological heritage the road to that new identity would, at best, have been a long and rocky one.

There was one important challenge to the reigning Republican philosophy. At the turn of the twentieth century Teddy Roosevelt sought to modify the Republican doctrine and turn the party back in the direction of its earlier reformist tendencies. Although acknowledging the Republicans as the party of economic development, TR wanted to tame the energies of industrialization. He thought a benign federal government should intervene in economic matters and act as a referee, mediating between the interests of the haves and have-nots. Sounding a note reminiscent of Lincoln, Roosevelt said, "We are neither for the rich man or the poor man as such . . . but for the upright man." Although the "Rough Rider" did not attempt to lead the Republicans all the way to the left side of the political spectrum, he moved the party in the direction of the "left" and that was enough to weaken its economic growth agenda and threaten its alliance with the business interests of the country.

Warren Harding rescued the GOP from the clutches of the progressives and reset the party back on its traditional path as the agent of industrialization and friend of the rich. But, unfortunately for the Republicans, they were at the helm, in 1929, when the deepest and most traumatic economic collapse in the nation's history occurred. Their punishment was banishment from the center stage of American politics and out into the political wilderness for nearly 50 years.

Ronald Reagan modernized the Republican creed, since it was last dominant in the 1920s, and brought the party back to the lead role in American politics. He broke ranks with his GOP peers and accepted the Democrats' core social programs, Social Security and Medicare, as a basic and untouchable part of American soci-

ety. The Gipper remade the GOP as more than a party just for the
rich. He dressed the conservative party up in populist clothing
and, in the Clay-Lincoln tradition, emphasized the new paths of
opportunity his program would open up to ordinary Americans.
Furthermore, he totally divorced the party from any remaining
relics of its prior flirtation with mercantilism and married it fully
to a free-market philosophy.

Reagan boldly adopted a new and untried economic theory,
"supply-side" economics, which practically all Democrats and
even most Republicans were skeptical about, and incorporated it
into the Republican doctrine. It was to provide the theoretical
underpinning to a program of providing an environment conducive to economic growth and entrepreneurship.

Although in many matters the GOP has changed its stripes
over time, it has remained steadfast in its determination to provide policies thought to encourage economic development and to
be a faithful friend of the well-heeled. A wealthy class perched on
the top step of the social ladder does not disturb Republicans.
They deem it healthy to reward the most productive members of
society, even though these happen to be the wealthiest as well.
The Republicans also believe in law and order. Without public
order there would be social chaos and businesses could not operate. They thought the best way to ensure public order was to
encourage the cultural and moral values derived from the Protes-
tant tradition, which, in turn, would provide the moral glue
needed to bind a diverse society together.

The Democrats have been the party on the "left" side of the political aisle. Their primary goal has been, and remains, **to alter
the way society is organized** in a fairer, more egalitarian manner. Today the party marches behind banners that spell out
SOCIAL JUSTICE, FAIRNESS, and INDIVIDUALISM. And
throughout their long existence they have joined hands with society's underdogs. At the Democratic convention in 2000, Al Gore
stood at the podium, raised his arm in a half-salute, and shouted

that his party "puts people first." To emphasize, he proudly repeated, "I'm for the people, not the powerful."

The prime Democratic visionary was Thomas Jefferson, who thought, that given the proper environment, people could develop in healthy ways the rigid Old World society had not permitted. To Jefferson the Old World was infested with a corrupt and decadent "upper crust," which was able to use artificial privileges to lock out the have-nots. It was a world that bred dependency relationships and robbed people of their freedom.

Jefferson wanted to change that and create a fair society in which all citizens would begin "the race of life" on equal footing, one that would allow free rein to individual talent and energy. In the New World it would be merit or ability, not birth, that mattered. Sure there would be an aristocracy, but it would be a natural one based on ability, not an artificial one. No matter their birth, individuals would have an equal opportunity to participate and succeed. They would not be doomed to be what their fathers had been.

To create the conditions for a fair society Jefferson and his followers turned the government's focus in an agrarian direction and extended the boundaries of "individual freedom." Andrew Jackson came next and extended the meaning and scope of democracy by stressing the superior moral authority of majority rule, **democracy,** over all forms of elitism. All white men were given access to the ballot box, and Old Hickory would see to it that government would hear their voice and respond. Naturally, the voice Jackson would hear the clearest was that of the "little guy," whom he recognized as the natural ally of the Democratic Party.

Jackson, like Jefferson, fought tooth and nail to keep the government's hands off the economy. Both thought a government that was granting subsidies and special charters would inevitably favor certain groups and thereby put ordinary citizens under the thumb of the rich and powerful—as was to happen in the late nineteenth century under the impact of industrialization.

By mid–nineteenth century the contradiction within the Democratic Party that advocated the utmost individual freedom while supporting slavery opened up a wedge for an opposing party to take up the cause of the blacks and attack the Democrats from the "left." Following the Civil War, the Democrats were stripped of their legitimacy and sent off to spend decades wandering the political desert.

But more important, it was clear Jefferson's political formula was hopelessly inadequate for operating in an industrial economy. It had been designed with an agrarian society in mind. The rise of industrialism required a reorganization of society for economic development, and Democrats were at a loss at how to respond, within their philosophical construct. How could they answer to the needs of mammoth business enterprises that depended upon large numbers of low-paid workers and still espouse a vision that promoted social equality? It was highly unlikely that humble wage earners would be hobnobbing at tea parties with ultra-rich capitalists. In post–Civil War America class distinctions reemerged . . . and with a vengeance.

Two prominent Democrats played an important role in helping the Democrats reconcile Jeffersonian values with an industrial society. First came William Jennings Bryan, the "Boy Orator of the Platte," who captured the hearts and souls of the Democratic conventioneers in 1896. He wanted to use the powers of the federal government to protect those who had been left behind. However, the "Boy Orator of the Platte" was marching backward. He offered a return to the bygone agricultural world with the toilers of the soil as the top dogs. He refused to believe that the United States had become an industrial society and there was no turning back. Although he ran three times, Bryan never became president. But many of his ideas were to become legislation during the progressive era: more stringent railway regulation, currency reform, women's suffrage, a federal income tax, popular elections of U.S. senators. And his concept of "social justice" was to win the allegiance of twentieth-century Democrats.

Woodrow Wilson, the other key Democrat to play an important transitional role to modern liberalism, wanted to liberate American society from the rule of both big business and big government. Wilson, "The Great Idealist," initially believed he could clip the wings of the "big" federal government that had emerged during the Roosevelt-Taft administrations and renew the nation from the bottom up. But in the end Woodrow Wilson outdid Teddy Roosevelt in fostering government intrusion and regulation of the economy. Wilson's programs extended the power of government into nearly every phase of American life and tilted heavily in the direction of labor and the have-not class.

Wilson, together with the "Boy Orator of the Platte," helped take the Democratic Party several steps further down the road to a new vision, one in which the government was to play a key role in taming the marketplace and shoring up the ordinary classes. Yet unlike Bryan, Wilson realized that the United States no longer was an agricultural society but had become a nation of business enterprises. And above all, he rescued the fundamental progressive principle, that "the capitalist economy required government intrusion in order to preserve it," from Teddy Roosevelt's clutches and handed it over to the Democratic Party to become one of their bedrock precepts.

FDR recognized that an industrial economy required an overclass and accepted the fact that an egalitarian social system was simply not a realistic option. The government, however, could intervene on the side of society's underdogs and ensure them a basic elementary level of security. It could intercede to help provide the ordinary classes with a larger share of the national economic pie. This would be **social justice** and would become the rallying cry for the modern liberal ideology.

To attain a healthy and just society, a "big" intrusive federal government was necessary. There had to be programs to provide a safety net to those left behind. There had to be regulations to prevent businesspeople from using their power to exploit workers and shortchange consumers. Big government would be the instrument **to protect and empower those born without advantages**; to promote "social justice."

Democrats realized that although they could not provide society's have-littles with economic freedom, they could extend the boundaries of freedom into the personal and social realm. They removed social restrictions so that people would have more choices in their everyday life. Today the American people can shop on Sundays, drink alcohol in restaurants and bars, or frequent a porn shop if they like. "Good taste" handcuffs on sex and violence in the media were removed, and people can now turn on their TV or go to the movies and watch a story unfold in a "no holds barred" fashion. Woman can abort unwanted fetuses on demand. And the right to privacy is defended at any cost. The party of Jefferson, Jackson, and FDR believes human life will flourish only when the individual has been liberated from all sources of authority external to himself.

Under Franklin Roosevelt's tutelage Jefferson's vision of individual freedom metamorphosed into an ideology that preached "social justice." Rather than promoting a totally egalitarian society, modern Democrats lowered their bar and set their sights on the less ambitious goal of rebalancing society so there would be less of a gulf between the well-to-do classes and those at the bottom of the social pyramid. The Democrats of today reign supreme as the party of reorganizing society in a *more* egalitarian direction.

So . . . **Which of the two visions is correct?** Should society be organized around the principle of promoting economic growth or should the nation use the leverage of government to stress "social justice" above all else?

The Answer: **Both!**

Since the beginning of our modern epoch in the mid–eighteenth century, those two great traditions, economic growth and social rebalancing, have propelled mankind forward to higher stages in the democratic revolution that is at the very essence of the American experience. And each of America's two major political parties has taken on the responsibility of standing guard over one of these traditions. The Republican Party stands ready at all times to water and nurture the economic spirit. To them, all other things pale in importance. At the other end, the Democrats have been the guardian angels of society's underdogs, faithfully trying to improve upon their position in the social order.

Up until quite recently, "economic growth" was not the natural order of things. It was not until the mid–eighteenth century in Great Britain that an economic sphere, which had a high degree of autonomy from political control, emerged. Up until that time commercial activity and the merchant class were at the mercy of the crown. Whether in Asian, Islamic, or Western civilization the state viewed commercial society with scorn and suspicion and tried to keep it under its control and restrict its activities. Merchants had to deal with an arbitrary authority that at any given time was capable of confiscation, forced loans, debt repudiation, irregular levies, expulsions, and even judicial murder. For members of the commercial class existence was precarious, and history is replete with stories of kings confiscating their money and, at times, taking their lives as well. Take the case of Jacques Coeur, the richest merchant in all of France in the fifteenth century. Coeur, who was the largest creditor of the crown, was arrested on trumped-up charges. His properties were taken over in what amounted to a royal debt repudiation and he had to flee the country in order to save his life.

In premodern times a speedup in the tempo of economic activity usually aroused the envy of the ruling class, which would intervene to crush the merchant class and smother the emerging economy. The classic case is China, circa A.D. 1000. At about that time it was the richest and most powerful country in the world and appeared to be undergoing a commercial revolution, similar to what was to occur in the West hundreds of years later. Great merchant cities, which were primarily emporiums of trade, sprouted. China seemed poised for economic takeoff. But it never came! Although it isn't entirely clear what happened, most world historians place a lot of stock in the idea that the aristocrats felt threatened by a rich merchant class and wanted to rein them in.

If increasing the material wealth of society is to be the chief priority of a nation, the business sphere needs a political party to water and nurture it, to make sure that every possible pathway to bolster economic growth be opened and left open, to protect the merchant class from greedy politicians, who, in times past, had been quick to dip their hands into the gains of this sector and rob it of its lifeblood. The Republican Party has taken on that role. Their tactics to accomplish this goal have undergone change during that time span. They have progressed from "quasi" mercantilist policies to today's all out espousal of free trade.

Yet, both then and now, the Republican Party has been adamantly opposed to any form of government regulation. The economy was to be given as free a hand as possible. It was also very important that capital be kept mobile so that people would not hesitate to withdraw it from stagnant industries and businesses and deploy it in newer ones where prospects appeared the brightest. Naturally that meant a low tax on gains derived from the use of capital. Then, in order to attract people to become businessmen and women the overall business environment had to provide incentives. That required a tax structure that allowed commanders of the great commercial enterprises to keep the lion's share of what they earned. Also, it was important that the price level remained fairly stable so that the value of tomorrow's dollar could be relied upon. When the Republicans were the majority party in the late nineteenth century, in the 1920s, and in today's New Economy those conditions for economic growth were present and huge numbers of people were willing to brave the odds and risk their assets in new business ventures. All three periods were "economic growth" paradigms wherein business surged ahead at breathtaking speed. A crop of new industries sprouted, which changed the nature of America's and the world's economies. They were times of enormous economic creativity and soaring stock values. And with the outpouring of new goods helping to keep prices low, they were also times of low inflation.

In the late nineteenth century invention after invention broke through long-established technological bottlenecks and sent productivity soaring. Out poured telephones, typewriters, sewing machines, calculating machines, Bessemer converters, McCormick reapers, Elisha Otis's new elevators, and scores of other inventions. Most were on display, along with countless others, at the Centennial Exposition of 1876, held in Philadelphia. In the most popular building of the Exposition, the great Machinery Hall, stood the supreme symbol of industrialization, the giant Corliss steam engine, which dwarfed everything else in the hall. It alone supplied the power for eight thousand other machines, both large and small, on the exposition grounds.

Between the end of the Civil War and century's end the output of manufactured goods increased fivefold, more than 150,000 miles of railroad tracks were laid, and American steel mills, which had hardly been a factor in the world market for finished steel at the beginning of the period, were outproducing their British counterparts by more than 50 percent. It was during that time that the president of one of the major railroads asked his fellow citizens, "Have not the great merchants, great manufacturers, great inventors, done more for the world than preachers and philanthropists?"

Again in the 1920s another burst of robust and innovative economic growth took place. At the beginning of the period only about 20 percent of U.S. households had electricity, but by decade's end more than two-thirds of American families were plugged in. The decade turned into a consumer paradise for countless middle-class American families. They were introduced to lamps, washing machines, toasters, and above all the radio, along with numerous other appliances and gadgets. To the astonishment of contemporary economists, output per working hour increased 35 percent, just about double the gains of the prior period. It appeared that America had solved the riddle of economic growth, and delegations from abroad streamed into the country in hopes of discovering the secret of American productivity. The stock market commemorated those achievements by soaring from peak to peak throughout most of the period. Although the economy was to grow more complex, it was during that time the national economy acquired its basic twentieth-century infrastructure, and that essential form would not change for more than 50 years.

Today we are (or as of 2000 were) in the midst of a third burst of economic energy led by high tech, biotech, telecommunications, and the Internet. Like the previous two, this growth spurt is fundamentally changing the nature of American business. In celebration, the stock market partied throughout the 1990s and created amounts of new wealth that stagger the imagination.

Some might argue economic well-being is not only a GOP phenomenon; it also occurs during Democratic Party–led paradigms. The period from the end of World War II to the early 1970s, a span of more than 25 years, was certainly a time of remarkable and expanding prosperity. But do not confuse the economic growth that occurs during Republican Party "economic growth" paradigms with the prosperity that occurs when the Democrats are calling the shots. There is a clear difference in the two parties' approaches to the economy, and it goes back to the beginning of the republic.

When they are in charge, Republicans usher in new and innovative growth that gives fresh life to the economy. On the other hand, the prosperity that occurs when the Democratic Party is the ruling power is mostly a result of helping those industries that have already been created to expand further. There is not a great deal of new blood, and eventually the economy loses the ability to expand its output to meet the public's demand for goods and services. The sign of this: an inflation that rages out of control.

This is because the Democrats tend to take the economic sphere for granted. In their worldview it does not have to be constantly nurtured and looked after. The merchant class does not have to be coddled with low taxes. In fact, just the opposite; because of the industrialists' greater wealth they should be taxed more. The idea that gains on capital should be taxed at a lesser rate than labor leaves Democrats red-faced and foaming at the mouth. They are not bothered by the fact that a tax on capital gains locks huge pools of money into stagnant businesses and makes them unavailable to back promising new opportunities. The Democrats are quick to regulate business activity and relationships, thinking it necessary to prevent the moneyed interests from running roughshod over the public.

Naturally this attitude toward business does not produce a spirit of entrepreneurship; it does not motivate the nation's brightest youths to flock to Wharton and other leading business schools. This attitude eventually paralyzes the energies of the business community so that the nation's output of goods begins to flag and new business innovation becomes rarer and rarer. And, of course, we are soon visited by the demon of inflation.

The same could be said about the communist utopian vision of constructing a society of equals. The Soviets, in putting theory into practice, utterly failed to appreciate that dynamic economic growth requires a flourishing commercial class that must be stroked every so often. Naturally, as time went on, the Russians were unable to match the economic advances occurring in the West. They were unable to fulfill the aspirations of their citizens or stand tall in the community of nations.

There were two "social reorganization" type paradigms in the twentieth century. Although this type of political pattern is typically the province of the Democrats, the Republicans were the majority party during the progressive era. But it was a Democrat,

Woodrow Wilson, who carried the programs of that era to their natural conclusion. Near the end of both the progressive and the New Deal–Great Society eras the American economy was overwhelmed with a Great Inflation. During the last five years of the progressive era, the price level more than doubled. Again during the last decade of the New Deal–Great Society era consumer prices inflated by about 125 percent, far outdistancing any prior 10-year span during the twentieth century. These were clearly the two worst and longest periods of inflation during the twentieth century. Both were signs that the nation's economy was in trouble. And in each case, the Republicans were called in to put out the fire.

On the other hand, during "social reorganization" type paradigms, a great deal of mileage can be had from supporting and pushing the economy along pathways that have already been conceived. Several decades of economic growth can take place based on a wider distribution of the new goods that were introduced during the previous innovative period. The Democrats' programs to expand the public's purchasing power and spread it out among more of the nation's families provide the underlying support. And the party's pro-regulation stance makes it likely they will pass legislation to make many of the newer industries more consumer-friendly. Also, they are likely to help fix up some of the businesses that have been broken during the last phase of wealth destruction. Yet, make no mistake about it, this type of prosperity is built upon the economic gains made during the earlier period. It lives off inherited wealth, while the other type creates new wealth.

It does not seem outlandish to applaud the Republican Party for its role in the greatest takeoff in material abundance the world has ever seen. This prosperity has made possible the alleviation of suffering and want, which is a precondition of moral advancement. Certainly it seems possible that without a political party focused expressly on economic development and protecting the interests of a merchant-industrial class the immense increase in wealth and living standards that took place over the past 150 years might well have been far more modest, like in, say, Italy or Spain . . . or perhaps not have happened at all.

The Democrats have also stood guard over a great tradition. Just as the Republicans have been successful in providing for giant leaps in the nation's wealth, the Democrats, when they have been the majority party, have been every bit as successful in refashioning society in a more egalitarian manner and improving the position of those classes of people who were getting the short end of the stick. They have ensured that union workers, blacks, ethnics, women, and (now) gays were included in the mainstream. They have provided a "safety net" so that old age, illness, or handicaps do not leave ordinary citizens destitute. Listen to Al Gore in election 2000, trying to arouse and inspire his underclass constituency: "There is one thing you can be sure of . . . no matter how powerful the opposing interests . . . I will fight for you." Gore was telling society's underdogs that he would man the barricades to protect their educational system from Republican vouchers and Social Security from GOP treachery. Furthermore, he would carry the battle to the streets and alleyways of the enemy to secure for his people prescription drugs and patient rights. He would protect the little guy from the malign influence of big corporations.

We can thank the Democrats for extending a fairly close approximation of the lifestyles and freedoms enjoyed by the top class downward to the ordinary classes. Most middle- and working-class families own their home, can vacation abroad, and can find a lawyer willing to protect their interests. When the party of FDR has been in the driver's seat they have protected the purchasing power of the nation's middle and lower classes, and this in turn has helped prop up the economy and ensure it has legs. And by including new groups of people that were formerly left behind, the party of Jefferson and FDR opened up the social system so that another crop of human talent could be harvested to refresh American democracy.

Above all, Democrats have prevented the social system from slipping back into the mode of premodern rigid hierarchies, with a new top-dog class, the big industrialists, riding roughshod over the others. In times past, societies have had a strong tendency to stratify. Those who considered themselves the "better kind of people" have set themselves off from the masses by distinctions of dress, speech, manners, and education. They formed elites and put up institutional barricades to protect their wealth and power and block anyone else in society from joining in on the fun. But America in the nineteenth and twentieth centuries did not revert to a stratified society, reminiscent of seventeenth-century Europe, because there was a Democratic Party to check the GOP's tendency to favor an elite class. The Democrats have put forward measures to provide for an expansion in the middle layers of society and to cut the top class down to size, making sure it paid a greater share of society's costs. Under the Democrats' prodding, America has become the first predominately middle-class society in the history of the world wherein a majority of its citizens are able to partake in the material benefits society has to offer. Just as the miraculous economic growth did not just happen, the monumental social achievements of the past two hundred years resulted because a great political party stood their ground and actively intervened on behalf of the little guy who was in danger of being left out. The social innovations of the Democratic Party have made for a more humane and civil society.

However, there is a glitch. Each party, after ruling for a period of time, loses its magic to propel society upward to a higher level of civilization. Instead, the machines of society clog up and appear to verge on breakdown. After a period of Republican rule there are a large number of corporate abuses, multiplying business mistakes, and an increasing inequality of income. Furthermore, to many, the culture seems too devoted to a vulgar worship of money, too dependent on greed, and too deeply founded on adversarial individualism. On the flip side, when the Democrats have held the reins of power for too long, business stagnates, inflation takes off, and there is a whopping increase in social disorder. The sense of individual responsibility falls by the wayside, and the culture takes on a "something for nothing" aroma.

The first flaw in the GOP creed is that the economy cannot tolerate ultra-fast business growth generated by a loose, relatively unregulated environment for too long. These periods breed a free-wheeling, "anything goes" business atmosphere wherein powerful business interests are able to get away with many abuses and as time goes on they become more frequent. The industrialists of the Gilded Age made a mockery of the ideals of those who imagined that the nation's development could take place with dignity and restraint under the regime of laissez-faire. Furthermore, "economic growth" periods begin to appear so risk-free that business-people become overconfident and throw caution to the wind. They can, and usually do, build a "bubble" into the stock market. Yet people recognize the economy has moved on to a faster growth track at about the time the low-lying fruit of business opportunities has been picked clean. The more difficult higher-branch food is all that is left. Businesspeople turn their attention to the higher-risk endeavors, and that will make for a good number of business mistakes.

A second major GOP flaw: The affluent are likely to get a disproportionate share of the new wealth being generated. It was estimated that during the Gilded Age the top 1 percent of the population received a greater share of the national income than the bottom 50 percent combined. That income disparity, besides threatening to reshape the nation's social system into a rigid hierarchy, saps the purchasing power of the middle and lower middle class so their spending cannot keep pace with business growth. This removes the economy's underpinnings.

These flaws multiply the chances of an unpleasant surprise, such as a severe economic bust during which a great deal of the newly created wealth is destroyed. When that happens large numbers of people who had joined in on the nation's dash to riches become disillusioned and dump their assets, putting further downward pressure on the economy, ensuring that it becomes stuck in the mire for a long, long time. And the Republican Party, because of its ideology and its constituency, is unable to deal with the problems that are spreading to multiple fronts.

What to do! Luckily, another political party with a different ideology and a different constituency is sitting on the sidelines, prepared to deal with those type problems. The Democrats because they operate from the bottom up will have the right prescription to correct the Republican flaws. They will pass legislation to regulate and rein in the freewheeling "anything goes" economy, which will ameliorate business abuses and force some of the newer industries to modify their conduct so as to conform to long-held ideas of fair play.

Also remember, even after allowing for the destruction of wealth at the end of Republican economic growth eras, much still remains. And the Democrats are able to redistribute it in ways that seem fairer. They will pass laws aimed at **helping those who had been left behind,** which will enhance the aggregate purchasing power of the underclasses. Taken together these measures will render the economy more orderly and stable. The Democrats play a key role in checking and counteracting the Republican flaws and, in so doing, lay the groundwork for another period of vigorous economic growth. But that will be a while in coming.

Furthermore, the Democratic creed embraces a "devotion to the public good" ethic, wherein people are encouraged to surrender personal desires and commit to something greater than themselves—a higher "social" purpose. Status is conferred on those who make significant contributions to the common good, i.e. helping others. This encourages a community "we-are-in-this-together spirit," which treasures cooperation and knocks the props out from under a brutal and adversarial competitive social system that had valued selfishness, obsessive moneymaking, and luxury.

The Democrats' style of governing, like the Republicans', inevitably leads to intractable problems that the party will not be able to deal with. The great social upheavals during "social rebalancing" type paradigms produce a culture of unbridled individualism, wherein breaking the rules becomes the "rule." Yet society needs rules that are accepted by most all its members in order to permit cooperative endeavors. Without rules our sense of community is undermined. We trust others to keep commitments and avoid opportunistic behavior only when we can expect them to behave and act according to rules. When that level of trust is lowered it weakens the bonds holding families, neighborhoods, communities, and nations together. Social cohesion becomes less achievable, all forms of authority are eroded, the legitimacy of established institutions is undermined, and public order breaks down. There are dramatic increases in the level of crime, illegitimacy, alcohol and drug usage, and divorce. American society appeared on the precipice of social crack-up near the end of social rebalancing paradigms, as in the 1840s–1850s and again in the 1960s–1970s and, in a lesser way, during the 1917–1920 period.

Also not to be overlooked is the other Democratic flaw already mentioned. Their tendency to regulate the economy and to tax business and the wealthy ultimately leads to an overregulated and overtaxed economy wherein enthusiasm for entrepreneurship is thwarted and the movement of capital is deadened. A regulatory economic environment builds barriers to entry that allow many older, less efficient businesses to remain alive and block the entranceway for newer and more promising companies. The supply potential of the nation is sapped. But the same Democratic philosophy will also have produced policies designed to lift the purchasing power of the working and lower classes, which practically guarantees outsized increases in overall demand at the very time that the economy's productive power has atrophied. The result: The phoenix of inflation rises from the ashes.

The Democrats cannot deal with the problems that arise during their reign. Their philosophical construct will not permit them. Naturally they will recognize the growing problems within their political model and propose solutions. When crime and drugs arose as major social problems in the late 1960s the Democrats put American flags on their lapels and talked the talk about programs to stop crime and drug usage. Again when inflation burst out in the late 1970s President Jimmy Carter came out with a plethora of proposals to curb the beast. But his party was unable to walk the walk. Because of their constituency and party ideology, they will underestimate the problem and propose painless and halfhearted fixes. Their proposals may help soothe the concerns of constituents, but nothing concrete is likely to come of it. That is because their mindset does not enable them to recognize that their basic policies are contributing to the burning problems. While one hand is sprinkling water on the tribulations, the other will be pouring gasoline on the troubles.

After a while the Democrats' program also breaks down on multiple fronts, but luckily there is another party in the bullpen awaiting their call. The Republicans, because of their ideology, will be able to correct the Democrat type problems and bring the nation back to its senses. The Grand Old Party will be able to generate specific policies that can deal with inflation and public disorder. They will introduce programs that will spawn a new crop of bold, ambitious, and energetic young men, who will make the investments and provide for the necessary supply increases. You can also count on the GOP to cut back on the programs pandering to the lower orders of society, and this will cool demand.

The fundamental Republican philosophy also has a second side, which is maintaining public order. They are quicker to make common cause with traditional religion and together to impose or suggest institutional constraints on human behavior, for example, moral standards, Sunday blue laws, and school prayer. Republicans are more apt to fire the whole group of air controllers if they go out on strike. This puts union members on notice that they have something to lose if they break the law and strike against the public interest. The Republican Party also places more emphasis on individual responsibility, and this will go a long way toward quelling the excessive individualism of the previous period. Kiss good-bye to inflation, and welcome in public order. Yet, in doing so, the GOP will be preparing the way for another period of social leveling, but again, that will be a while in coming.

As the Good Book says:

> *To everything there is a season,*
> *And a time to every purpose under the heaven;*
> *A time to be born, and a time to die,"*

and so on.

May we add:

> *A time for fast economic growth, and a time for social rebalancing;*
> *A time for idealism, and a time for realistic government;*

And above all:

> ***A time for the Republicans to rule, and a time for the***
> ***Democrats to govern.***

When the policies of one party put the American ship of state in danger of careening off course, the other party steps in and

checks the excesses of their adversary party. The two parties
have developed a symbiotic relationship wherein each develops
policies to offset the other's weakness. The Democrats ride to the
rescue and tame a disorderly economy, while reducing social barriers. The Republicans, on the other hand, bring order to a disorderly social system, while removing the barriers to economic
growth. Neither can live without the other. Each is a piece of the
whole—but not the whole.

Both major parties stand guard over one of the two great modern traditions. The Democratic Party has been the vehicle for
rebalancing the social system. We can expect its standard-bearers
to tilt the system in favor of the have-less classes. The Republicans are the party that encourages economic development. It has
enabled society to ensure that every possible pathway to enhance
material prosperity is opened. We can count on presidents of that
party to promote programs that are conducive to economic
growth. Together the Democrats and the Republicans have created the wealthiest, the most humane, and *yes*, the fairest society
yet, in the history of the world. This more than 200-year duel
between competing visions has made for the **Great Game of
Politics.**

—◈◈◈—

X

The Nine Political Paradigms

America, since its beginning, has alternated between two basic types of paradigms. First is the "economic growth" type, wherein the economy is pushed to its limit and there is a large redistribution of wealth to the affluent. It propels the nation toward the right. During the "social rebalancing" type the government stabilizes the economy and launches an assault upon the privileges of the well-heeled, while reaching out a helping hand to those left behind. It moves the nation in the direction of the left. A summary of the nine political paradigms follows. (See table 13.)

Paradigm #1: The Federalists

The Federalist paradigm, led by George Washington, came first. The Federalists attempted to redefine the American Revolution and turn the egalitarian "spirit of 76" into a quest for material betterment. Washington and Hamilton set the new nation in a pro-commerce direction. The nation's finances were put in order, a national bank was established, and federal taxes were imposed to support government endeavors. Furthermore, the strength of the army and the navy was increased. After a second term George

TABLE 13

Nine Paradigms

Paradigm-Setter	Paradigm	Began	Governed
1. Washington	Federalist	1789 Pro-commerce	from the right
2. Jefferson	Democratic	1801 Individual freedom/agrarian	from the left
3. Madison	New Nationalism	1815 Pro-commerce	*toward* the right
4. Jackson	New Democracy	1829 Individual freedom/agrarian	from the left
5. Lincoln	Post–Civil War	1861 Economic growth	from the right
6. T. Roosevelt	Progressive	1901 Social justice	*toward* the left
7. Coolidge	New Era	1921 Economic growth	from the right
8. F. Roosevelt	New Deal	1933 Social justice	from the left
9. Reagan	New Economy	1981 Economic growth	from the right

Washington made a grand exit from the American political scene, which featured an eloquent farewell address. He voluntarily gave up power, something kings in the past were not inclined to do, setting a precedent that most future presidents would adhere to. John Adams succeeded Washington.

However, the Federalists stood in the way of democracy as it was emerging. Their interference in economic life to help the rich via tariffs, taxation, banks, privileges, and bounties made it seem as if the American nation was being transformed into a rank-organized commercial society that was taking on the form and spirit of the British monarchy. Adams was defeated in the election of 1800.

Paradigm #2: Jeffersonian Democracy

Thomas Jefferson, a Democratic-Republican, took control of the government and made an about-face in its direction—to the left—so as to recapture the egalitarian spirit of 1776. Jefferson and his crowd were appalled by the elitism of the Federalist era and sought to break up the politically supported privileges of the New England gentry. The national bank was scuttled, government expenditures were trimmed, the hated excise duties were abolished, the government refused to subsidize internal improvements, and the size of the army and the navy was substantially reduced.

The Jeffersonians were determined to return to a world in which trade and commerce played a relatively minor role. They forged an agrarian alliance with the powerful Southern planters and turned the government's focus to extending the nation's frontier, to pushing the Indians farther back into the interior, and to lowering the purchase price of frontier land. This agrarian agenda was part of Jefferson's grand design to expand the boundaries of individual freedom.

In 1812, at a time when the federal government was weaker than at any other time in its national history, James Madison, who had succeeded Jefferson, let the expansionists egg him into a second war with England. The war went badly, and Madison recognized that the Republicans had gone too far in uncoupling the nation from its important stabilizing institutions. In late 1815 he reversed course.

By the time the second paradigm had come to a close it was apparent the Jeffersonians had laid the foundation for a fluid social system, which was shunting aside the "New England" gentry and upsetting social hierarchies that had been frozen since the Revolutionary War.

Paradigm #3: The "New Nationalism"

Although remaining true to Jefferson's agrarian program, Madison shifted to the right and advanced policies that would also encourage the buildup of a commercial sector. He provided for a high protective tariff, reestablished a national bank, increased the size of the army and navy, and made sympathetic sounds as to federal funding of internal improvements. A market revolution was launched; industries began to take root, creating new opportunities for many American families. An economic boom followed but ended with a bang as a general financial panic struck in 1819. James Monroe, who won voter approval for the "New Nationalism" policies in 1816 and then again in 1820, gets an assist in providing paradigm leadership.

The "New Nationalism" paradigm was also unusual in another respect. Changes in political direction of that magnitude are usually engineered by the opposing party. But in this case the Federalist Party was impotent and unable to dislodge Jefferson's party. As a result, once Madison recognized that some of Jefferson's positions had been too extreme, he was able to maneuver his party to the "right," instituting needed reforms to nudge the nation in a commercial direction without tossing aside its devotion to agrarian pursuits. Because the Democratic-Republican Party presided over the modification of the Jefferson agenda, change was kept within bounds.

In 1824 John Quincy Adams took over and proposed the "American System," which threatened to extend the Madison-Monroe agenda much further in a pro-commercial direction than the citizens of the United States were ready for. His crushing defeat in the election of 1828 was a repudiation of economic nationalism and marked the end of the third political model.

Paradigm #4: The New Democrats

The next political pattern, the fourth, was the "New Democratic" era. General Andrew Jackson reclaimed the White House for the Democrats and rededicated the party to its old agrarian policies. And, like Jefferson, Jackson fought to overthrow the institutions of power and open up the gates of opportunity for the little guy. Martin Van Buren, Old Hickory's successor, never had a chance. Depression struck shortly after Van Buren took the helm, and in the following election the Whigs won the right to occupy the White House.

Once the majority paradigm party fails to win a plurality of the votes, it indicates the mini-revolution has gone too far, at least for the moment. Either the country will turn and march in the other direction or some of the excesses will be tempered so that the mini-transformation is able to proceed at a more moderate pace. The paradigm will either end or begin a period of political equilibrium. If the minority party is able to win the public's approval for a program to redress the nation's grievances, it will transform into the majority party of a new political model. However, the historical moment is not always conducive to "big" change. When the minority party has gained enough new voters to effectively challenge the ruling party, but not enough to back a full-scale change in the government's direction, it indicates there is no clear consensus as to the nation's priorities. The mini-revolution has stalled and the nation has **entered into a political stalemate.**

When the minority party reaches the White House during a stalemate it is in a difficult position, as it is operating in an enemy political model. Minority presidents must walk a tightrope between not attacking the main paradigm agenda and not angering their own constituency, which will be calling for an honest-to-goodness change in direction. Thus minority party presidents usually attempt to satisfy their followers with modest and incremental changes, while being careful not to veer too far off paradigm course. The changes they make are not very serious, nor long-lasting; they leave few footprints. Keep in mind: Bill Clinton! He remained sympathetic to the Reagan economic policies of free trade and less government regulation while trying to distinguish himself on social issues, such as gays in the military or portability of health-care insurance.

During a political standoff the minority party usually has only a one-to-two-term fling in office before the populace becomes disenchanted with them also. Meanwhile, the majority party will benefit from their time out of office. They will put a new face on their program, tempering unpopular and objectionable policies, and thus render the party voter-friendly once again. Keep in mind:

George W. Bush and "compassionate conservatism." After a short period of minority party rule the dominant paradigm party will be able to muscle their way back into the White House and begin a restoration. Interestingly, in all four of the "first restoration of the paradigm" presidential contests (three paradigms also had a second resurrection) the two major candidates were separated by less than 1½ percent of the total vote. Those close elections were essentially ties, as voting irregularities, or imprecise counts, could have accounted for much of the difference. But remember: the majority party, because it normally controls the election machinery (and also the Supreme Court), is usually able to turn tie into victory—and in all four cases they did.

Restorer presidents typically serve a term or two before running into deep trouble. Herein lies the difficulty. The public disenchantment that caused the majority party's hold on power to loosen, some years back, is a sign the mini-revolution had solved much of what was ailing society. Meanwhile, that very success is creating a new set of problems, but troubles best handled by the party from the other side of the political spectrum. The minority party, whose agenda is more attuned to the emerging problems, will be gaining adherents. However, after recapturing the White House, resurrection type presidents govern according to the blueprints for the prevailing political model. They rally their forces to complete the unfinished paradigm business, and for a while it appears they have broken out of the political stalemate. But they press too hard in pushing their agenda. It upsets the political balance and the "new" type problems become more urgent. So instead of jubilation for the implementation of additional paradigm programs the forces of opposition are aroused and the majority party loses its popular support. A **time of paradigm troubles** usually begins. From the time the sun is about to set on the restorer presidency until a new mini–political revolution has begun, neither party is likely to be able to deal effectively with the nation's overriding problem (or problems).

The Democrats' defeat in 1840 marked the beginning of America's first political stalemate. The Whigs took over the federal government, and by the end of their first term it was clear that they were unable to move the nation onto a new path.

In 1844 James Polk restored the Democrats to power. Just 5,000 votes in New York State could have given the White House to his opponent, Henry Clay. And there were over 15,000 votes in that state that went to the Liberty Party candidate, most of which originally were thought headed Clay's way. Polk steered the government back in its "New Democratic" direction. But in so doing he pushed core policies beyond the public's comfort zone and stirred up sectional controversy once again, beginning **a time of paradigm troubles,** which would last until the Civil War. Trying to open new pathways to industrialism while at the same time appeasing the big Southern planters would be the chief problem. By the time Polk left office in 1849, he was unpopular enough to take a circuitous route to his Tennessee home in hopes of avoiding unfriendly crowds.

The Whigs got another chance to try their hand at governing in 1849, but again they were unable to change the course of government. After a second Whig one-term fling in office, the Democrats regained the White House and began a "second" restoration. By the time a second resurrection begins, the political, economic, and social backdrop, which originally had been so favorable for this mini-revolution, will, most likely, have changed considerably. Standard paradigm policies will no longer be very effective; in fact, they very well may be sailing against the wind and exasperate the mounting problems.

When the Democrats returned to power in 1853, things went badly for the party right from the start. The Democrats tilted further in favor of their Southern constituency and tried to give the South a chance to extend their peculiar institution of slavery into areas where in the past it had been excluded. But rather than an extension of slavery, the nation got Bleeding Kansas, Dred Scott, and a grand finale to the Jacksonian political model with cannons and guns blasting away on the battlefields of Bull Run, Gettysburg, and Cold Harbor.

The Jacksonian political equilibrium lasted 20 years, from 1840 to 1860, and during that time the Democrats were able to lose a couple of elections and still remain the majority party. The beginning of a stalemate is clear only in retrospect. If the minority party loses an election before they have put through a far-reaching program to change the direction of the government, it indicates their term in office was the beginning of a stalemate, not a paradigm shift.

The period from 1801 to 1861 may actually be viewed as a singular whole, with a temporary interruption in the middle "New Nationalism" years, when the Democrats (or their predecessor party, the Democratic-Republicans) backpedaled on some, but not all, of their key issues. During the whole of this period the party of Jefferson and Jackson dominated the political landscape. They won 12 of the 15 presidential elections held during that time. The central political thread throughout the whole of this period was an unrelenting agrarian program, which featured territorial expansion, Indian removal, and the continual cheapening of the price of a homestead. The price of establishing a homestead, which had been $1,280 at the beginning of the century under the Federalists, was reduced to about $200 by the 1850s.

The party of Jefferson and Jackson championed policies to remove government restraints and privileges and pushed the boundaries of individual freedom further and further so as to give free rein to individual ability and enterprise. American society reached its high-water mark in egalitarianism as the rich and powerful could no longer bend the acts of government to their selfish purposes and there was a notable absence of deference to the rich and wellborn. Observers from all over the world noted that in American society distinctions based on social class didn't count for much. For perhaps the first time in human history, a large society was formed around the idea a nation's institutions should serve the individual, not the other way around, as it had been throughout human history. The **individual was primary!**

To be sure, the early Democrats largely ignored groups such as women and blacks, who had been assigned lower positions in society. But that was the beginning of the nineteenth century and the level of social consciousness was ... well, nineteenth-centuryish. How can you condemn an ancient (older) society for failing to measure up to ideals that have only recently been conceived?

Paradigm #5: Late-Nineteenth-Century Transition

Abraham Lincoln won the election of 1860 with less than 40 percent of the popular vote. The Republican "Lincoln" political pattern began with a great Civil War, which decided the nation would stay together. "Honest Abe" adopted the Whig pro–economic growth program, but because all eyes were focused on the war it was not clear in which direction Mr. Lincoln was aiming to take the country.

A fight for succession began. Lincoln's vice president, Andrew Johnson, took the first stab, but a Republican Congress blocked the former Democrat from claiming Lincoln's mantle. It was the only time the president directly following a pattern-setter was not a "true" successor. Andrew Johnson was America's "accidental" president.

General Ulysses Grant was Lincoln's "true" successor and settled the matter as to Mr. Lincoln's "after the war" design. Grant steered to the right, choosing business growth, and led the Republican Party into an alliance with the winners in the race to industrialization. Naturally the gap in income between the rich and poor would become enormous. In resolving the confusion as to paradigm direction Ulysses Grant deserves an assist as pattern-setter. Also, the general was one of only three successor presidents who were able to win reelection in their own right.

In 1876, after two Grant terms, the Democrats captured a majority of the votes but failed to win the White House. Nonetheless, this indicated problems outside the Republicans' scope of competence were developing and another political stalemate, much like the one from 1841 to 1861, was beginning. During most of the 24-year span from 1877 to 1901, the two parties would appear as two equally matched armies.

Although the GOP tenaciously held on to the White House in five of the seven presidential elections, two victories were accomplished in the face of a Democratic voter plurality. Another was achieved with a 9,000-vote margin out of 9 million cast. The chief problem at this time was how to tame "big" business so that it would not run roughshod over the rest of the populace, while, at the same time, ensuring the pathways to industrialization remained open.

The GOP was able to hang on to the White House until 1885, when the Democrat Grover Cleveland beat his Republican opponent. The chief paradigm problem appeared to be beyond Cleveland's competence also, and in the following election Benjamin Harrison restored the GOP to the White House. In one of the most corrupt elections in America's history, Benjamin Harrison, with about one hundred thousand fewer votes than Grover Cleveland, won a majority in the Electoral College in 1988. The Democratic New York City Tammany Hall "machine" was upset with reformers, for taking away their perks, and threw their powerful political organization behind the Republican candidate. The state of New York went for Harrison by less than 15,000 votes—which a loyal Tammany Hall could easily have made up—and with it went the election. Again, as in 1844, a tie had become a win for the majority party. Harrison announced that "Providence" had awarded his party a great victory. "Providence hadn't a damn thing to do with it," retorted campaign manager, Matt Quay. Harrison, Quay added, would never know "how close a number of men were compelled to approach the gates of the penitentiary to make him president."

Like Polk, in the mid-1840s, Harrison pushed traditional GOP policies too far for a nation that was basically sitting on the fence. He presided over a steep increase in tariff duties, and his administration championed a slew of costly new measures, such as granting pensions to Union army veterans and their widows and children. The public was outraged by what it saw as a ransacking of the nation's treasury and provided the Democrats with an overwhelming congressional victory in the 1890 mid-term election. In the following presidential contest Grover Cleveland, the Democrat, won back the White House and was given another shot at governing. But it would also be the beginning of another **time of troubles.**

A depression struck shortly after Cleveland reclaimed power. Like the Whigs after they retrieved the White House in 1849, Cleveland's Democrats spent all their time trying to straighten out the mess the country had gotten into. After more than three years of deep depression the two parties lined up for the important 1896 election. William McKinley won the presidency by selling the public on the idea that the GOP was responsible for America's post–Civil War economic growth. It was to be the Grand Old Party's third chance at governing, its second restoration, during this political model. But McKinley was killed shortly after his second term began, and the paradigm ended.

Paradigm #6: The Progressives

Following McKinley's assassination, Teddy Roosevelt took the reins of government and guided the country down a new path. It was the sixth, the "progressive," mini-revolution. The colonel veered off the traditional Republican model and led the government to intervene in antitrust matters, environmentalism, labor relations, and consumer safety. Taft succeeded TR but seemed to waver too much for the progressives, so much so that Teddy Roosevelt came off the sidelines to oppose his reelection, ensuring a Democratic victory.

Woodrow Wilson, who became president in 1912, formed a left-of-center coalition with workers and liberal reformers and extended the government's intrusion into the economy much further than Roosevelt had dared go.

All three progressive era presidents used the mighty hand of the state to curb the growing power of industry, to impose order, and to protect the ordinary citizen. The business excesses of the late nineteenth century lessened, the nation rediscovered its "devotion to the public welfare" ethic, and the middle class was able to attain status and a greater portion of the nation's income. Differences in wealth between the rich and the middle class, which had been so glaring in the late nineteenth century, narrowed.

Most mini-revolutions begin following an election in which the "out" party captures the White House. The new president begins to move in another direction immediately. Twice, however, the "in" party began the transformation. Teddy Roosevelt's progressive era was quite similar to James Madison's "New National" paradigm. In both, the minority party was on the ropes and the field was left wide open for the ruling party to appropriate some of their rival party's policies to use in modifying their own program.

Madison, reeling from the failures during the War of 1812, reached back into the dustbin of American history and retrieved some of the Federalists' old policies. He moved in the direction of encouraging a buildup of commercial growth but did not go all the way back to the right. Eighty-six years later Teddy Roosevelt maneuvered the Republican Party in the direction of reform. He brought the government into the picture as a counterweight to corporate power. But when a party espouses a program more suited to the competing party's ideology, they are unlikely to pursue their program with passion. The transformation is unlikely to become total; it becomes a major modification of their traditional doctrine. Madison's shift to the right stopped well short of leading his party into becoming a pro-business party. And a similar thing happened during the Roosevelt administrations. TR led the charge to reform the economy and aimed to steer a middle course between favoring the plutocrats and the masses. He never intended to upend capitalism. He only wished to curb its excesses and heal the most conspicuous sores on the body politic to make sure that socialism didn't gain a foothold in America.

When the majority party attempts to steer the nation in a direction incompatible with its basic creed, the passion is likely to be supplied by the minority party once they take over the reins of government. They view their election victory, even if attained with considerably less than 50 percent of the popular vote, as the country calling on them to lead because they are ideologically suited for the path the nation is already traveling along. They refuse to interpret their narrow win as a sign that the American public is unsure of its priorities. Instead, egged on by their constituency, they attempt to extend the mini-revolution further. But usually this will provoke a huge reaction. It happened in 1825 when John Quincy Adams, a 31 percent vote gatherer, refused to recognize the election of 1824 as an indication that the public was growing weary of economic nationalism. Instead he tried to push the nation further down the path of industrialization than the electorate was bargaining for and aroused a backlash.

Woodrow Wilson, when he took up the cause of progressivism, fell into a similar trap. Like John Quincy Adams nearly a century before, Wilson emerged from the election with considerably less than half the popular vote and failed to recognize that his political model was about modifying the power of business so as to smooth the transition to an industrial economy. Instead, he turned Roosevelt's attempt at evenhandedness between the haves and have-nots into a pro–little guy stance and a government on the left side of the political spectrum. Like J. Q. Adams, Wilson had gone way beyond the public's level of comfort and elicited a backlash. Yet in crossing the important threshold that separates right from left both Woodrow Wilson and J. Q. Adams ultimately defined their paradigm, *more so than the pattern-setter.*

In both cases the ruling party was so successful in modifying its core doctrine and stealing much of what should have been the opposing party's agenda that the minority party lost legitimacy and the majority party was able to extend its political domination for well over a half-century. Madison's flirtation with nationalism drove the Federalists from the political playing field and allowed the Democrats' period of political leadership to last 60 years— from 1801 to 1861. In much the same way, Teddy Roosevelt's modification of the Republican agenda permitted the party to extend their reign as the dominant force in American politics until 1933—which was 72 years after Lincoln moved into the White House in 1861.

Paradigm #7: The New Era

In 1920 the Republicans picked Warren Harding to lead the party back to its traditional pro-business roots. He swamped Wilson's stand-in, James Cox, in a landslide of monumental proportions. The election was reminiscent of 1828, wherein Andrew Jackson swept past John Quincy Adams by a big margin and led the Democrats back to their agrarian roots.

A Republican Party dedicated to promoting economic growth was back in the saddle and a seventh mini-revolution which would move the country to the right, began. The tariff was raised, regulations were wiped off the books, taxes were cut, and the government backed away from meddling in the affairs of the economy. Calvin Coolidge, who came next, adopted Harding's program wholeheartedly. Although Coolidge gets credit for this political model, his debt to Harding was large and the latter certainly deserves a considerable assist.

These paradigm policies encouraged people to undertake productive activities, to innovate, to invest, and to economize. The economy was unleashed and began a "New Era" of mouthwatering growth. Marvelous new business opportunities opened up, and the stock market soared year after year. The government was clearly tilted in favor of the rich, and much as in the post–Civil War span, the wealth gap between rich and poor widened considerably. But in the fall of 1929 the economy hit a speed bump and slowed, sending the stock market on a downward course. Soon the economy followed suit and both entered into a race for the bottom. Herbert Hoover, who was unlucky enough to have succeeded Coolidge just before the turn, was held responsible for pauperizing much of the nation and for decades to come was deemed the great presidential failure. Americans came to regard the twenties as frivolous, wasteful, and even amoral, and the Republican Party was banished from its perch at the top of the political heap to begin a long period of wandering in the American political wilderness.

Looking back from the vantage point of the mid–twentieth century, the 1920s were seen as Indian summer to a dying old order, and the Republican presidents who ruled during that time would not be forgiven for another fifty years. Most historians blamed the New Era politicians for not taking the problems of the 1920s, such as an agricultural depression and the lagging income of the working class, to heart. Coolidge and Harding were criticized for turning their backs on the activist reform and restructuring presidencies of Teddy Roosevelt and Woodrow Wilson.

Wait a minute: There is something social scientists call hindsight bias. It is the tendency to think that if one had been present at an earlier time, he surely would have known of future events that had not yet taken place. This bias encourages a view of the world as more predictable than it actually is. Remember, in 1920 the American people voted overwhelmingly to bury the prior progressive policies and unshackle the hands of businessmen. Harding had gathered an even larger majority of the voters than FDR was to attract 12 years later during the heart of the depression. In 1924 and 1928 the American people, who were riding on an enormous wave of prosperity that appeared without end, saw no good reason not to believe the current Republican policies were correct and would continue to deliver. Besides, their opponents promised policies not all that different. Who could doubt, in fact who did doubt, that the nation's businessmen had earned the country's respect, as well as a free hand! Should the presidents of that time be held to a higher level of prescience than others?

The Republicans called the shots from the White House in 56 years of the 72-year period spanned by a Civil War on one side and a Great Depression on the other. The party of Lincoln and Grant won 14 of the 18 presidential elections held during that interval and 10 with over 50 percent of the total vote. The Democrats, on the other hand, were able to top the majority mark only once during the whole of that period, and Tilden, the candidate who accomplished the feat, didn't even get to sleep in the White House.

The chief article of faith during America's age of industrialization, up until the Great Depression, was an abiding belief that a "high tariff" was indispensable for prosperity. The Morrill Tariff, the Dingley Tariff, the Fordney-McCumber Tariff, each raised duties substantially and was followed by a long period of increasing prosperity. The high tariff, during that time, was the third rail of politics; mess with it as Chet Arthur, Grover Cleveland, and William Taft did, and you were politically dead. Not even Teddy Roosevelt, a progressive whose creed favored lower tariffs, attempted to take on the high-tariff forces during his presidency.

During that long span America clearly became an industrial society and the Jefferson-Jacksonian social revolution was tamed. A social reformation back in the direction of a stratified society, which had been under way since the Civil War, was completed. Public order was firmly reestablished. The excess of democracy, evident in the 1850s, with but one brief flare-up during Woodrow Wilson's reign, was put to rest as the indicators of social disorder, crime, divorce, illegitimacy, and strikes, all rising during the early nineteenth century, were now pointing down or stuck at low levels.

Paradigm #8: The New Deal/Great Society

Paradigm number eight, the New Deal era, belongs to Franklin Delano Roosevelt. After the stock market crash of 1929 and the subsequent economic collapse, Americans were ready to embark on a "new age of social responsibility." FDR tilted the government back to the left, forged an alliance with the "little guy," and initiated a series of bold new reforms, a New Deal, which made America a more humane industrial society. Labor relations were soothed, the racial caste system was overthrown, and the extremes of wealth and poverty narrowed—the top 1 percent of American families earned nearly 19 percent of the national income in 1929, but that figure dropped to only 7.7 percent by 1946. And by the time the curtain rolled down on the paradigm, the state had taken on the responsibility for the health and vigor of the nation's economy and many of those who formerly had been left behind, workers, blacks, ethnic groups, and women, would be given special rights to help bring them into the mainstream. Although economic restrictions grew during the era, social constraints were loosened considerably.

Harry Truman inherited the presidency from Franklin Roosevelt and stuck by his predecessor's domestic policies. But FDR's foreign policy, adopted during the confusion of World War II and steeped in Wilsonian idealism, proved too naïve for the postwar period. Truman led the Democrats in adopting the policy of containment to check Soviet expansionism, and this became the central theme of American foreign policy until Jimmy Carter took over the White House. Because he recognized the Soviet challenge and committed the nation to the policy of "containment," Harry Truman played the main role in establishing America's postwar international stance and deserves a partial assist to FDR.

In 1952, after 20 consecutive years of Democratic rule, Dwight Eisenhower won the presidency for the Republicans. This GOP win indicated the bloom was off the rose of the Democratic mini-revolution. Another political stalemate was beginning and would last until 1980. And during that 28-year span the Democrats would prevail in only three of the seven presidential elections, although they would maintain an iron lock on Congress.

Eisenhower took a tougher approach to foreign affairs and blocked ambitious new social programs. This slowed the momentum of change, enabling the political model to have a longer life. Interludes wherein the minority party gets a chance to tame some of the excesses of paradigm policy help extend the dominant political pattern. After an eight-year Republican intermission, the country was ready to turn back to the Democrats.

John Kennedy restored the Democrats to power in 1960, though by a razor-thin margin—118,000 votes out of nearly 69 million cast. The Democrats were the majority party and in control of the election machinery, and many political observers thought the election had been stolen. A switch of less than 30,000 votes (out of 7 million tallied) in Illinois and Texas, the two states where a great deal of voting irregularities were alleged to have taken place, would have shifted 51 electoral votes and produced a different outcome.

During the 1960 battle for the presidency John Kennedy pledged a new commitment to the cold war, vowing he would lead the nation to victory over the Soviet Union. This undermined the Republican position, but also made American entry into Vietnam more likely. After Kennedy was killed Lyndon Johnson took charge and in the following year won a stunning election victory. He pursued a very ambitious social program, the "Great Society," which took the New Deal to a higher level. But at the same time, adhering to the Democratic sacred doctrine of "containment," he upped the ante in Vietnam and conducted a "guns and butter" program, which let the genie of inflation out of the bottle. Soon it would become obvious he had pushed paradigm policies too far.

In pushing an aggressive social program on a nation that was beginning to feel that "enough was enough" he elicited a lower-middle-class backlash. That class, which earlier had been the core of the Democratic Party constituency, felt that they were to be the losers in this new social realignment. Blacks were bused into their children's schools, exposing their offspring to ghetto values; affirmative action denied jobs to many members of that class whose credentials would have gotten them the job in the past; their taxes were upped to pay the welfare costs of an underclass that, at least in some instances, was gaming the system; and when long-standing laws governing punishment were changed in ways that favored the perpetrators of crime, their lower middle class neighborhoods became unsafe. By the time LBJ left office, it seemed as if the country was being torn apart. As in the late 1840s, as in the early 1890s, a **time of troubles** began.

Beginning about 1968 a series of mishaps and failures took place. A shortcoming of American might, in Vietnam and later Iran; Watergate; a cultural insurgency by the youth of our country; the reality that our most important resource, oil, was limited and outside our control; and a Great Inflation would all serve to shake American's faith in the New Deal–Great Society paradigm.

Richard Nixon assumed the presidency in early 1969 and tried to mend the country. He tried to end the war in Vietnam, he tried to stop the inflation, and he attempted a cutback of social programs. But, like minority party presidents in earlier political models, he was only partially successful. This provided fuel to Nixon's "liberal" critics, who blasted away at him. In frustration, Nixon and his administration resorted to extralegal activities in hopes of silencing some of the opposition. Instead he got caught and had to resign. By 1976 the country was ready to give the Democrats another shot at putting things back together.

President Jimmy Carter made a halfhearted attempt to reposition the Democratic Party in the middle ground of American politics. In an effort to narrow the budget deficit and alleviate inflation he submitted a proposal for a modest increase in government spending, which also included small cuts for many sensitive domestic programs. It placed him on a collision course with the party's vocal liberal wing. In a direct challenge to Carter, Senator Edward Kennedy told the faithful to "sail against the wind" of public opinion and reject "drastic slashes" in domestic spending. As a result Carter did not, and probably could not, go far enough in modifying the Democratic agenda. His administration, like that of Buchanan more than a century earlier, was fated to be the end of the line for a Democratic "social rebalancing" paradigm.

The central liberal tenet throughout this paradigm was the belief that a government, which was willing to spend big taxpayer bucks, could design programs to cure most any of the nation's pressing problems. Big-money social programs became the Democrats' theme song.

Paradigm #9: The New Economy

Once again the political wheel turned and a ninth, "Ronald Reagan" paradigm began in 1981. Reagan's program to cut taxes, reduce domestic spending, and rebuild America's defenses awakened a sleeping economy, which in turn provided the liftoff to a stock market that by century's end had soared to unimagined heights. During this era of the "New Economy," the government steered to the right side of the spectrum and displayed a pronounced tilt toward the wealthy. Yet most people didn't seem to mind, because an expanding number of Americans were joining the ranks of the overdogs.

After eight Reagan years, George H. Bush took the helm for four more. Successors to a paradigm-setter often have a troubled presidency. By the time the successor takes charge the model builder has usually taken his agenda to the permissible edge of the envelope or even beyond. A modest readjustment may be necessary. Yet, by that time, the majority party will have become fully indoctrinated in the paradigm-setter's program and deny the heir the flexibility to readjust policy back in the other direction. If the successor, who does not have the political capital his popular predecessor enjoyed, dares backpedal, even slightly, party loyalists are apt to turn on him.

This was the difficult position that Bush found himself in. Reagan had cut taxes to the bone, and a swelling deficit was catching the attention of the American public. Leading citizens, such as Ross Perot, were pelting the president with criticism, posing doomsday scenarios, and attracting followers. Had Bush done nothing to stem the tide of red ink he might very well have lost the next election for being impervious to the ballooning deficit. But when Bush backtracked from his "read my lips—no new taxes" pledge, it cost him dearly. He became the fifth successor to a paradigm leader to drop the mantle, failing to win a term in his own right. John Adams, Martin Van Buren, William Taft, and Herbert Hoover were all ensnared in similar type traps and were defeated when they ran again. Adams, Van Buren, and Taft backtracked from their predecessor's policies, offending large parts of their political base. Hoover went the other way. He didn't backtrack, and that didn't work, either. He stuck by policies even when they clearly weren't working any longer. These presidents couldn't avoid a "damned if you do and damned if you don't" situation. (See table 14.)

On the other hand, successor presidents who find a role to play

TABLE 14
Successor Presidents

Pattern-setter	Successor	Reelection attempt	Win—lose	% of vote
1. G. Washington	John Adams	1800	Lose	47%*
2. T. Jefferson	James Madison	1812	Win	59%*
3. J. Madison	James Monroe	1820	Win	98%*
4. A. Jackson	Martin Van Buren	1840	Lose	47%
5. A. Lincoln	Ulysses Grant	1872	Win	56%
6. T. Roosevelt	William Taft	1912	Lose	23%
7. C. Coolidge	Herbert Hoover	1932	Lose	40%
8. F. Roosevelt	Harry Truman	1948	Win	49%
9. R. Reagan	George H. Bush	1992	Lose	37%

*Percent of Electoral College.

in further defining their political model fare much better. James Monroe, Ulysses Grant, and Harry Truman all assisted the pattern-setting president in setting the course of their paradigm, and each was successful in winning a new term in his own right. Grant and Truman filled in important blanks in the model-builder's program. Monroe carried the ball for the emerging "New Nationalist" mini-revolution. Madison, the remaining successor president, was able to win a second term during wartime and then, several years later, switched gears to begin a new political model.

Tax cutting had become the chief political mantra during this paradigm. Like the Jefferson-Jackson agrarian program, like the high tariff during the age of early industrialization, like the FDR tax and spend programs, it was the article of faith that could rally the majority party faithful. And more times than not it could win over the bulk of the nonaligned voters. It was not a good idea for a president of the majority party to mess with this success formula. On the other hand, minority party chief executives could tinker, as Bill Clinton would soon do, but the operative word was "gently."

After G. H. Bush's defeat, Clinton reclaimed the White House for the Democrats, beginning another political equilibrium. Like Eisenhower, in the earlier paradigm, Clinton tamed the excesses of the mini-revolution, thereby granting it additional life. But Clinton remained true to the main outline Reagan had etched; in fact, so much so that many Democrats took to referring to him as Republican "lite." He reappointed Alan Greenspan as chairman of the Federal Reserve Board and pushed welfare and trade policies at odds with his Democratic Party's black and labor constituencies.

At the turn of the millennium George W. Bush, defining himself as a "compassionate conservative"; faced off with Vice-President Gore, who had repackaged himself as what appeared to many a "government knows best" liberal. Bush honed his message to inclusiveness, a concern for the downtrodden, and portrayed the Republican Party as more open to minorities than it had been in the past. Like JFK, who scolded Nixon in 1960 for the Republican's neglect of America's defense position, "Dubya" neutralized a key Democratic strength, "compassion," so as to leave the Republicans less vulnerable to attacks from the left.

In an election that was strikingly parallel to the 1960 Kennedy-Nixon contest—or, for that matter, the one in 1844, between Polk and Clay, or the Harrison versus Cleveland match in 1888—W. Bush was able to turn a tie into an Electoral College victory. The Republicans, as the majority party, controlled most of the election machinery, and the Supreme Court had a conservative tilt. It allowed the GOP to pull out all the stops and make sure their "mighty" 537 Florida vote advantage would stick. Although Dubya received almost 550,000 fewer votes nationwide than Al Gore, many more men and women, when questioned in exit polls, claimed to prefer small government and market-based solutions over big-government answers to the nation's problems. The people, it seems, were still sympathetic to the core philosophy underpinning the ninth political paradigm.

Bush Junior is a "first restorer of the current paradigm" president, and this type chief executive usually has a tough time of making a go of his presidency. These leaders are operating in a friendly political model and attempt to extend the proper paradigm program. Bush Junior entered the White House with the Gipper's game plan in his hip pocket. It read "cut taxes, reduce domestic spending, pour more money into defense, and curtail regulations." His rhetoric, "the axis of evil" and Osama bin Laden as "the evil one," sounded Reaganesque, reminiscent of the "evil empire."

Yet the prior defeat of the majority party some years back was a sign their program had gone about as far as most people felt comfortable with. Further policy success is likely to upset the delicate political equilibrium and provoke a backlash. Case in point: Polk's extension of America's frontier brought the slavery issue to the forefront. Case in point: Harrison's pursuit of a high tariff also helped out the big industrialists, encouraging them to adopt an even more arrogant attitude. Case in point: Lyndon Johnson's reform legislation shunted aside the lower-middle-class whites, leaving them feeling alienated. And his increased spending for these new programs, along with his Vietnam adventure, helped set off a virulent inflation.

Initially all three were able to enact some of the remaining items on the paradigm agenda and *appeared quite successful.* Yet by the following election, or two, the public was clearly disenchanted with the majority party, and a time of troubles soon followed.

All the above "first restorers of a paradigm" ended their presidencies badly. (LBJ finished Kennedy's first term and therefore gets the nod as "first restorer.") About George W.'s presidency . . . we shall see. He took office just as the biggest "bubble" in U.S. history had popped. "Economic growth" paradigms, with loose regulation and bruising competition, such as the present one, normally run into problems after a period of fast growth. Typically there is a speculative "bubble," during which an infectious greed takes hold and breeds great corporate excesses along with a gross mispricing of financial assets. Usually the result is a vast misallocation of resources, diminished corporate profitability, and a plethora of financial scandals and corporate abuses.

A long period of wealth destruction normally follows, as debt undertaken on assumptions of ever-swelling stock market and business gains is liquidated, setting off disturbing and uncontrollable forces in the American economy. Lifestyles and spending habits are adjusted downward. Innumerable attempts are made to resuscitate and reenergize a faltering economy and prop up the values of people's shrunken savings. And all the while the public's love affair with free markets is being reevaluated. This occurred either at or near the end of each of the last three "economic growth" paradigms—in the 1820s, again in the late nineteenth century, and still again following the "New Era" of the 1920s. It is not inconceivable that another time of troubles may start before Bush Junior finishes his presidency.

To date there have been nine political paradigms in American history and each has brought about a much-needed political, social, and economic realignment. Each introduced either a "new" **economic model,** wherein wealth creation becomes the nation's top priority, or a "new" **social model,** during which the government intrudes to rebalance society in favor of those in the lower layer of the social pyramid.

During wealth-creating paradigms large numbers of people are encouraged to become entrepreneurs, and they hit the ball out of the park lighting up the economic scoreboard. After a while, however, fundamental cracks begin to appear. In the giddy atmosphere of rapid economic growth, abuses by the business sector multiply and an increasing portion of the nation's income and wealth gravitates to the top classes. The purchasing power of the "not-so-well-heeled" classes lags, which undermines the prosperity, and the nation becomes vulnerable to an economic meltdown.

There have been five of these patterns, including the present one. All, except for the James Madison "New Nationalism" era, were engineered by Republican or Federalist presidents.

The weaknesses of this type political pattern will be corrected by the strengths of the social realignment model. The second type model is usually, but not always, presided over by the Democrats or, in the early 1800s, the Democratic-Republicans. The exception was the "progressive" era, initiated by the Republican Teddy Roosevelt but reaching its zenith under Woodrow Wilson. During social rebalancing eras the government steps up to the plate and regulates the economy, while underwriting programs to redress the balance between the haves and have-nots. This is just the remedy society needs.

Problems eventually surface during the rebalancing type model also. Societal restrictions have been reduced just as the gates of social mobility have swung open and a new, overly "individualistic" middle class comes pouring through grabbing for more material goods. Meanwhile, the producing classes have been put in the straitjacket of market regulation and are unable to rev up the engines of business to meet those exploding demands. It bumps into an inelastic supply and sets off an enormous and defiant inflation.

The opposing party, usually the Republicans, will ride to the rescue and turn the nation's attention back to the economic race once more. And you can bet that a rapidly growing economy will soon be able to meet the needs of the masses. Meanwhile, the nation will have been prepared for another bout of rapid economic growth. The prior period of reform, of taming the economy, and of helping those who had been left behind will have narrowed the difference between the haves and have-nots so that the latter class, armed with a greater purchasing power, is able to keep up.

There have been eight completed paradigms, so far in the history of the American Republic, and **all have ended badly.** All "economic growth" models, but for the first, Federalist one, ended with a long period of hard economic times along with the destruction of a great deal of the previously created wealth. Naturally, in each of those times mankind thought it was smarter and had learned the correct answers and . . . it wouldn't happen again. But keep in mind, following the bursting of the 1920s "bubble," policy makers responded in what they, and most everyone else, thought was the correct and appropriate manner. It didn't work! In late 2002 Allan Greenspan, chairman of the Federal Reserve Board and according to many the architect of the 1990s prosperity, said, "History teaches us that no matter how well intentioned economic policies and decisions may be, policy makers never can posses enough knowledge of the complexities of the economy nor sufficiently foresee changes in the economic environment to avert error." Amen!

As for America's first "economic growth" paradigm, near its end the United States became embroiled in a society-destabilizing "quasi-war" with France.

Social realignment paradigms have their problems also. To date there have been four and all ended badly. The first ended with the War of 1812; next came the social chaos of the 1850s and the approaching Civil War; then there was the intense social disorder along with raging inflation that followed World War I; and in the more recent "FDR" model America suffered throughout the 1970s as it fought a long and draining war in Southeast Asia while on the home front a "Great Social Disruption" together with a Great Inflation nearly brought the country to its knees.

Take your pick; war, social disorder, wealth destruction, or inflation or some combination thereof seems to be lying in wait to mug us at the end of each paradigm. Yet it is, in fact, these crises, major or more modest in scale, that tell us the old policies, the old way of doing things, are no longer working and a correction in the way we think and act is necessary. It is time to sidestep the politicians and populace who are stuck in the old rut, in the old mind-sets, and move on—to a new paradigm.

To be sure, the economic growth models are not exact replica-tions of one another. Nor are the social rebalancing models. Each builds on the significant achievements of the prior paradigm. This has been one of the major insights of the pattern-setting presi-dents. They accept some key provisions of the prior political model and then move on. For instance, Jackson accepted the idea that commerce would play an important, though not the leading, role in American society. Lincoln lowered the cost of a homestead to practically nothing, allowing people to acquire a piece of prop-erty, thereby neutralizing the Democrats' agrarian issue. Franklin Delano Roosevelt accepted an industrial society and built his reform programs around a business structure. Ronald Reagan declared the core safety net programs of the Democrats, Social Security and Medicare, off-limits and avoided tampering with them. Even Thomas Jefferson, who more than the other model-setting presidents wanted to undo his predecessor's program, did not do so completely. He did not try to dismantle the Federalists' nation-building work. Nor did he attempt to tear up a Constitution that he thought had betrayed the spirit of 1776. These great paradigm-setting presidents recognized the major achievements of the prior era and incorporated them into their grand design.

Since 1865 the American nation has been on a long and ardu-ous campaign to increase the level of society's material prosper-ity, expand its wealth, and improve its living standards. But at times growth gets out of balance. Just as conquering armies must stop every so often to recuperate, tend to their wounded, and bury their dead, it is necessary for a rapidly transforming society to pause and bring itself back into better social alignment so that the nation may resume its dash to new economic heights. It paused twice, once during the "Progressive Era" and again during the "New Deal" paradigm.

The Civil War was the great demarcation point in American history. It was the watershed event that opened the way for the nation to embark on industrialization. Prior to 1860 the republic was treading down a different path. It was moving in the direction of becoming an agricultural society of numerous small units and narrowing the social distances between the classes. But at times the movement toward equality got out of hand. A buildup of commerce provided the necessary backdrop to support and refresh an agricultural economy. But when business threatened to dominate, the nation regenerated its efforts at agrarianism, by providing greater opportunities for land ownership.

The ability of each of America's two major political parties to shift the nation's priorities, while correcting the other's weaknesses, has provided for a stable social system. When things look bleak and the country appears to be off course, as it did in the late 1970s, the nation is able to renew itself and take on new life. This is because each paradigm shift destroys old encrusted habits and relationships and releases new energies so that the body politic is able to regenerate itself.

———∞∞∞———

XI

Political Stalemate and the Role of Third Parties

Most presidents fall into one of four categories; paradigm-setters, successors, minority party presidents, and restorers. (See table 15.) These labels refer to the role they played in establishing or maintaining a paradigm. Add in Warren Harding and John Kennedy, who died before completing their first term, as assisters. Rutherford Hayes, Chet Arthur, and Andrew Johnson do not fit into any category. They are the three exceptions. (The three presidents, William Harrison, Zachary Taylor, and James Garfield, who served less than half a term are not counted.)

We have already discussed paradigm-setters and successors. Model-builders blaze a new trail and stir up a mini-revolution, which proceeds at full speed ahead. Successors try to follow in their footsteps, but problems usually appear sometime during their reign and it appears as if the transformation is running out of steam. Perhaps the mini-revolution has accomplished its task, curing society's festering sores, and the nation may be ready to march off in a new direction. If that be so the political model ends at this point. Or, on the flip side, perhaps, some of the policies have become objectionable to many, yet there is still unfinished business to complete. If this be so, rather than an end to the mini-

TABLE 15

Presidential Type

Phase	1st paradigm	2d paradigm	3d paradigm	4th paradigm
1. Paradigm-setter (PS)	G. Washington	T Jefferson	J. Madison*	A. Jackson
2. Successor / sometimes assist (S)	J. Adams	J. Madison*	J. Monroe (A)†	M. Van Buren
3. (1st) Minority president (M-1)			Q. Adams	J. Tyler
4. (1st) Restorer (R-1)				J. Polk
5. (2d) Minority president (M-2)				M. Fillmore
6. (2d) Restorer (R-2)				F. Pierce / J. Buchanan

	5th paradigm	6th paradigm	7th paradigm	8th paradigm	9th paradigm
1. (PS)	A. Lincoln	T. Roosevelt	W. Harding (A) / C. Coolidge	F. Roosevelt	R. Reagan
2. (S)	U. Grant (A)	W. Taft	H. Hoover	H. Truman (A)	G. H. Bush
3. (M-1)	G. Cleveland	W. Wilson		D. Eisenhower	W. Clinton
4. (R-1)	B. Harrison			JFK (A) / LBJ	G. W. Bush
5. (M-2)	G. Cleveland			R. Nixon / G. Ford	
6. (R-2)	W. McKinley			J. Carter	

Don't fit any category
1. A. Johnson
2. R. Hayes
3. C. Arthur

Not considered: Served less than one-half a term
1. W. Harrison
2. Z. Taylor
3. J. Garfield

*James Madison was both a successor and a pattern-setter.

†(A)= Assist: W. Harding assisted C. Coolidge; J. Kennedy assisted L. Johnson.

transformation, it is likely to go into a stall and a political stalemate begins.

Minority Presidents

When the minority, "opposing," party wrestles control of the Oval Office from the grip of the dominant party, it means either the American public will march off with the new party in a different direction or the nation is in political equilibrium. The oppos-

TABLE 16
Minority Party Presidents (at Time of Their Election)

| Elected/% of vote | | Following election becomes or is: | |
		New Paradigm—Political Stalemate	
1. **Thomas Jefferson***	1800/53%†	Win/92%*	
2. J. Q. Adams	1824/31%		lose/44%
3. **Andrew Jackson**	1828/56%	Win/54%	
4. Harrison/Tyler	1840/53%		‡ Clay—lose/48%
5. Taylor/Fillmore	1848/47%		‡ Scott—lose/44%
6. **Abraham Lincoln**	1860/40%	Win/55%	
7. Grover Cleveland	1884/48%		lose/49%
8. Grover Cleveland	1892/46%		‡ Bryan—lose/47%
9. Woodrow Wilson	1912/42%		Win/49%
10. **Harding/Coolidge**	1920/60%	Win/54%	
11. **Franklin Roosevelt**	1932/57%	Win/61%	
12. Dwight Eisenhower	1952/55%		Win/57%
13. Richard Nixon	1968/43%		Win/61%
14. **Ronald Reagan**	1980/51%	Win/59%	
15. Bill Clinton	1992/43%		Win/49%

*Bold = becomes majority party.

†Percent of Electoral College vote.

‡President didn't run again/replacement is listed.

ing party knocked off the dominant party 15 times over the course of American history. A mini-revolution followed six times. The other nine marked either the beginning or the continuation of political standoff. (See table 16.) Although we do not know which outcome will follow, we can get a hint of it.

When the changing of the guard takes place with majority approval, the chances it will become a paradigm shift improve considerably. Seven times (including Jefferson's electoral majority before popular elections began in 1824) a majority of the voters called for a change of the political guard, and five resulted in a shift of the political pattern. Only the elections of William Henry Harrison in 1840 and Dwight Eisenhower in 1960 did not prove meaningful. On the flip side, only one of the eight minority party victories, with less than half of the total vote count, turned out to be the beginning of a new mini-revolution. Abraham Lincoln did it in 1860. In the other seven there was no fundamental shift in the main theme of the political pattern. They were part of a political stalemate. The minority party also outpolled the dominant party in 1876 but didn't move into the White House. Nevertheless, it too was the beginning of a political equilibrium.

A political standoff indicates the easy part of the revolution has been accomplished and the majority party is having trouble getting the public to swallow its harder, more undesirable parts. A readjustment is usually required, but "successor" type presidents do not have sufficient leeway to accomplish the mission. There are two other types of chief executives who will deal with that task. They are the "minority party" and the "restorer" types of president.

In a political stalemate the public is not objecting to the general direction in which the country is traveling but merely to some of its more unappealing aspects. The role of the minority party president is to readjust paradigm policy so as to remove its more unsuitable features and bring the political model into a more proper balance. Yet if the opposing party president is successful in taming the mini-revolution, his party is not likely to reap a reward for a job well done. It will, instead, set the stage for an extension of the mini-revolution. The main paradigm agenda, with its hard edges smoothed, will appear relatively more attractive to voters once again, and the majority party will oftentimes be able to muscle its way back into the White House—but just barely.

Minority party chief executives, who, of course, are not aware of the role they are destined to play, initially have high hopes of marching off in a new direction. But during a stalemate they soon learn they don't have the public mandate to do so. For example: Eisenhower began his administration with a strong desire to balance the budget and dismantle some parts of the New Deal. When recession struck soon after "Ike" took office, he was inclined to let the nation work its way out without government assistance;

much as pre-1930s presidents did. But the hue and cry that spread across the nation was too great and the Eisenhower administration quickly dropped its conservative stance and put through some contra-cyclical programs to aid the economy. And from that point on his administration recognized that it would make its mark by holding the line on government spending, preventing additional New Deal type programs, and taking a new approach to foreign policy. Most minority presidents make small readjustments backward, reversing a bit of the mini-revolution and then adopting a "hold the line" posture. They end up reshaping their political party as the party of the center. Bill Clinton resigned himself to becoming a centrist president after his attempt to install a comprehensive health-care program didn't fly. He readjusted the Reagan tax cuts marginally upward, prevented big new reductions, trimmed defense spending, and kept Republican hands off core New Deal entitlement programs.

The second period of minority party rule during a political model is generally more difficult because it comes after a "time of troubles" has begun. It will not be so easy to bring the paradigm back into balance. Presidents who govern during this phase hit the deck with problems rushing at them and have a difficult time coping with them. The Taylor-Fillmore administration was greeted with a defiant "South" threatening succession over the issue of slavery in the territories. The second Cleveland administration met a depression coming at them head-on. And Nixon, poor Nixon, faced an incubating Great Inflation, inherited a highly unpopular war in Southeast Asia that had to be brought to an end, and oversaw a general breakdown of law and order. All of those heads of state were in trouble right from the start, and the public soon turned its back on them and gave the dominant party one more shot at governing.

Not one "centrist" president was able to create a line of succession, that is, a legatee who wins an election while embracing the program of his predecessor. (Gerald Ford inherited the White

House but was unable to win an election in his own right.) While "hold the line" presidents are often quite successful personally, their defensive strategy makes it hard to generate a legacy, as it is difficult to attract new followers without offering to take them somewhere they have not yet been. Every candidate who followed a "hold the line" chief executive was defeated, and over the course of two centuries there were seven of them. (See table 17.) Two others, J. Q. Adams and Cleveland, lost reelection attempts. However, this "centrist" type leader was considerably more successful than successor or restorer presidents during the twentieth century. "Centrist" presidents were reelected in every one of their four tries, although two such reelections were accomplished with less than half of the votes cast. On the other hand, it seems that nineteenth-century "minority party" presidents had not yet caught on to their "hold the line" role. Millard Fillmore, once he became president in 1850, took up the traditional Whig economic issues.

TABLE 17

Minority Party

	Reelection	Legacy
1. J. Q. Adams	1828 L	
2. W. Harrison/J. Tyler	DR*	1844 Clay L
3. Z. Taylor/M. Fillmore	DR	1852 Scott L
4. G. Cleveland (1st term)	1888 L†	
5. G. Cleveland (2d term)	DR	1896 Bryan‡ L
6. W. Wilson	1916 W	1920 Cox L
7. D. Eisenhower	1956 W	1960 Nixon L
8. R. Nixon/Ford*	1972 W	1976 Ford L
9. B. Clinton	1996 W	2000 Gore L

*DR = Didn't run.

†Won the popular vote.

*Ford took over after the first minority party reelection had already taken place. Ran in 1976 as a successor to a minority president.

‡William Jennings Bryan ran away from his legacy and proposed a program that was totally different from Cleveland's. Also, both Cox and Gore did, to some degree, try to separate themselves from their predecessor.

Instead of moving toward the center, he requested a new higher tariff and made an impassioned case for the necessity of federal subsidies for internal improvements. But those pleas got nowhere, as did Fillmore. He could not win his party's nomination for a try at another term.

Also to keep in mind: Minority party chief executives oftentimes have to navigate without a friendly Congress to go along with them. Overall the minority party governed in 52 of the 214 years (till 2003) of our republic. But in 30 of those years—58 percent of the time—they did so without also controlling at least one House of Congress to buttress their presidency. The majority party, on the other hand, held the White House for 162 years and in only 10 of those years was their presidency blocked by not also being in charge of at least one house of Congress; that was about 6 percent of the time.

Restorer Presidents

Restorer chief executives know where they are going—to complete the unfinished paradigm business or extend it into new areas. But, during a political equilibrium, the majority party will also fail to derive any lasting benefit from its success in rekindling the mini-revolution. This is because, in the face of a heavily divided electorate, any further extension of paradigm policies will shift the nation either too far to the left or too far to the right side of the political spectrum. After the first restoration of a political model a "time of troubles" usually begins and the opposing party's agenda will again appear more attractive. Yet from this point on neither party will have much success in governing.

JFK, who won the White House back for the Democrats during the New Deal paradigm, put together an agenda that included the long-overdue Democratic reforms in health care and education, along with a civil rights program, and labeled it the New Frontier. Lyndon Johnson, who adopted Kennedy's policies and finished his term, gets the nod as the restorer president. Their administrations broadened the concept of inclusion, beyond where FDR had left off with labor and the aged, to also embrace blacks and women.

We have already touched on "first restorer of the paradigm" chief executives and how difficult their time in office is. Yet the "second resurrecter of the political model" president is likely to experience an even more difficult time. By the time these heads of government reach the White House, the environment will have become unreceptive to traditional paradigm policies. Most of what had originally ailed the country will have been cured, and the nation will now be suffering from new maladies that do not respond to the old medicines. Solutions, which were fashioned with the old background in mind, are likely to backfire. Yet it is difficult for restorers to switch gears, as they were chosen to lead their party because they seemed to be "true" believers in party dogma. Pierce's, Buchanan's, and Carter's presidencies were in trouble right from the start. It seemed they couldn't do anything right.

McKinley was a different story. His first term was successful, but the pages of what would have been his second have been left blank. The fact that Teddy Roosevelt was able to take the nation in a new direction implies there was a great deal of sentiment to change the course of government.

Not counting John Kennedy, who was killed before his political judgment day, there were seven restorer chief executives and only two, William McKinley and Lyndon Johnson, were reelected. (See Table 18.) James Polk had pledged not to run again; Franklin Pierce failed to win his party's endorsement to run for another term, the only elected president to have done so; and there was no chance for James Buchanan to get his party's nod for another try at governing. The remaining two, Benjamin Harrison and Jimmy Carter, were knocked off in reelection attempts. Except for McKinley, who was killed shortly after his reelection, none

TABLE 18

Restorer Presidents

		Reelection attempt	
1. James Polk	(1)	DR*	
2. Franklin Pierce	(2)	DR	
3. James Buchanan	(2)	DR	
4. Benjamin Harrison	(1)	1892	Lose
5. William McKinley	(2)	1896	Win
6. Lyndon Johnson	(1)	1964	Win
7. Jimmy Carter	(2)	1980	Lose
8. George W. Bush	(1)	2004	?
(1) = First restoration period of political model			
(2) = Second restoration period of political model			
*DR = didn't run.			
John Kennedy was not considered, as he did not get the chance to finish his term.			

left office well thought of, and most left with their reputation in tatters.

This war between "minority party" and "restorer" presidents rages during a political stalemate and for a long time it appears not to be winnable.

The political models that begin with a pattern-setter touting a program better suited to the opposing party (the Madison and Teddy Roosevelt models) take on a bit different shape. The minority party president, instead of taming the excesses, fans the flames by aggressively pursuing policies that attempt to finish what has already been started and take the paradigm all the way to the other side of the political spectrum. But that usually proves fatal. Both John Quincy Adams's and Woodrow Wilson's presidencies sank in a stormy "sea of troubles."

Paradigms actually come in all sizes. Some collapse before a political stalemate is reached. Some may go on a bit longer. And some last until a second restoration is achieved. Yet if the paradigm has lasted that long it becomes extremely vulnerable at that point—in fact, so far, none have gone beyond it.

Third Parties

Third parties have played a limited but important role in American politics. Since popular elections began in 1824 at least once during each paradigm a new third party has sprung up, as if from nowhere, and mounted a serious challenge, which threatened to upset the balance between the two major political parties. What counts as a strong confrontation? Certainly the 8½ percent vote the Populists received in 1892 was taken quite seriously by the two major parties. On the other hand, John Anderson's 6½ percent in the 1980 election did not prevent Ronald Reagan from capturing a majority of all the votes cast and was not perceived as an important attack on the major party balance. Split the difference and we can consider a third party vote count of *about* 7½ percent or more as a grave challenge.

Spontaneous third party revolts usually arise at the beginning of or during a political standoff when the popularity of the dominant party is flagging. They tap into a reservoir of public discontent and call the nation's attention to the simmering paradigm problem, which neither of the two major parties seems willing or able to address. The first important third party challenge came in 1848 with the birth of the Free Soil Party in response to the controversy over slavery in the new territories. The Free Soilers attracted 10 percent of the vote, but, more important, they split the Democratic vote in New York, giving the state to the Whigs and possibly costing the Democratic Party a nationwide electoral victory. Yet neither the Democrats nor the Whigs paid much attention to the Free Soilers' rising star. Neither adopted its antislavery message into their party agenda. The result was a rapid disintegration of the two-party system. Northern Whigs, along with a batch of antislavery Democrats, joined with Free Soilers to form a new "major" party, the Republican Party. As we know, this new party instantaneously replaced the Whigs as the Democrats' major rival. During the period of party realignment the new Republican Party was able to beat back further challenges mounted by other third parties—the American (Know-Nothings) in 1856, the National Democrats and the Constitutional Union Party in 1860—and hold on to their position as one of the nation's two major parties. This episode has, ever since, served as an object lesson to the two major parties as to what fate may await them if they refuse to listen to the voters and adopt the message a serious third party delivers.

Since the Republican Party first won the White House in 1860 there have been five other important challenges by a new third party. (See table 19.) Each was in response to a growing paradigm problem. Each delivered their message and then quickly faded from the political scene. The Populist Party offered "free silver" in 1892 as the remedy to the depressing business conditions that were burying the farmer. In 1912 the stalling of progressive reform motivated Teddy Roosevelt and his merry band of progressives to break free from the Republican Party and form a progressive "Bull Moose" Party. The third party movement in 1924 was atypical. First, it was not a spontaneous new movement as the previous three had been. Rather, it was a flare-up of a revived

TABLE 19

Important Third Parties

(Captured 8 Percent or More of the Popular Vote)

Birth		Important issue
1. Free Soil	1848	Slavery
2. Populist	1892	Free silver
3. Progressive	1912	Stalled progressive legislation
4. American Independent	1968	"Big" liberal government and maligned working class
5. Independent/Reform	1992	Debt reduction.
6. American "Know-Nothing"	1856	Anti Catholics and immigrants
7. National Democrats	1860	Pro-South
8. Constitutional Union	1860	Holding the Union together

Progressive Party, which had first emerged 12 years earlier. Second, unlike the others it occurred while the mini–political revolution was still in full swing. The time was not yet ripe for a stalemate to develop. Consequently, it did not undercut the majority party. The Republicans, in fact, did quite well, gathering 54 percent of the voters to their side. In 1968 George Wallace led his American Independent Party on a crusade against a liberal elite, whom he thought responsible for "big" government type solutions, which were undermining the position of the lower middle class. "I'll throw all those phonies and their briefcases into the Potomac," he promised. In 1992 Ross Perot bankrolled the Independent Party (later to become the Reform Party) to fight against a profligate federal fiscal policy.

In each of the six political models since 1828, a new third party issued a serious attack to the party system. (See table 20.) The 1924 election, which came only four years after a new paradigm program had been initiated, was the only one that did not threaten to upset the political balance. In the other five the majority party went down to defeat during the first third party challenge of the paradigm. On the other hand, important third party attacks that came after a first challenge to the prevailing political model seem to pack somewhat less punch. All three came late in the "Jackson" paradigm after the political upheaval that saw the Republican Party replace the Whigs as the main rival to the Democratic Party. They were essentially challenges to replace a still fragile Republican Party as the nation's number two political organization.

Nonetheless, by the following election or two, one of the two majors had incorporated the challenging party's core message into its program. But adopting the third party message did not guarantee success to the party that embraced it, nor was it necessarily the proper solution to the paradigm problem. In the mid-1890s the Democrats bought the Populist message and rode it . . . to a crushing defeat. No matter: Once the message was adopted, it meant the process of seeking a resolution to the paradigm prob-

TABLE 20

Elections with a Serious Third Party Challenge (over 7½ Percent)

following election	Third Party				next election
First challenge of paradigm	% of vote	Minority party		Majority party	% of Vote
1. 1848 Free Soil	10%	**Whigs***	47%	Democrats 43%	5%
2. 1892 Populists	8½%	**Democrats**	46%	Republicans 43%	… †
3. 1912 Progressive	27½%	**Democrats**	42%	Republicans 23%	…
4. 1924 Progressive	16½%	Democrats	29%	**Republicans** 54%	…
5. 1968 American Independent	13½%	**Republicans**	43%	Democrats 42%	…
6. 1992 Independent/Reform	19%	**Democrats**	43%	Republicans 37%	8½%

Later paradigm challenges	% of vote	Minority party		Majority party	% of Vote
a. 1856 American (Know-Nothing)	21½%	Republicans 33%		**Democrats** 45%	…
b. 1860 National Democrats	18%				
Constitutional Union	12½%	**Republicans** 40%		Democrats 29%	…
c. 1980 Independent‡	6½%	**Republicans** 51%		Democrats 41%	…

*Bold = winner.

† … third party disappeared.

‡Less than 7½%, not serious but close.

lem had begun and the reason for the third party's existence was eliminated. The third party soon faded from the political landscape.

Take Ross Perot and his Independent Party's challenge in 1992. He called the nation's attention to the alarming budget deficits and was able to attract 19 percent of the vote. During the following midterm election, the Republican congressional leader, Newt Gingrich, made a balanced budget amendment the first plank in his "Contract with America." The GOP won a congressional majority and prodded Clinton into accepting a balanced budget deal. In the following presidential election, the Reform Party's (the Independence Party's new name) vote tally fell by more than one-half and Ross Perot's party was on its way to extinction. Shortly afterwards the American public learned that the long-feared budget deficit had turned into a whopping surplus. In the next presidential election, of 2000, the Reform Party was unable to pick up even 1 percent of the vote.

To many Americans a new third party, which merges the compassionate Democratic social vision with the Republican economic growth mission, sounds attractive . . . but which of the two traditions would the party really stand for? When the issue comes down to man versus the dollar, as many issues do, which way does the party go? Would we have to levitate General Grant from his final resting place to settle the issue once again?

A third party if it was to gain a permanent foothold on the American political scene might very well impede the self-correcting process that enables the nation to regenerate itself. Most likely it would lessen the attraction of the two majors as it took attributes from each, diluting each major's core message and interfering with its ability to offset the other's weakness. Electoral majorities would become less likely and the mini-revolutions that have propelled the nation's political shifts from right to left and back again to right might not be so clear-cut. During those shifts a party has to plunge full steam ahead, while practicing the **"art of avoiding compromise."**

WE MAY NEED TWO MAJOR PARTIES. And we may need them partisan as they are, and we may need them fully biased toward what they see as the "correct view of the world."

Another Observation

The question that many Americans ask themselves before going into the voting booth to cast their vote for president: Which is more important, the **party** or the **candidate**? The answer: It depends!

A vote for the majority party candidate usually means an aggressive pursuit of the party agenda. The new president, along with his advisors and most of the supporting staff, comes to the Oval Office carrying a set of preconceptions based on the rich heritage of their political party. In addition, they are beholden to a constituency of "true believers" in the party creed. This tends to keep presidents in tow with party ideology. Consequently, voters, in general, know what policies to expect when they elect the standard-bearer from the majority party. They can count on Democratic presidents to aggressively pursue a Democratic agenda and nudge the nation further along the path to the left and Republican presidents to hew closely to the traditional Republican programs and tug the country to the right.

Not so when the new president is from the minority party. He (or someday she) may attempt a major shift back to the other side of the political spectrum or, on the other hand, may simply aim to pull his own party in the opposite direction . . . toward the center. A president who initiates a "big" shift is usually one who has campaigned for major change and received voter permission to go ahead.

However, when the country is not ready for a major transition to the opposing direction the job of a minority party chief executive requires a great deal of political skill. Opposing party presidents who move to the center must bob and weave. Besides trying to slow the momentum of the majority party–led mini-revolution, they must throw token offerings to their own constituents to keep them in line. Take Bill Clinton, again, as a typical example. He held the line against the Republican agenda and protected the crown jewels of the Democratic entitlement programs. Meanwhile, his own constituents received an earned income tax for the working poor along with some modest additional programs for education and job training.

The rule of thumb is: Pay more attention to the party doctrine and less to the candidate from the majority party. On the flip side, assess a candidate from the minority party very carefully and give less credence to party philosophy.

The exception to this majority/minority party rule occurs during a major modification when a president, such as James Madison or Teddy Roosevelt, moves his party toward the other side of the political spectrum, but not across the line. However, in both cases the voters did not get advance warning. Neither president laid out his program to the public prior to the election. Rather, both presidents took advantage of special circumstances to shift direction during a presidential term. Teddy Roosevelt, who filled in after McKinley's death, began the shift well after the voters had cast their ballots in November 1900. (Interestingly, both major modifications were launched during a second term, or what was to have been a second term, *after* the majority party had reclaimed the White House. Quite likely a majority party cannot engineer a swing toward the other side of the political spectrum, away from its constituency, until after it has gotten a clear-cut voter endorsement to govern for four more years.)

Following a major modification by the majority party, the minority party is thrown off balance. Its options become limited. It is unable to move back toward the center, as that space is already occupied. Its only viable choice is to complete the job the dominant party had started and move even further in the direction of its own party creed, as J. Quincy Adams and Woodrow Wilson did. In the case of a dominant party moving toward the center, the party/candidate rule is turned upside down. The candidate from the majority party moves in the opposite direction from party orthodoxy and toward the center, while the minority president actively pursues his party's main agenda.

———⊶∞⊷———

XII

The Role of Power

To understand a society, keep your eyes on just three things . . . power, power . . . and power: How is it distributed throughout the society? How is it used? What serves as its chief instruments?

In the beginning, when humans were emerging from the jungle, the law of "tooth and claw" prevailed. Yet human beings were able to survive an environment based on brute strength and build a civilization that allowed them to ascend to the top of the food chain because they were able to create new instruments of power and increasingly complex power arrangements. Beginning with the club, they built bigger and better instruments of force, scaling up from sword, to chariot, to warship. And today airplanes, nuclear weapons, and electronically guided missiles determine who is boss nation.

Early on, humans learned there was strength in numbers. Thousands of men and women acting in concert were able to build cities, ward off enemies, and ensure a reliable food supply. Civilization was organized by allowing the most able to take charge, setting goals and coordinating group efforts. Monarchs put on crowns and took their seats as head of state, providing direction to society. Army commanders planned the attack or the defense and made sure fighters acted in unison. Within the family the male assumed the dominant role as leader. Civilization today is organized around an elaborate set of power arrangements, extending from a top class, to the boss of a business, to the head of a household.

Power arrangements and instruments of power play an important role in human life. Yet Democrats and Republicans disagree to the core on how power should be used, what its chief instruments should be, and how it should be distributed throughout society. Republicans, in general, remain faithful to the "traditional" power structure of society. They do not wish to tamper with a foundation that has enabled humans to climb up the ladder of civilization to their present lofty perch. The exception is in the economic sphere. Shifts in money and status based on valuable economic and technological contributions to society's material well-being are quite all right. For those very contributions had enabled the eighteenth-century takeoff into modernity and economic prosperity.

The Democrats, on the other hand, believe power arrangements set during an agrarian and feudal society are decomposing under pressure from the industrial way of life, and they aim to make sure this process proceeds full speed ahead. Their hope is to eliminate the inequities founded on the patterns of the past and make sure clout is distributed more equally. They want to take it away from the reigning contemporary institutions and elites and, as Al Gore told the Democratic conventioneers in 2000, transfer "power to the people." Democrats too have their exception: An increase in the authority of the federal government is an absolute must. That is because they have assigned the state the supreme role of ensuring a fair and equitable distribution of clout among society's members.

These contrasting attitudes toward power and its use underlie the two parties' approach to foreign affairs. Although conducted mostly offstage, international relations, at times, moves to center stage to become the main attraction, when, say, war threatens or national honor hangs in the balance.

The traditional approach to foreign affairs can be traced back to George Washington, *who understood power and how to use it.* He wanted to use it to improve the strength and reputation of the United States. And he was not timid about wielding it. When some western Pennsylvania farmers rebelled against a federal excise tax on whiskey, Washington recruited about fifteen thousand militia troopers to put down the rebellion. Jefferson and his faction were appalled at the overwhelming use of force, but Washington wanted to make sure the effort would be a success and also send a message to the outside world that the U.S. government was serious about supporting its laws.

Washington also recognized that power should have its limits. The Revolutionary War general stunned a world that assumed victorious military leaders automatically set themselves up as Caesars, at the head of government. Imitating Cincinnatus, the legendary Roman hero, who raised an army, saved the city, and then relinquished his sword and returned to his plough, Washington handed his sword back to Congress and retired to private life at Mount Vernon after the war. When learning of this, King George III of England observed, "If he does that he will be the greatest man in the world." Then, nearly 14 years later, Washington did it again, voluntarily surrendering the presidency after two terms and setting a precedent that would hold until FDR broke it in 1940. George Washington showed Americans how to handle power gracefully . . . by *giving it up, TWICE*—something kings and other rulers in the past refused to do.

As president, Washington began a tradition of using the nation's military force **sparingly**. In the mid-1790s, when Britain challenged America's notion of neutrality on the high seas, there was a public clamor to take up arms. Washington, however, kept a cool head. He ignored the war hysteria and endorsed a pro-English version of American neutrality, avoiding war with England at a time when the United States was ill-equipped to fight one. "Sparingly" has meant different things at different times in America's past. To Washington it meant the commander-in-chief, regardless of public opinion, should not wage war when it was not in America's best interest to do so. Yet at other times it has meant remaining faithful to the spirit of the Declaration of Independence and not shoving weaker nations around. **Sparingly** plays an important role in American foreign policy; in general the nation limits its exercise of force to times when its vital interests are clearly threatened.

George Washington's professional demonstration of power and diplomacy provided the basic precepts of traditional foreign policy. The leading role goes to military power, the strength of a nation's armed forces, and its willingness to use it. A strong military presence is primary. It is essential to a nation's security. It is also the ultimate form of power and the supreme arbiter in world politics. More of it enhances the likelihood of a favorable outcome when the nation resorts to force, but most important, a strong army and navy is likely to intimidate potential adversaries, so much so that many will back off from challenging you. In the words of Queen Victoria, the nineteenth-century British monarch, who presided over "Pax Britannica," "If we are to maintain our position as a first-rate Power . . . we must . . . be Prepared for attacks and wars, somewhere or other, Continually."

Willingness means when force is required, don't be afraid to use it—unabashedly. A cardinal rule of diplomacy: Don't look weak. "Weakness invites challenge," according to statesmen of the traditional school. Other nations have an amazing ability to sniff out countries that are uncertain about exercising their power, and take advantage of it. Second- or even third-rate powers with a superior determination to fight, and accept causalities, often prevail over stronger nations that lack the will to fight to their utmost ability. Example: The American Revolutionaries, low on food, shoes, coats, and ammunition but high in spirit, prevailed against the world's greatest military and naval power of its day. England was not willing to commit a major part of its military resources to subduing the determined colonists. Vietnam was another example: the United States, who deliberately refrained from using their military might to the fullest and, faced with a determined foe, lost heart, pulled up stakes and left.

In a democracy there is a well-kept secret, not fully appreciated by historians, journalists, and the public, that when conducting foreign policy it is necessary for chief executives to stretch their constitutional authority to the limit, and sometimes beyond. We live in a world of nations where anarchy rules and many do not observe the niceties of international law. Conducting foreign relations, in an arena that does not respect the rule of law or the "sanctity of human life," depends upon keeping highly sensitive information secret; not telegraphing your moves to an adversary; acting in a timely fashion; and performing the highly unpopular task of risking the lives of the nation's youth in an international showdown. Democratic procedures do not work well in a setting where the "law of the jungle" rules. Alexis de Tocqueville, the nineteenth-century French observer of American society, commented, "It is especially in the conduct of foreign relations that democracies appear . . . decidedly inferior to other governments." A raucous deliberative body of 100 highly egotistical members, many of whom think they know better than the chief executive, is incapable of handling that task with the necessary aplomb. Congressional participation is not only inconvenient but impractical. A nation must be able to speak with one voice; if not, that reflects on its **willingness** to exercise power.

Nonetheless, we are constantly reminded that according to the Constitution the chief executive is supposed to collaborate with the Senate in the conduct of foreign policy. Furthermore, American tradition holds that ends, however laudable, do not justify the means. Yet the American public is willing to overlook these inconvenient maxims. It recognizes that it is the president's role to keep the nation out of harm's way and lawmakers should not interfere with his efforts to operate in a lawless world—as long he appears to be successful at it. If he fails, the voters will remedy the situation in the following election.

Chief executives have understood this problem of a democracy, and throughout our history they have fought against restrictions on their authority to conduct foreign affairs. George Washington refused a congressional demand to see the state papers relating to Jay's treaty. Instead he lectured Congress "that the nature of foreign negotiations depends on secrecy." Thomas Jefferson put his constitutional scruples aside and paid little heed to the Federalists, who were faulting him for "tearing the Constitution to tatters" when rushing the Louisiana Purchase through Congress. Teddy Roosevelt took great pride in the Panama Canal. In 1911, years afterwards, he said, "If I had followed the . . . Methods, I would have submitted a dignified state paper of 200 pages to Congress and the debate on it would have been going on yet; but I took the Canal Zone and let Congress debate, and while the debate goes on the Canal does also." Franklin Roosevelt cut the corners of American neutrality laws in order to support Great Britain at a crucial time before America's entry into World War II. He traded destroyers for naval bases, *without* the advice and consent of the Senate. Noninterventionists were up in arms, but the administration's stock answer was that Congress was slow and windy. While they deliberated, Britain's very existence would be at stake. More recently Ronald Reagan may have supported an attempt by a group of dissident Nicaraguans, in disregard of congressional limits on his authority to do so, to overthrow the "leftist" Sandinista government and prevent what could have become another communist beachhead in America's backyard. Illegal? Perhaps . . . but if so, he was also following a time-honored tradition of American presidents, to wrestle away from Congress the authority to conduct foreign affairs.

A reliance on force, actual or threatened, is the centerpiece of "traditional" foreign policy, and the Republicans are in tune with this. They recognize that one of mankind's oldest verities is that pain and punishment are the most effective means to influence people and nations to change or modify their behavior. The way Republicans see it, when dealing with other nations it is better to be feared than loved. To be sure, Democrats sometimes approach foreign affairs in this realistic manner. But oftentimes they veer off course and forget the important role that power plays in the real world.

Thomas Jefferson sought an alternative to the traditional use of force. He thought that republics were naturally peaceful and that economic sanctions, "peaceful coercion," he labeled it, would be an adequate substitute for military force as America's chief instrument of power. Consequently he believed the United States did not need a traditional army and navy to defend its interests.

When faced with a French and English challenge to America's neutrality rights on the high seas, he responded with an embargo, thinking he would teach Europe a useful lesson, "showing that there are peaceful means of repressing injustice, by making it to the interest of the aggressor to do what is just." Jefferson's lesson to the Europeans proved to be a nightmare for Americans. Much of the nation's commerce was thrown into chaos, and Jefferson's government was forced to resort to ever harsher measures to enforce the embargo. As one congressman bluntly stated, it "was a miserable and mischievous failure."

Shortly thereafter, in 1812, the Democratic-Republicans led the nation into another war with England. They overlooked the fact that the weak, highly decentralized government Jefferson championed was incapable of waging an expensive war against the world's number one sea power. On the eve of war many Jeffersonians opposed all efforts to strengthen the government's capacity to wage war and the regular army was cut back in favor of the militia. Some even urged a reduction of the navy, abolition of the army, and opposition to the taxes needed to finance the war.

Following that era of diplomatic failure Madison recognized Jefferson's approach to the role of force in foreign affairs was naïve. Madison reversed course back toward a more realistic and traditional foreign policy. During the following century the United States stayed out of European affairs and told the Old World to stay out of its backyard—the famous Monroe Doctrine. America was then able to focus on exploring and exploiting a continent without foreign interference.

By the late 1880s, when the Great European powers—Great Britain, France, and Germany—were scooping up colonies in a scramble for markets and resources, the United States fell under the spell of Alfred Thayer Mahan, the head of the Naval War College, who sought to prepare the country for national greatness. He influenced a generation of policy makers to build up the nation's naval superiority, gain control of the world's sea-lanes, and pursue an aggressive foreign policy, which would let America play a larger political role on the world scene. The precept of **sparingly** was put on the back burner as the nation rushed headlong into war with Spain.

A liberal anti-imperialist crowd, led by William Jennings Bryan, arose and argued America would be betraying its most cherished principles embedded in the Declaration of Independence if it followed Europe in an imperialistic direction—which meant controlling peoples of other nations. While their voices were effective in toning down the rush for empire, the beginning of the twentieth century witnessed the United States under the aegis of Teddy Roosevelt stretching its military might and becoming a regional power.

Woodrow Wilson issued the first successful challenge to America's early-twentieth-century aggressive pursuit of power. The terrible destruction and loss of human life in World War I soured him on the power politics of traditional diplomacy. He wanted to replace the Old World's system of international order where power had been king with a new kind of international politics that would promote peace among nations. His new world order would be a more enlightened one based on moral force, an appeal to reason, and the rule of international law. And because he thought the road to international peace was through democracy he advocated populating the world with those "good" states, which would in turn put the rights of man before their own selfish pursuit of POWER.

The centerpiece for his new Wilsonian world order was to be a League of Nations, which would extend the rule of law into the international sphere and put an end to anarchy among nations. The League, like the United Nations, which was to follow, was a general association of nations, which would guarantee one another's sovereignty and independence. But was the United States ready to go to war to protect Britain's frontier in India or Japan's right to Shantung Province in China, its spoils from WWI?

Wilson thought America, which had become the world's strongest nation, should lead by moral example, not with guns and tanks. He stated, "There is such a thing as a nation being so right that it does not need to convince others by force." In his view, strong nations, such as the United States, should seek the approval of mankind. They should help the less favored nations. According to "The Great Idealist" it is far better to be loved than to be feared.

Wilson wanted to create a principled, ethical world, which would put human rights above all other rights, where militarism, colonialism, and war would be brought under control. But he was naïve to a fault on the role "power" played in the world of his day. He tried to initiate so-called "cooling off" treaties, in which nations would agree to submit all international disputes to a commission of investigation. Neither party could declare war or increase armaments until the investigation ended. Naturally these treaties didn't work. Twice he initiated embarrassing and confused excursions south of the border, which brought America close to war with Mexico. His Fourteen Points for an honorable peace, following

World War I, failed to satisfy the wartime emotions that sought vindication, and stood little chance of being implemented. According to Georges Clemenceau, the French premier, "God gave us the Ten Commandments, and we broke them. Wilson gave us the Fourteen Points. We shall see."

This same mindset had Wilson order military commanders not to make war plans prior to America's entry into World War I, because it would violate neutrality. According to "Black Jack" Pershing, head of the American Expeditionary Force, after war was declared and "the acting Chief of Staff went to look at the secret files where the plans . . . should have been found, the pigeonhole was empty."

Following World War I Wilson could not get Congress to go along with his grand design and the United States did not join the League of Nations. And during the following election American voters soundly repudiated Wilsonian policies. Yet, notwithstanding the Democrats' rejection in the election of 1920, the politicians apparently paid attention to Wilson's ideas and a shift in the rules and behavior of the international community soon began, though hesitantly at first.

The 1920s saw American activity shift in support of international law and disarmament. In 1922, at a Naval Conference in Washington, D.C., the world's leading sea powers agreed to limit the size of their naval fleets. Then, in 1928, 62 nations, including most all the major powers at the time, signed the Kellogg-Briand Pact committing them to renouncing war *forever*. Of course, provisions for enforcement were not included.

FDR, who served as undersecretary of the navy in Wilson's cabinet, was very much in tune with this emerging new structure of world order and indicated it to be his blueprint for the post–World War II era. Shortly before he died, FDR said, "In the future world the misuse of power as implied in the term 'power politics' must not be the controlling factor in international relations." However, after the war it became apparent that his outlook was too idealistic in a world wherein the United States had an expansionist rival who was growing stronger by the year. Harry Truman recognized the Soviet threat and toughened up American foreign policies, though remaining true to the Wilsonian international outlook. Democrats, ever since, have flirted with moral force and a global rule of law as guiding principles of a foreign policy more suitable for today's modern world. They emphasize and pursue the "rights of man" hoping to aid the new egalitarianism, which they see breaking out in the world. In Wilson's words, America will "guide the feet of mankind to the goal of justice and liberty and peace."

The party of Jefferson and Wilson is suspicious of presidential authority and adamantly opposed to the idea a chief executive should be given a "free hand" to conduct foreign relations. Rather, they want to extend the say-so of the deliberative bodies to make sure the head of state is held accountable for his actions outside of the nation's borders.

But above all, Democrats are reluctant to use force to settle conflicts between nations. They prefer softer measures, such as economic sanctions, trade embargoes, and arbitration, to change an adversary's behavior. Consequently, they place less dependence on traditional instruments of power, a big army and navy. Their goal is not the strongest possible national defense, rather a strong enough defense and a vigorous enough use of force. The result is that they are apt to err on the side of too little force and invite foreign challenges. But they fail to recognize that nations armed to the teeth with advanced weaponry are usually less called upon to use it.

Let us return to the story of American statecraft. The United States emerged from World War II as the world's leading power. Almost immediately a Soviet-led communism attempted to expand beyond its protected sphere of Eastern Europe and presented a major challenge to the American and other Western nations. With the Democrats calling the shots, the United States responded with the policy of **containment**. America and its allies would use *enough* force to prevent further expansion by communist regimes but would not risk war by challenging their right to exist. It was to be a long and cold war—not a hot one. Its main outline follows.

The Cold War

The Soviets began their challenge by blocking the United States and the other Western powers' access to Berlin, which lay deep within the Russian sector of Germany. It was a test of America's resolve. Truman rejected a proposal to send an armed column down the main highway to Berlin and instead chose an airlift of food, fuel, and supplies to the people in West Berlin. Even though Russia had not yet become a superpower, Truman rejected hot war and set a precedent that would be followed for most of the cold war. *Power was to be used in a restrained and moralistic manner.*

In 1949 Russia denonated an atomic bomb and several months later signed a mutual assistance treaty with Mao Tse-tung's Communists, who had just come to power in China. With the know-how to produce nuclear weapons and a strong ally by their side, the Soviets became a superpower and a legitimate rival to the United States in the eyes of the world. Russia felt strong enough to provide an umbrella to other communist regimes that wanted to probe the edges of the Western perimeter and find "soft" spots that could be exploited. North Korea's attack on South Korea followed. Truman, now fully committed to the policy of containment, thought the free world must not relinquish one single piece of territory—no more Munichs, no more Chinas—and came to the aid of the South Koreans. But the president chose to apply strict limits on the use of military force in Korea and the conflict soon boiled down to a stalemate. During the presidential campaign of 1952, the Republicans painted a picture of a growing communist menace, a global map that was becoming increasingly red. They blamed the Democrats for losing China, for allowing Russia to get the bomb, and for the stalemate in Korea.

In 1953 Dwight Eisenhower, who had been Supreme Allied Commander in Europe during World War II, took possession of the Oval Office and brought with him a change in America's strategy. Eisenhower was well aware the balance of power was still strongly tilted in favor of the United States and reasserted the threat of "unrestrained" force into the diplomatic equation. He dropped subtle hints to China about the possible use of nuclear weapons, and it helped break the stalemated peace efforts, bringing the Korean conflict to an end. Then again when the Chinese Communists threatened to seize a couple of small coastal islands occupied by the Nationalists, Eisenhower rattled the nation's nuclear weapons cage, and China backed off.

Furthermore, "Ike" allowed the CIA to subvert foreign governments and assassinate foreign leaders in order to prevent "leftist" governments sympathetic to the communists from coming to power in Iran and Guatemala. In the first case it helped protect America's oil supplies, and in the other it denied the Soviets a possible foothold in the Western Hemisphere. Although not in conformance with today's moral practice of foreign diplomacy, the cost in American lives and resources was miniscule compared to the price we were soon to pay in Vietnam.

Eisenhower also understood "sparingly." He knew when not to challenge the communists. He refused to intervene to prevent a French defeat in Indochina (part of which was to become Vietnam). As he later explained, "The jungles of Indochina would have swallowed up division after division of United States troops." Again when Soviet tanks and troops rolled into Hungary to put down an indigenous uprising, the Eisenhower administration took a cautious approach and made it clear they were not going to intervene and upset the status quo.

Eisenhower used American power considerably beyond what

the Democrats were likely to do, and when he left office in early 1961 he was able to boast that during his eight years of steward-ship "we lost no inch of ground to tyranny . . . [and] . . . incipient wars were blocked." But he ignored Cuba. Nonetheless, communist inroads, which at the beginning of the decade had appeared so threatening, were halted and America did indeed seem a safer and more secure nation.

In the late 1950s Ike shifted gears and sought to relax tensions with the Soviets. He stopped testing nuclear weapons in the atmosphere, and the Russians soon followed suit. Soon afterwards Eisenhower met with his Russian counterpart, Nikita Khrushchev, at Camp David. For the first time since the cold war had begun tensions between the two superpowers appeared to be easing, and there was a great sigh of relief in the United States and Europe.

In early 1961 John Kennedy was handed the keys to the White House after waging a tough-talking presidential campaign that took the Eisenhower administration to task for permitting a "communist satellite," Cuba, to arise on "our very doorstep." JFK emphasized his standing as a cold warrior with the ringing declaration: "Let any nation know, whether it wishes us well or ill, that we shall pay any price, bear any burden, meet any hardship, support any friend, oppose any foe . . . to assure the survival and the success of liberty. We will do all this and more."

Kennedy sought to change America's military posture. He did not want to rely on threats of massive retaliation alone to deter communist aggression. He and his advisors wanted to add into the military equation conventional forces that could fight limited conflicts. They thought it would lessen the chance for nuclear confrontation. However, it also implied the United States was taking a nuclear response off the table, and this may have rendered conventional warfare more thinkable.

In office Kennedy acted with considerable restraint. He gave the go-ahead for an ill-equipped Cuban émigré force of 1,400 to go ashore at the "Bay of Pigs" in hopes of toppling Castro's government. But, at the last minute, he cancelled plans to provide air cover, dooming the mission to failure.

At the beginning of Kennedy's presidency, anticommunist governments in both South Vietnam and Laos were in jeopardy. Eisenhower's parting advice to the incoming president was that Laos was key to all of Southeast Asia, and urged intervention, unilateral if necessary, to keep it out of communist hands. Kennedy ignored the advice and instead negotiated the neutralization of Laos, which included communists in the government. *Time* magazine editorialized: "Kennedy declared he would 'pay any price to assure the survival and success of liberty.' But its price in Laos seemed too high."

Then, in the summer of 1961, the Kremlin boss threatened to sign a peace treaty with Germany, giving them authority over access routes to Berlin. Although Kennedy called up more than 200,000 reservists and national guardsmen to active duty, his response seemed vacillating and indecisive. He also slashed a requested extramilitary budget by about 25 percent and did not ask Congress for an immediate mobilization of America's armed forces. Soon afterwards the East Germans erected a barricade, the Berlin Wall, separating East from West Berlin and halting the flow of skilled workers to the West. The best response the United States could muster was to add 1,500 men to the tiny force of 5,000 already garrisoned in Berlin.

By 1962 Khrushchev had taken Kennedy's measure and found him sufficiently lacking in strength and resolve. Khrushchev decided to make a bold gamble to erase America's enormous lead in nuclear striking power. The Soviets, at that time, had only a small number of intercontinental ballistic missiles (ICBMs), all based on Soviet territory and known to be highly inaccurate. Khrushchev reasoned he could close the strategic gap in nuclear striking power in one stroke by deploying a larger amount of more precise intermediate missiles in Cuba, pointed at the heart of America. It was clearly the most direct and intense challenge to the United States during the whole of the cold war. Had it succeeded, future American presidents would not have the confidence of clear military superiority, and some, no doubt, would have been reluctant to oppose Soviet belligerency elsewhere.

President Kennedy sought an appropriate response to the Soviets, not so strong as to provoke war, but not too weak so as to encourage the Russians to make further aggressive moves. He refrained from ordering a surprise attack to take out the missile sites, which, besides blemishing the name of the United States in the pages of history forever, might have evoked a countermove by Khrushchev elsewhere, say Berlin. Instead, Kennedy set up a blockade, calling it a "Quarantine," and allowed the Russians time to back down. Furthermore, in discreet negotiations he offered to dismantle obsolete missile bases in Turkey, thereby permitting the Kremlin boss to save face. Kennedy's combination of toughness and restraint allowed for a peaceful resolution of the Cuban missile crisis. Although not the nation's finest hour, which was still to come, it was a triumph for Kennedy and the Democrats.

Next came Vietnam, America's most important post–World War II foreign adventure. The Democrats, wedded to their policy of containment and still mindful of Khrushchev's Cuban challenge, accepted the notion "weakness invites challenge" and marched directly into the Vietnam conflict, chanting "no more appeasements." The Democrats were convinced they could stamp out the communist threat in Southeast Asia via a rational application of American economic and military power. The Vietnam War was fought with the intention of doing just enough but no more than was necessary. President Johnson insisted he would not heed "those who urge us to use our great power in a reckless or casual manner . . . we will do only what must be done." Limits were placed on the use of American power; the air force could not bomb vital targets in the North, nor could American ground forces pursue the enemy into Cambodian or Laotian "sanctuaries." The Democrats overestimated the ability of U.S. military forces to deliver while being held in check from using their full might, and the war dragged on with no apparent light at the end of the tunnel.

In 1969 the Republicans were returned to the White House with the understanding they would bring the conflict to an end. Nixon's aim was to withdraw from the fighting in Vietnam without having it appear a humiliating defeat, suggesting weakness. This meant the South Vietnamese, after taking over the fighting, would have to hold off the North Vietnamese for a reasonable length of time. To that end Nixon repaired relations with the two top communist powers, gambling that Russia and China, once having tasted the fruits of détente, would not undermine his plan.

When North Vietnam seemed reluctant to accept the generous peace terms Nixon proposed, he removed restraints on the military and unleashed American B-52s to rain terror over Hanoi, initiated a naval blockade of North Vietnam, and mined Haiphong Harbor, the port through which Soviet and Chinese arms flowed. The harbor had been off-limits to American military forces during the Johnson administration. Soon afterwards North Vietnam gave Nixon the agreement he had wanted. In the meantime, the two superpowers signed the Strategic Arms Limitation Treaty (SALT I). It was a symbolic first step toward control of the nuclear arms race, indicating the two leading nations were trying to achieve a settlement of their differences by peaceful means.

So far so good; Nixon's strategy of covering a strategic retreat from Vietnam with a relaxation of cold war tensions with the Soviets and China appeared ingenious. But then Watergate interfered! Vietnam had fractured the cold war consensus, and Congress used the occasion of Nixon's disgrace to assert authority over foreign policy and then pulled the rug out from underneath the South Vietnamese feet. Financial aid promised was denied. Shortly after Nixon resigned, a besieged South Vietnam fell to the Northerners and communist governments now ruled most everywhere on the mainland of Southeast Asia. Meanwhile, détente was proving fruitful. President Ford and his Soviet counterpart were preparing a more ambitious SALT II treaty.

In 1977 the Democrats, under the leadership of Jimmy Carter, retrieved the keys to the White House. Carter brought with him a new foreign policy heavily tinged in Wilsonian moralism. "We can never be indifferent to the fate of freedom elsewhere," declared the president. "Our commitment to human rights must be absolute." But to the Russians, who were sensitive to criticism about the absence of civil liberties in their country, Carter's focus on human rights appeared to be a direct repudiation of détente.

Carter set out to win Soviet goodwill by allaying their fears. Shortly after taking office he announced that he was scrapping the B-1 bomber program and deferring the neutron bomb project, without asking for reciprocal concessions. Instead of responding to the president's conciliatory gestures the Soviets increased their arms buildup, deployed a bevy of intermediate missiles aimed directly at Western Europe, and used Cuban troops to extend their influence in Africa. And the president looked the other way. U.S. resolve became suspect again, and soon America's antagonists were on the move.

The Sandinistas, a "socialist guerilla force," came to power in Nicaragua and moved steadily to the left, welcomed Soviet assistance, developed close ties with Castro's Cuba, and served as a supply base for leftist guerilas in nearby El Salvador. Carter, unlike LBJ, who had sent twenty thousand American troops to the Dominican Republic to block the possible emergence of a Castro type government, didn't seem to care about another leftist government in our backyard. Soon afterwards Russia moved into Afghanistan and, once more, the color of the world map was bleeding red. In the aftermath, SALT II was scrapped. To further add to Carter's distress, Iran took a group of American diplomats captive and refused entreaties from the world's most powerful nation to release them.

The American people called in the Republicans in 1981 and the rest is history. Ronald Reagan played the part of diplomatic maestro. He called the Russians an "evil" empire and challenged them with a buildup of American military might until the Soviets lost heart and decided to turn their swords into ploughshares. In a stunning triumph for traditional foreign policy the United States won the cold war without firing a shot. It was America's finest hour on the field of foreign affairs.

Interestingly, by the end of the three periods of Republican reign tensions with the Soviets were easing and the two superpowers were agreeing to limits on the arms race. On the other hand, the three periods of Democratic leadership witnessed a deepening chill in relations. This seems counterintuitive, unless one accepts the fact that when dealing with countries who view foreign relations through the lens of the "reality of power" concessions seem to work *after*, but not before, you win their respect by demonstrating your resolve.

There are clear differences between the Democratic and Republican approaches to foreign diplomacy. Democrats, because they are suspicious of the role of power, often tend to use it ineffectively and without conviction; this has led to a series of mishaps and national humiliations. Take Jefferson's naïve embargo; a barely visible army and navy on the eve of the War of 1812; the ill-fated "Bay of Pigs," wherein the United States failed to provide critical air cover. Then there was the humiliation of a desperate attempt to rescue 52 American hostages that ended in failure when two helicopters collided in the Iranian desert.

And not to forget that fateful day in October 1993 when the Defense Department refused an urgent call to reinforce a group of outnumbered and underequipped American Rangers in Somalia. Later that same day, eighteen Rangers lost their lives, and the body of one was unceremoniously dragged through the streets of Mogadishu while the world watched on TV.

Liberals tend to forget how difficult it is to subdue an adversary in a restrained and morally acceptable way. The restraint Democratic presidents put on the use of military might probably allowed two third-rate Asian countries, North Korea and North Vietnam, to hold the mighty United States to a draw. Still today when presented with foreign provocation, Democrats prefer sanctions or international diplomacy to military conflict. Example: When voting in 1990 to grant Bush Senior authority to go war with Iraq only 10 of 55 Democrat senators voted in the affirmative. Most of the naysayers favored economic sanctions.

In contrast, Republican leaders have not been timid about using America's power. They favor a muscular foreign policy and take a dim view of appeasement, trade embargoes, and collective security because they feel it undermines the perception of willingness. This "traditional" approach to foreign policy seems to have worked quite well. Republicans were at the helm in 1991 when the United States, in conjunction with an alliance of other nations, unleashed a barrage of weaponry on Saddam Hussein, subduing Iraq in a matter of days. They came to the aid of the Democrats and restored military force, or the threat to use it to the fullest, to its central role in world affairs and dug the nation out of the mire of Korea and Vietnam. During Eisenhower's tenure the Republicans prevented further communist inroads into the free world, allowing time for economic prosperity to win over the hearts and minds of Western Europeans, many of whom were flirting with communist parties following World War II. Nor is it likely the Republicans would have sanctioned an invasion of Cuba without adequate air cover or attempted a rescue mission in the heart of Iran with only eight broken-down helicopters.

Traditional foreign diplomacy, as practiced by the Republicans, did not result in national humiliation or a deep setback to American interests. During the past century the worst military embarrassment a Republican administration suffered occurred during Ronald Reagan's excursion into Lebanon as part of an international peacekeeping mission. A bomb explosion cost the lives of 241 American marines. The president soon reversed course and removed the remaining force from harm's way. However, in that case the troops had been part of a multinational operation rather than a projection of American power.

From the point of view of winning the respect of the other nations in the international community, the practice of traditional statecraft has been a resounding success and has allowed the United States to stand tall in the community of nations. It seems it is good to be loved but better to be feared. Is the Republican approach to international diplomacy superior to that of the Democrats?

To understand and appreciate the role the Democrats play, we must look at foreign affairs from another point of view. As the Democrats see it, "traditional foreign policy" works until . . . well, it no longer works; prime example: the Great War. In a world where nations are armed to the teeth with weapons of mass destruction, we can no longer afford the periodic breakdown in international civility that happened in 1914 or in the mid-1790s. Those were the two no-holds-barred multination Great Wars of modern times. (World War II is considered a resumption of World War I, similar to the different phases of the Napoleonic Wars.) As the liberals see it, the problem is *finding a way for modern man to live in the "New World,"* which is coming into being under a cloud of nuclear weapons, *without destroying all mankind.* To do so, they think it necessary to take a nation's approach to foreign affairs to a new and higher level beyond the power politics of the old agrarian world.

Democrats are seeking to change the rules guiding the way nations behave toward one another. They are trying to substitute policies of collective security, trade embargoes, and, yes, even appeasement in place of traditional policies. George McGovern, Democratic Party candidate for president in 1972 who advocated appeasement in Vietnam, was asked the question by a delegate to the Democratic national convention. "You want us to do all they demand and then beg them for our boys back?" McGovern's reply. "I'll accept that. Begging is better than bombing."

The party of Woodrow Wilson hopes that by substituting moral force, an appeal to reason, and the establishment of an international rule of law for military force they will be able to change mankind's behavior and prevent war. Theirs is the more difficult task, as they focus on a New World that can only be dimly imagined and with no blueprints to point the way. They are left to experiment and make up the rules as they go along. Under the circumstances, perhaps, it is necessary to cut them some slack and allow for a measure of confusion.

Democrats have been responsible for elevating the foreign policy debate to one that now takes into account morality and international approval. Increasingly nations around the world, along with Republicans at home, have come to pay attention to the moral force of world opinion. It has played a part in the collapse of apartheid in South Africa. Colonialism is gone, stronger nations no longer brush aside the rights of smaller nations with impunity, and Republican hard-line policies have been toned down. Liberal voices played an important role in preventing the United States from acquiring a colonial empire during the late nineteenth century and in halting the growing U.S. domination of Latin America in the early part of the twentieth century. And from the backbenches they applied steady pressure on Richard Nixon to get out of Vietnam as promised. These were not insignificant feats.

The Democrats' use of restraint has not led to an all-out general war and, on the positive side, may have checked "traditional" policy from reaching too far. Their willingness to limit America's use of power during both the Berlin blockade and the Cuban missile crisis may well have prevented a nasty confrontation and probably did the country no long-term harm.

The same symbiotic relationship that prevails in the social and economic realms also seems to occur in international relations.

Example: The Democrats set the framework of how the cold war was to be conducted. America's military might was to be used cautiously so as to keep the big-power rivalry within bounds. It bought time to allow the Soviet system to decay from within. Then the Republicans came in and delivered the knockout punch, although no punch was actually thrown. All it took was a menacing fist and the cold war was history.

The Republicans link us to the traditional policies of the Old World, while Democrats nudge the country ever closer to a new foreign policy that *may* be more appropriate in an emerging New World. As Democrats experiment with new ways to neutralize the destructive potential of mass warfare, they oftentimes become confused as to the use of force and out of tune with the world "as it is." Republicans then get a turn and take a realistic stance, applying the old tried and true muscular policies, which are more appropriate for the world of the present. They reassert the use of force, making sure that no permanent harm is done to the nation. Together the two parties have edged the United States toward a more humane foreign policy, and both deserve credit for smoothing a transition into the New World.

Why do the political parties act as they do? Why do Republicans line up uncompromisingly on the side of tradition and the Democrats favor undoing the power arrangements of the past five thousand years? Because they entertain contrasting assumptions concerning the nature of man, and this has led to different approaches to politics, economics, and society.

The "optimistic" view of human nature maintains **MAN HAS BEEN BORN GOOD and made bad by society.** In this worldview Man's fall from grace, his social ills, are rooted in an outmoded and corrupt social system. However, not to despair! Help is on the way because Man's ability to comprehend reality by the use of abstract reason produced a fundamental change in the course of civilization that took place in the eighteenth century. Because they have the **power of reason,** humans are not condemned to remain victims of an "unjust" social system. Reason transcends custom and tradition and will light the way to a society with institutions that conform more closely to widely held ideas of egalitarianism and fairness. These optimists applaud self-government, democracy, as the opening shot in a global struggle against all forms of oppression.

But they are quick to remind us, there is still a long way to go before we reach our destination. This tender-minded, idealistic view of the world underpins the Democratic liberal philosophy.

Liberals are **"haunted by visions of what will be."** It is a utopian vision of a new humane political and social order based on reason and science; a world without war, without poverty, and overflowing with social justice. Democrats, in their hearts and souls, believe they can usher in a New World, as it "ought" to be.

Conservatives do not confuse utopian dreams with the world "as it is." They are more interested in how men actually behave, not how they ought to behave. The great sixteenth-century Princewatcher, Machiavelli, warned us. "He who studies what ought, rather than what is done, will learn the way to his downfall rather than to his preservation." The conservative worldview is based upon a rather pessimistic assumption about the nature of Man. Human beings, as conservatives see it, are in constant warfare with their passions, which at times overrule reason. And without a controlling authority, whether it be government or religion, passion would trump reason even more. Accordingly, **Man is born bad (or flawed), an unregenerate rebel, and it is SOCIETY THAT MAKES HIM GOOD.** From the pen of the eighteenth-century British philosopher Edmund Burke: "Men are qualified for ... liberty ... in exact proportion to their disposition to put moral chains on their own appetites ... Society cannot exist unless a controlling power upon will and appetite be placed somewhere, and the less of it there is within, the more there is without."

These pessimists claim Man does not, and cannot, know everything and when he acts as if he did, he invites trouble. They argue that institutions, which have stood the test of time, have been the building blocks of our civilization. They have a reason and purpose inherent in them. According to Irving Kristol, one of the founding fathers of neoconservatism, "the fact that human beings don't perfectly understand or cannot explain why they 'work' is no defect in them but merely a limitation in us." In other words, custom and tradition transcend reason. The Republican philosophy of governing is built upon the foundation of this tough-minded, no-nonsense view of human nature, and its holders like to think themselves realistic.

The battle between Democrats and Republicans as to the proper way to view the world, "what will be" or "as it is," rages on. Republicans are in tune with the verities of the past, while Democrats reach for the future as they imagine it. Democrats favor lessening dependence on the "traditional" instruments of power, such as a citizen's right to own guns, police power to bully suspects, and the electric chair. They want to change society's most basic power arrangements: employee-employer, husband-wife, etc., in favor of those who are on the lower end. Furthermore, they aim to curb the influence of the churches and synagogues, which preach a personal morality deeply rooted in the past.

Republicans, on the other hand, are skeptical of just how much power people can handle responsibly. They are not afraid of asserting the authority of a leadership class. They are against pampering criminals, against giveaways to an idle class. They are in favor of the death penalty, the right to own guns, law and order, a greater role for religion—school prayer—in contemporary life, and more money for national defense. Likewise, they are not too keen on same sex marriage, affirmative action, and measures that undermine the prevailing power structures.

Today's liberals are grooming the power of reason and moral force to become the chief instruments in their new power arsenal.

Their hope is to replace the conventional instruments of force in the world they are trying to birth.

Liberals worship at the altar of reason. To them, brains are replacing brawn as one of the chief engines of power. Because of their willingness to use cause and effect logic when making decisions, Democrats often think themselves more intelligent than the opposition. John Stuart Mill, the British philosopher-economist writing in the nineteenth century, called the conservative party "the stupid party." To the liberal way of thinking, the typical conservative is not very enlightened, because he is apt to place a great deal of stock in things that work, even though he doesn't understand how or why they work. In their hearts, Democrats believe theirs is the party of **reason**. They KNOW the "root" cause or causes for society's ills and how to correct them. They have the ability to reason people and nations into the correct positions. It is only natural that they, the Democrats, should be the arbiters of what is reasonable and what isn't. And they can get rather arrogant about it. Picture candidate Al Gore during the presidential debates sighing at each unenlightened Bush answer.

To some extent the Democrats *have* gained control over the rules of logic. Take, for instance, the idea that without the champion of the left Ralph Nader playing the spoiler role in the presidential race of 2000 Al Gore would have been sitting in the White House on January 20, 2001. Most Democrats and even some Republicans agree that in a two-way contest enough Nader votes would have gone to Al Gore to have put the Democrat over the top in Florida and probably a couple of other states to boot.

Yet it is not all that cut-and-dried. Life is more complex and mysterious than a belief in simple reason implies. According to Nobel economist and social philosopher Friedrich Hayek, "It may indeed prove to be by far the most difficult and not the least important task for human reason to rationally comprehend its own limitations." The idea of Nader playing the spoiler in the Bush-Gore presidential contest is simplistic. Without Nader in the contest the Bush campaign would have been handled differently. Ralph Nader's candidacy put normally Democratic-leaning states Wisconsin, Washington, Oregon, and Minnesota into play for the Republicans. The Bush campaign, looking for votes, poured money and time into those Nader friendly states and tilted their candidate's message more toward the center. Without the "champion of the left" in the race those resources would have been deployed elsewhere and very well might have produced a treasure lode of additional Bush votes and perhaps a significant amount would have been in Florida.

However, as in real life, the situation becomes even more complicated. Gore's strategy would, in all probability, also have changed. Quite likely he would have felt that he did not have to tailor his story to the hard-core left and could have campaigned as more of a centrist. But keep in mind that from 1999 throughout the primary season polls consistently showed Gore having trouble winning over the Democratic left wing. While a more centrist message might have swung more of the independent vote his way, on the flip side, more of the left-wing Democrats, who actually did come back to him in the end, might have boycotted the election. Because these new variables do not lend themselves to precise measurement, it is by no means certain that sans Nader, Gore would have won! In actuality there was probably just as much chance Bush would have done better without Nader than Gore would have. A change in one part of an equation does not necessarily lead to a predictable change in the outcome.

Humans, no matter how hard they try, cannot get a crisp picture of cause and effect. Their activity is multifaceted and circuitous, not neatly linear. One-way causality does not take into account feedback, interconnectedness, and dynamic interpretations. There are variables that we cannot measure but that still exert a large influence on outcomes. During the last half-century we have learned that increased bombing does not always lead to more deaths and that antibodies are not always a cure for disease.

And many "well-intentioned" policies of the 1960s did not work in the way they were supposed to. For example, during those years the Democrats raised welfare benefits to lift the burden of poverty from the backs of the poor. Poverty rates did fall. But to the nation's bewilderment, dependency also grew, employment rates declined, and family life eroded. There is an unreasonableness in modern rationalism, and Democrats are loath to confront it. Their **faith** in causal reason is often misplaced. William Jennings Bryan, champion of the underdog and three-time Democratic nominee for president, was to remark, "It is a poor head that cannot find plausible reason for doing what the heart wants it to do."

Think of the "law of gravity." In a pre-Galilean/Newtonian world simple logic would imply the earth was indeed flat and the center of the universe. Before the *concept of gravity* was embedded into our brainwaves, it seemed quite logical to thinking people that the earth was *not* a sphere spinning around the sun. Try telling a five-year-old the earth is a round ball suspended in space. The first question will be, "How come we don't all fall off?" That is your cue to first explain the concept of gravity. For if there was no gravitational pull between the worldly bodies and the earth was a circular ball, twirling in space, we would, indeed, all fall off. What could seem more logical to the average person? (The official thinkers about this matter had an elaborate theory called the geocentric system, which was more complex, yet earth stood at the center.) But when Newton convinced his late-seventeenth-century world that there was a natural "law of gravity" based upon the magnetic pull of bodies it forever changed the way humans saw their world. What had previously seemed logical no longer appeared so. What about all those new laws of nature that have yet to be discovered?

Marching hand in hand with the power of reason in the liberals' new power arsenal is moral force. Liberals are shoving aside traditional religion and taking over the leadership role in man's epic struggle for freedom and human dignity. As the liberals see it, they, not the church, not the synagogues, not the mosques, are going to take us—all of us—to the Promised Land, a land without poverty, a land at peace, a land overflowing with compassion, humaneness, fairness, and social justice—*a heaven on earth.*

Yet they may be overlooking the important role traditional "Judeo-Christian" religion has played in the building of Western Civilization. It was the church that told us what thou shall not do . . . and what thou shall do. It pointed the way to what was right and what was wrong, providing mankind with a code of conduct to soften the edges of what was a brutal civilization. In defining morality it helped curb man's appetites, brought order to a world of moral anarchy, and, in so doing, made it easier for men and women to govern themselves.

Prior to the advent of organized religion, people lived in a state of moral laissez-faire, wherein, according to Thucydides, a Greek historian who lived in the fifth century B.C., "the strong did what they had the power to do and the weak accepted what they had to accept." It was a world without a conscience, without a moral compass, a place wherein people had to make their way without guidelines on how to conduct their life.

It was into this moral jungle that organized religion arrived more than 1,600 years ago. Religious authorities supplied a code of conduct, which chiseled all sorts of no-nos and yes-yeses into mankind's conscience. They provided answers to morally ambiguous situations, which heretofore individuals had bent to suit their personal agenda. Example: What is the ethically appropriate thing to do when a spouse suddenly becomes incapacitated? Easy! Refer to the marriage vows, which emphatically state "in sickness and in health . . . till death do you part" Better yet, society internalized those moral teachings and stood on the sidelines ready to render a harsh social judgment on violators.

In fact, because traditional religion has been so successful at resolving moral ambiguity, contemporary men and women have a hard time recognizing it. But take away this church dictum, allow a few decades for society's internalization to evaporate, and many spouses would be tempted to flee, especially so if incapacitation occurred while the marriage contract was still warm. Without a code of conduct, it becomes hard to prevent moral anarchy.

In the Western world the church became a junior partner to temporal authorities in the creation of a secular government and religion-based society. Religious officials made moral dictums, and secular leaders enforced them. Neither was to transgress on the other's territory. No less an authority than the father of our country, George Washington, in his farewell address to the nation, reminded the young country of this secular–religious bond. In his words, ". . . religion and morality are indispensable supports."

Yet the United States staked its claim to liberty on nature's laws rather than the laws of God. Its mission was to pursue the rights of man and individual freedom, *unfettered by religious sentiment.* Liberals take this ideal of a secular state quite seriously, and their aim is to neuter traditional religion by denying it a voice in determining right and wrong in a society. Scientists will replace priests as the arbiters of moral truth. As an example, we need look no further than the issue of abortion, which has become the most contentious domestic issue since abolition.

Legally sanctioned abortion depends upon accepting the idea life begins at "birth," but in truth there is a great deal of ambiguity as to when it actually begins. Conservatives muster a strong case that "conception" is the proper beginning of life, while liberals make equally powerful arguments that it starts at "breath of life." And to date neither side has been able to present overwhelming evidence that will quiet the other side. So objectively, how can we truly know? Some authority must make the call, and that determination must then take on the force of moral law. Traditional religion, in fulfilling its moral arbiter role, had decided that life begins at conception.

However, in granting women the "right to abort" the state has gone way beyond previous encroachments on the church's moral authority. Even though science had not made a convincing case as to when life begins, government allowed women the moral freedom to make their own choice. God's gift to humanity, a religious-based morality, was given back and the door to moral chaos has swung open. Traditional religion, especially the "religious right," whom liberals see as the barbarians at the gate, recognizes the challenge to its moral authority and fights for its life on the battlefield of the abortion issue.

Today liberals have their own religion, "Secular Humanism," and it attempts to fashion a belief and moral system based on reason and science, which they think more suitable to a modern world. This secular religion does not consider itself in the business of saving individual souls. Personal moral behavior is more or less irrelevant to it. People are left to make up their own minds as to morality. Anything goes, as long as "it makes you feel good."

It is social morality, doing good for humanity, that Secular Humanists are concerned about. It is a morality that empowers the weak and seeks to rid the country and the world of guns and weapons of mass destruction. Believers are the good guys because they have a higher purpose than merely grubbing for money. It is the causes you believe in that define the "man or woman." Democrats were able to rally around Bill Clinton during his impeachment trial and overlook his personal moral failings because "he" stood for, fought for, and would continue to battle for the "right" causes—and "that" was what was truly important.

The "religious left" of the Democratic Party aims to make it the "conscience" of the world, the source of light for an emerging New World, and, quite importantly, the basis for a new international rule of law, one that will reject the use of violence by nations. Naturally, not all Democrats march with the Secular Humanists, but those quasi-religious ideas are becoming a growing force within the party.

Liberals, seeking a morality that transcends traditional religion, are nudging us ever closer to a religion of Secular Humanism. Yet two looming "big" questions remain unanswered. Without traditional religion will people continue to think and act ethically, not tomorrow but decades into the future after the internalization from traditional religion has worn off, so that self-government is able to work? Will the West and its Secular Humanism write the rules for a new "conscience of the modern world?" There are three other major civilizations, along with related satellite societies, and each sees morality and values in a somewhat different light. Because those other civilizations may not accept a Western-driven universal morality so easily, the shape of what eventually emerges, when the world becomes fully interconnected, may be quite different from what the Secular Humanists had in mind. It may not be the liberal values of the West that rule the moral world.

To sum up: Up until the present time **power,** in the traditional sense of military strength and hierarchical positions in society, has enabled mankind to prosper. But now, according to the Democrats, because of weapons of mass destruction mankind's future is uncertain. In order to survive, civilization must make a revolutionary leap in the way it operates. It must replace the use of force with the exercise of reason and moral power. Yet much of what occurs under the rubric of reason in its present mode is improper. The Democrats have forayed into the realm of morality and threaten to allow individuals the freedom to make moral choices, opening up the Pandora's box of moral anarchy. Allowing for some adjustments—a fine-tuning in the makeup of the new power weapons—the fundamental, but **unanswered,** question becomes: Can they adequately replace force as the modus operandi by which civilization marches forward?

The Democratic and the Republican Party each play a different, but necessary, role in politics. Together they maintain the world "as it is" but "*maybe*" **inch it** ever so slightly toward the world "as it is" but "*maybe*" **inch it** ever so slightly toward the world "as it ought to be." Republicans are pleased with the existing power structure of society and wish to uphold it. They see the world "as it is" and use models from the past as their guide. It is the safer route. They do not harbor visions of a distant world of peace and egalitarianism. Rather, their vision of the future is one of greater material abundance. Yet to the Democratic way of thinking the Republicans have aligned themselves with the wrong side of history.

Democrats stand for the triumphal arrival of modernity. They want to sweep away forever all laws and human relationships dependent on coercion and find replacements. They are on the path that promises to change our conception of humanity so that the world of, say, **2300** will, in all probability, be as unrecognizable to the men and women of today as agricultural societies would have appeared to the hunters and gathers who preceded them.

But at times the speed of Democrat-induced change exceeds society's readiness to handle it, and confusion results. Just as we need Democrats to bite into the "cake of custom" and move society toward a distant goal, when things go wrong it is necessary to have Republicans, at the ready, to provide a dash of realism. They keep a tight leash on the Democrats' utopian aspirations and bring them into a more fruitful and harmonious relation with reality. Republicans make sure that the speed of travel to that unknown future place is measured in **"inches"** rather in than miles. In America each of the two parties keeps the other within bounds.

———∞∞∞———

XIII

9/11 and Stirrings of a New World Order

Dateline: 12/31/2002

On September 11, 2001, Americans turned on their TV sets and looked on, in horror, as they saw three commercial airplanes hijacked by a group of suicidal terrorists being flown into the World Trade Center and the Pentagon, killing more than 3,000 civilians. Suddenly Americans realized **there were "somebodies" out there who wanted to kill them** . . . very badly.

And one must contemplate the "what ifs." A fourth plane, probably intended for the White House, didn't make it to its target. "What if" the terrorists had chosen a date when the president was in the White House and had taken him out? And "what if" the Pentagon plane had hit the Capitol building while Congress was in session, decapitating the American political system? Horrific as 9/11 was, what *might have been* simply boggles the mind.

We are engaged in a wholly new kind of war, and it is being waged against a dimly seen enemy. It has presented the Bush administration a unique opportunity to reshape the international order. The current structure of world order was set up following World War I and authored by Woodrow Wilson, who wanted to change the way nations behaved toward one another so as to prevent war.

Just as there are alternating domestic paradigms of "economic growth" and "social realignment," there appear to be reoccurring shifts in the rules and behavior in the international community. These global worldviews are satellite paradigms, which change very seldom. What is so interesting about the new Bush stratagems in the world arena is the possibility we may have a front row seat to a "once in a lifetime" phenomenon.

Prior to World War I, and during the eighteenth and nineteenth centuries, war was assumed to be the natural condition of a world system of states. The leading nations based their foreign policies on the notion that states were driven by a "lust for power." To tame war and maintain international order those nations adhered to a strategy called "balance of power," which meant adopting a game plan to prevent any of the others from becoming powerful enough to threaten the "balance." According to this strategy, sometimes it was necessary to make small wars so as to prevent "big" ones. Other tactics, such as buck-passing, which as the name implies meant trying to find another state to do the dirty work of checking the aggressor, were used as well.

This approach to international politics was called "realism." There were, of course, different shadings of realism, but at their core all were based on the belief that it made good sense for a nation to selfishly pursue power. And to be on the safe side it was best to stop an expansionist nation before it became a superpower.

Meanwhile, at the beginning of the nineteenth century the United States, which was off center stage, flirted with an alternative, "idealistic" foreign policy strategy, hoping it would enable them to avoid war. But America's embarrassing military performance during the War of 1812, which featured the British marching casually into the nation's capital to set the White House on fire, brought home the realization that Jefferson's policy of "peaceful coercion" was too naïve in a world community wherein the "law of the jungle" ruled.

Beginning with Madison's turn to the New Nationalism, the United States toughened its foreign policy and moved it back into line with European "realism." And with the arrival of Teddy Roosevelt in the White House, America began to flex its military muscle and strutted out onto the world stage.

During World War I, with its unprecedented level of carnage, Woodrow Wilson broke ranks with what had gone before and laid down the outline for a new world order. Although differing from Jefferson's proposal, it was based on the same **idealistic** vision that if the nations of the world would be willing to *surrender their power*, the result would be a safer, more humane globe, a world wherein war was to be avoided, not exalted. Wilson's grand design for a new structure of world order was to be built on a set of imposing pillars: human rights, international law, the worldwide growth of democracies, the force of world opinion, a voice for the less powerful nations, and, above all, a League of Nations.

It wasn't until after World War II that the implementation of the Wilsonian structure of world order shifted into high gear. Its centerpiece, the United Nations, successor to the League, was established to save "succeeding generations from the scourge of war." Colonialism was dismantled. The world population of democratic states grew. The protection of human rights became a priority. And slowly but surely, world moral opinion grew comfortable with the idea that it was morally unacceptable to fight wars merely to change or preserve the balance of power.

During the last half of the twentieth century, Democrats perpetuated Wilsonian doctrines, propelling them further into the calculus of America's approach to foreign affairs. Republicans, on the other hand, when they were at the helm, tried to infuse this overall strategy with a touch of muscular realism. Nonetheless, Republicans and Democrats both remained true to the Wilsonian ideal that relationships among states would be governed by international law, and this liberal approach to foreign policy became the reigning model. It now colors the way people throughout the Western world think about international relations. By 1992 Bill Clinton was able to state, "In a world where freedom, not tyranny, is on the march, the cynical calculus of pure power politics simply does not compute. It is ill-suited for a new era."

Although the highest expectations of its founders have not been met—wars have not been avoided—it does seem the United Nations has been, on balance, a force of moderation helping to tame war and to make the world a safer place. It appears to have played an important role in keeping the cold war in bounds. Each of the rival superpowers was able to use the United Nations to help muster world opinion, which may have offset the need for military action to check the other when it seemed on the verge of becoming too aggressive.

Now, however, George W. Bush and his foreign policy team seem intent on changing the way international relations are conducted. They want to downgrade the role of the United Nations and ratchet up the say-so of the United States. They have deliberately attempted to pursue a go-it-alone foreign policy and *threatened* to freeze the United Nations out of the decision on making war with Iraq (the United States relented and reluctantly allowed the United Nations a part in the process—but, as of this writing, it voraciously maintains that the decision of whether it's a "GO" is its and its alone), thereby setting precedents for future bypasses that may eventually marginalize the United Nations and its organizations. The United States walked out of the Kyoto Accords on global warming, abandoned the Anti-Ballistic Missile Treaty so that they could build a missile defense, and shunned a new International Criminal Court.

As the Bushies see it, the disparity of power between the United States and even its closest allies has never been greater. In fact, since the Treaty of Westphalia in 1648 no one nation has so outdistanced the others in terms of both economic and military might. There is no longer a rough "balance" among the leading nations as there was prior to 1914. According to *The National Security Strategy of the United States of America*, a 31-page report to the Congress by President George W. Bush, "The United States possesses unprecedented—and unequalled—strength and influence in the world."

Furthermore and most important, the Bushies are claiming there are states too dangerous to others to be tolerated in a world with weapons of mass destruction. They are jettisoning the American tradition of not starting wars and promoting, in its place, a radical new doctrine that endorses *pre-emptive military action* against threatening regimes. In May 2002 George W. stood before the West Point graduates and said, "We must take the battle to our enemy, disrupt his plans . . . before they emerge . . . [Americans must] be ready for preemptive action when necessary" This "Bush Doctrine" would allow superpowers to punish nations that harbor terrorists and prevent terrorists from acquiring weapons of mass destruction, just as nineteenth-century great powers tried to prevent expansionist powers from becoming a threat to the "balance." It looks as if we are back in the business of making small wars, in hopes of avoiding the "big" one.

No American president, including Teddy Roosevelt, has so flexed the nation's muscles. If the Bushies succeed, we can say "Good-bye" to the liberal Wilsonian world structure and "Hello" to an international community with new rules and norms—a Pax America wherein America asserts leadership on the world stage, even more so than Britain did in the nineteenth century. America, rather than the United Nations, would act as the chief arbiter of when war is justified. The United States would achieve world hegemony and its military power would be used to suppress or destroy threats to the stability of the global security system.

Why such a radical change in the way the United States wants to conduct its global relations? Had not the Wilsonian world structure successfully avoided all-out war? There were no mushroom clouds! But just as the War of 1812 brought home the naïveté of Jefferson's idealistic foreign policy, so too has 9/11 highlighted the shortcomings of the United Nations and the Wilsonian global order.

The Somebodies Out There

On 9/11 the West woke up to the realization there were militant Islamic terror organizations that had found a powerful new weapon to wage war on the West, "human" bombs aimed directly on innocent civilians, including women and children. We hardly paid attention when, way back in February 1998, Osama bin Laden, leader of the al Qaeda terrorist group, issued an incendiary fatwa authorizing the killing of "Americans and their allies, civilians and military alike." But we do now!

What is particularly worrisome is the very real possibility that 9/11 may have been the first explosions in what Harvard professor Samuel Huntington calls a "Clash of Civilizations." Islamic societies, which have been largely left at the gate in the world's race toward modernity and material well-being, nurse serious grievances and bitter anger. But their grudge encompasses much more than their relative backwardness in relation to the West. The threat that the seductive, "godless" Western materialism and individualism poses to their own nonsecular culture, which they are convinced is far superior to the West's, annoys them most. It is no wonder shadowy terrorist networks, which operate behind the scenes and are sometimes abetted by rogue states, are gaining influence and popularity throughout the Islamic world. Certainly the fault lines, Israel and Kashmir, where Islamic Civilization intersects with others, tremble with violence and reek of blood, suggesting, perhaps, the internal pressures within Muslim societies may be ready to erupt.

We know the level of anti-Americanism runs deep throughout the Islamic world. But in the fog of this war we are not sure if the enemy is al Qaeda and related terrorist organizations, or Muslim Civilization per se. It is difficult to ascertain how many more recruits are waiting in line to become martyrs. How much sympathy and support are the shadowy terrorist organizations receiving from Islamic governments? Will the popularity of those radical networks continue to grow until it reaches the point where they are able to gain the reins or backing of some Muslim state, and possibly one that has weapons of mass destruction—nuclear, chemical, and biological? Not to mention an "oil" weapon, which if used could bring Western economies to their knees. But we can be sure: We are engaged in a different kind of war and our *foe* is waging it with a new and very frightening weapon. And by directly "*targeting*" civilians he spits in the face of the West's most sacred ethic, "the sanctity of human life."

The United Nations evolved into an organization that was quite effective in helping prevent "all-out war" between competing superpowers that, more or less, shared a similar secular morality. But it seems ill-suited to handle this new threat to the security of the "West." This is because the Wilsonian world structure, including the United Nations, has taken on a distinct **"liberal" bias,** which inhibits the advanced states from responding effectively to this new challenge.

The pillars of "human rights" and the "force of moral opinion" created a climate wherein nations are precluded from taking the strong military actions necessary to cripple terrorist organizations. Attempts to do so are likely to provoke harsh criticism as violations of human rights. Give a hammer to a child and most everything becomes a nail. Give an abstract idea of "human rights" to an idealist with a "leftist" bent, most everything becomes a violation.

Witness the growing list of jurists the world over who at the beginning of the twenty-first century have become willing to make "moral" law, expanding the definition of war crimes against the people. A French judge issued a summons to former secretary of state Henry Kissinger so as to question him about U.S. policy in Chile more than 30 years ago. A Belgian court entertained a case charging Israeli prime minister Ariel Sharon with crimes against humanity in the 1982 massacres in Lebanon.

Most members of the United Nations fall into the category of the "less powerful" nations. In the parlance of a "social rebalancing" paradigm, they are the *little guys*. Their grievances, which are many—of course, they are less powerful—are heard and, at least to some extent, legitimatized. To redress the situation, world moral opinion gangs up on the top nations, pressuring them to surrender some of their . . . power. The Wilsonian world structure is reluctant to give first-tier nations its blessing to take the tough-minded responses necessary to shield their citizens. If those nations follow the rules of the international community they are prevented from making small wars, so as to preclude a major catastrophe. The Wilsonian world structure, along with its centerpiece, the United Nations, appears, much like a majority party at the *end* of an "economic growth" or "social realignment" paradigm, to have lost its punch and unable to deal with a new menace—a fresh way to wage war. So, perhaps, Mr. Wilson, surrendering one's POWER does not make for a safer world, at least not for the more advanced states. *What do we do now?*

Call In the Bushies!

The Bush team recognizes the liberal bias to the Wilsonian world structure and aims to dismantle it and turn the United Nations into less than an irrelevant debating society. They are attempting to establish a beachhead for an entirely different way of looking at global relations. And they are *not* tippy-toeing in. On the contrary, they are quite blunt as to their intentions! In their scheme of things, the United States is better able than the United Nations to take on the twin tasks of ensuring the safety of Americans and policing the world. While the United Nations shies away from confronting international lawbreakers (that is against its nature), the United States will not be afraid to use the full force of American might to do so. The Bushies do not intend to absorb the first blow and sacrifice thousands or perhaps millions of innocent men, women, and children to maintain an abstract ideal of world peace.

If, and to reiterate "if," this muscular new American realism takes on traction and lasts for many decades, George W. Bush—though not a domestic paradigm-setter—might well become a very important president, much like Woodrow Wilson, as the architect of a new world order. In that case, it will probably be Republican presidents who will be dotting the i's and crossing the t's of the emerging international order, providing it with more muscle, while Democratic presidents play the minority role, acting as an internal balance, much like the GOP during the Wilsonian world order. But in this case, during their time at the helm, the party of Woodrow Wilson will be working to tame and rein in the tough foreign policy after it has become *too* bellicose—although remaining true to the basic "realistic" doctrine. One possibility: A United Nations with a decided deference and toadying to America, i.e. the United States paying lip service to international institutions while claiming for itself the sole legitimate use of force anywhere, anytime it feels threatened.

The road to this new world order may be rocky at first—oftentimes new ideas to reshape long-standing ways of doing things are initially met with strong disapproval—yet it is probably best not to bet against the Bush blueprint winning out. But keep in mind: The success of the Bush doctrine does not necessarily spell the permanent demise of the United Nations. It may possibly be a way station to a new organizational structure for that body, one that enables it to function better in the emerging new world. So, Woodrow Wilson may yet have another day!

A Note on Diplomatic Niceties

In their rambunctiousness to establish a new world order, the Bushies often appear diplomatically clumsy—like bulls in a china shop. Eighty-some years ago, it was Woodrow Wilson who, hell bent on changing the world order, was thought diplomatically inept by his contemporaries. What goes? Do politicians of the United States lack the proper gene for diplomatic niceties?

As we saw, pattern-setting presidents must tear up old ingrained ways of doing things, and that usually requires practicing "the art of *not compromising*." In much the same manner, chief executives who set their sights on dismantling a world order must aggressively push their agenda on a recalcitrant world community. And this means pushing, shoving, arm-twisting, and blunt "in your face" talk. Their goal is to get the ball of a new international order rolling. Once done, successors can "tidy up" and restore an appreciation for diplomatic niceties.

———⊶⊷———

XIV

The "Rating the Presidents" Game

One of the favorite pastimes of political junkies and historical buffs is rating the presidents. Who was best, second best, third . . . and so on? Results are usually based on highly subjective evaluations. Instead, let's look at the presidents through the quantitative framework of voter approval or disapproval to determine how effective they were—that is, their ranking. The voters of their time will be the judges.

Rules of the game: Each president falls into one of six levels based on voter (or party) approval and the ability to establish a legacy. Then other criteria are used to unscramble them within their respective category. For instance, losers within striking distance (say 3 percent) of the winner are given a higher ranking than those defeated by a greater margin. Only presidents who served for at least half a term are ranked. This eliminates William Harrison, Zachary Taylor, and James Garfield, who died in office before serving two full years. On the other hand, both Warren Harding and John F. Kennedy served more than half a term before dying in office and receive credit for assisting their successors. All in all, 38 presidents, through Bill Clinton, are ranked. Keep in mind that the category to which the president is assigned is more objective than his placement within it.

Top level: The paradigm-setting presidents. The **9** presidents who had the most important and lasting influence on the nation's political culture. The size of their victory is not important as long as it was by a majority. To unscramble them I give credit for the length of their paradigm. For instance, FDR gets 48 years. I take the liberty of giving Lincoln and Jefferson credit for the entire length of their superparadigms. Furthermore, I give George Washington credit for all 214 years. How can we deny "America's one and only indispensable character," the person whom revolutionaries toasted as "the man who unites all hearts," the **"father of our country,"** acknowledgment for the whole American experiment? While it may be subjective, it's hard not to be influenced by his example of principled leadership, which provided "roots" for the revolutionary ideas to sprout into a new American political experience.

Level two: The contenders. The **6** presidents who were elected to a second term with a majority of the vote but failed to establish a legacy. How close the president came to establishing a legacy determines where he falls within the category.

Level three: The modestly successful. The **4** presidents who won another term, but without a majority of the vote. Again, they are unscrambled according to how close they came to leaving a legacy. Woodrow Wilson, whose legatee was on the losing side of the largest landslide in American political history, comes in behind both Clinton and Truman. Grover Cleveland brings up the rear; although receiving a plurality of the votes, he lost his bid for reelection. However, when he ran again four years later he won another term, but with only 46 percent of all votes cast.

These **19** were, according to the voters, America's most effective presidents. Eighteen won election to a second term as a sitting president, while one—Cleveland—reclaimed the office four years later. Voters, in that case, had already observed him in action as the chief executive. All served for at least a bit more than one term. On the other hand, none of the following 19 served more than four years, nor did they win voter endorsement.

Level four: The presidents of "the middle." These are the **4** presidents who were neither endorsed by the voters nor spurned by party or electorate. (Buchanan, who did not seek reelection, is not included, because he recognized the futility of obtaining the nomination.) Without any voter feedback to rely on, placement within this category is more subjective. Nonetheless, Warren Harding and John F. Kennedy rank higher because they laid the groundwork for a successor who easily won reelection. Harding ranks above Kennedy because he played a leading part in setting the policies of his paradigm. James Polk and Rutherford Hayes chose not to run again. Had they decided to do so, both would have had a good chance to win their party's nomination for a try at another term and, indeed, might well have prevailed in the general election. Polk's placement above Hayes is purely subjective. The author was impressed by Polk's achievements as president. Presidential scholars seemed to be also, as they placed Polk well above Hayes in a poll we shall review later.

The rejectees: The 15 presidents who were rejected by either party or electorate. Nine lost a reelection bid, while 5 failed to receive their party's nod for renomination. Buchanan is also included here. The 5 whose one term rang down a paradigm curtain are considered the great failures. The other 10 are the merely unsuccessful.

Level five: The unsuccessful. These are the 10 presidents who failed either to win election to a second term (excluding the great failures) or to be renominated by their party. Those who lost to the voters are ranked higher than sitting presidents rejected by their party. Unscrambling the 5 who lost their reelection bid was somewhat subjective. Those who came within striking distance (say 3 percent) are ranked higher. Taft, who lost out to both Wilson and Teddy Roosevelt in his bid for reelection, falls to the fifth spot of those who lost their reelection bid.

As for the remaining 5, Franklin Pierce was the only elected president who failed to win his party's nod for a try at a second presidential term. That drops him to the bottom of the unsuccessful list. Unlike the other 4 sitting presidents who were not renominated, he did not have the institutional constraints of being an unelected president. Millard Fillmore and Chester Arthur rank higher because they were able to mount a spirited fight for the nomination. Both James Tyler and Andrew Johnson had been Democrats almost up until the time they were selected as vice president for the Whig and Republican (National Union) Party, respectively. They fought with their newfound party, when in office, and at convention time their adoptive party snubbed them. They did not receive any consideration in the presidential balloting. (Johnson, however, did gather some support at the Democratic Party's convention).

Bottom level: The Great Failures. The 5 presidents whose one term marked the end of a paradigm. Those who left office with the country embroiled in, or about to be involved in, an important crisis are downgraded. In addition, consideration is given to how long the next paradigm, the one that followed, lasted. John Adams beat out his son, John Quincy, because the paradigm that followed the father's defeat lasted only 15 years, compared to the 32-year mini-revolution coming after John Quincy Adams's loss. On the other hand, while the paradigm that followed Buchanan's defeat was a bit shorter than the one coming after Hoover's loss, the impending Civil War places Buchanan dead last.

There you have it! The 38 presidents rated according to how the voters or, in a few cases, the party convention delegates saw it (table 21). While all the traditional favorites are on the most effective list, the custodians of presidential reputations are likely to raise their collective eyebrows at the inclusion of Calvin Coolidge and Ulysses Grant among the top 11. But mind you, both were

TABLE 21

Presidential Ranking: According to Stoken Voter Poll

Level One:	Length of their paradigm in years
1. George Washington ®*	212 (the entire history of the republic) and still counting
2. Abraham Lincoln ®	72 Superparadigm
3. Thomas Jefferson (D)†*	60 Superparadigm
4. Franklin Roosevelt (D)	48
5. Andrew Jackson (D)	32
6. Ronald Reagan ®	24 (through 2004) and still counting
7. Teddy Roosevelt ®	19
8. James Madison (D)	13
9. Calvin Coolidge ®	12
Level Two:	
10. Dwight Eisenhower ®	Came closest to establishing a legacy.
11. Ulysses Grant ®	Next closest to establishing a legacy/successor won in Electoral College.
12. Lyndon Johnson (D)	Successor fell way short of 50 percent, but it was a very close election.
13. James Monroe (D)	Successor got only 31 percent of the vote, though he won election in the House.
14. William McKinley ®	No chance for a legacy, as his successor, TR, began a new paradigm.
15. Richard Nixon ®	Resignation puts him at the bottom of this category. Lost chance for legacy.
Level Three:	
16. Bill Clinton (D)	Successor won a plurality of the votes/closest to a legacy in this category.
17. Harry Truman (D)	Successor does poorly . . . but . . .
18. Woodrow Wilson (D)	Successor does even more poorly than Truman. Is on the wrong side of the biggest landslide in American history (largest losing margin).
19. Grover Cleveland (D)	Marginally defeated in reelection attempt but won four years later.
Level Four:	
20. Warren Harding ®	Was an important paradigm assister.
21. John F. Kennedy (D)	His VP, LBJ, won big in following presidential contest.
22. James Polk (D)	Impressive accomplishments during his term/but subjective.
23. Rutherford Hayes ®	Was never able to attain legitimacy. Known as "His Fraudulency."

*® = Republican or predecessor party of the right (Whig or Federalist).

†(D) = Democrat.

Level Five:	
24. Benjamin Harrison ®	Tied/lost, but within striking distance.
24. Gerald Ford ®	Tied/lost, but within striking distance.
26. George H. Bush ®	Tied/lost.
26. Martin Van Buren (D)	Tied/lost.
28. William Taft ®	Loser/came in third in reelection attempt.
29. Chester Arthur ®	Tied/lost out on renomination attempt.
29. Millard Fillmore ®	Tied/lost out on renomination attempt.
31. John Tyler ®	Tied/no delegate votes to be the next Whig Party presidential candidate.
31. Andrew Johnson ®	Tied/no delegate votes to be next GOP standard-bearer.
33. Franklin Pierce (D)	Only elected president who failed to be renominated by his party.

Level Six:	Number of years the following paradigm lasted.
34. John Adams ®	15 No important crisis.
35. John Quincy Adams ®	32 No important crisis.
36. Jimmy Carter (D)	24 and still counting. Crisis: Great Inflation.
37. Herbert Hoover ®	48 Second worst crisis: Great Depression.
38. James Buchanan (D)	41 Biggest crisis: impending Civil War.

quite popular with the public of their time and each set in place, or helped set in place, policies that had a lasting impact on the political culture.

How does this ranking stack up to a more conventional one? On November 16, 2000, the *Wall Street Journal* published an article by James Lindgren and Steven G. Calabresi entitled "Ranking the Presidents." Unlike most prior studies, which had surveyed primarily either liberal or conservative scholars but not both, their study surveyed a panel of 78 experts, carefully chosen for political balance, from the fields of history, political science, and constitutional law.

The rankings are listed in table 22, with Stoken's Voter Poll (SVP) placements alongside. The third column records the differences between the two lists. A positive number in the differ-

TABLE 22

Wall Street Journal Poll vs. Stoken Voter Poll

	WSJ poll	SVP	Difference
Great			
1. George Washington	1		=
2. Abraham Lincoln	2		=
3. Franklin Roosevelt	4		(1)
Near Great			
4. Thomas Jefferson	3		1
5. Teddy Roosevelt	7		(2)
6. Andrew Jackson	5		1
7. Harry Truman	17		(10)
8. Ronald Reagan	6		2
9. Dwight Eisenhower	10		(1)
10. James Polk	22		(12)
11. Woodrow Wilson	18		(7)
Above Average			
12. Grover Cleveland	19		(7)
13. John Adams	34		(21)
14. William McKinley	14		=
15. James Madison	8		7
16. James Monroe	13		3
17. Lyndon Johnson	12		5
18. John Kennedy	21		(3)
Average			
19. William Taft	28		(9)
20. John Q. Adams	35		(15)
21. George H. Bush	26		(5)
22. Rutherford Hayes	22		=
23. Martin Van Buren	26		(3)
24. William Clinton	16		8
25. Calvin Coolidge	9		16
26. Chester Arthur	29		(3)
Below Average			
27. Benjamin Harrison	24		3
28. Gerald Ford	24		4
29. Herbert Hoover	37		(8)
30. Jimmy Carter	36		(6)

31. Ulysses Grant*	11	20
32. Richard Nixon*	15	17
33. John Tyler*	31	2
34. Millard Fillmore*	29	5
Failure		
35. Andrew Johnson*	31	4
36. Franklin Pierce*	33	3
37. Warren Harding*	20	17
38. James Buchanan*	38	=

*Zachary Taylor, who was #31 in WSJ poll, is eliminated, and the remaining presidents are moved up one notch.

ence column means a higher ranking by the SVP than the *Wall Street Journal* (WSJ) poll. This indicates that according to the SVP those presidents are underrated by the presidential scholars. On the flip side, a minus number (parenthesis) means a lower SVP rating than the WSJ poll, and these presidents are considered overrated. The WSJ poll ranked Zachary Taylor thirty-first, while he was not ranked in the SVP. To make the lists comparable Taylor is removed from the WSJ poll and the remaining presidents are moved up a notch so that the WSJ poll also has 38 places.

Amazingly, although different methodologies were used, the rankings for the SVP and the WSJ are, for the most part, comparable. Twenty-three of the 38 presidents (61 percent) were within 5 places of their ranking in the other poll. But several discrepancies stand out. According to the SVP, John Adams is the most overrated president (by 21 places) and Ulysses Grant the most underrated (by 20 places). Three other presidents were overrated by 10 or more places, John Q. Adams, James Polk, and Harry Truman. None of the 4 overrated presidents were reelected with a majority of the vote. Two, in fact, lost in their bid for reelection. Two of the 4 overrated presidents were Democrats, while the other 2 were from the parties of the right.

Meanwhile, 3 additional presidents were underrated by 10 or

more places, Warren Harding, Richard Nixon, and Calvin Coolidge. Three of the 4 underrated presidents won reelection with a majority of the votes, indicating that their countrymen seemed quite pleased with them at the time. The other, Warren Harding, died in office. But up to the time he died he had been quite popular. In fact, as the funeral train carrying his body passed through countless towns and villages, millions lined the streets to pay their last respects to him. Interestingly, all of the 4 most underrated presidents were Republicans.

The scholars appear to take Ulysses Grant, Warren Harding, and Richard Nixon to task for degrading the dignity of the office. The Grant and Harding administrations were immersed in scandal, and Nixon was caught in an illegal maneuver and forced to resign. I avoid a subjective judgment on those matters and rely, instead, on the voters to register their verdict. Both Grant and Nixon won a hearty voter endorsement at reelection time. Moreover, successors to both came within striking distance of capturing the popular vote. Hayes actually won in the Electoral College, while Ford, carrying the baggage of a Nixon pardon, lost in a very close election. In neither case does there appear to be a belated sign of *great* voter rejection of Grant or Nixon and their policies (at least no more so than of other contender presidents).

Based on the WSJ poll, the average placement of the 16 Democrats was 16.9, which was 4.5 places higher than the 21.4 average placement of the 22 Republicans and their predecessor parties of the right. The SVP's ranking gave Democrat presidents an average placement of 18.2, just 2 places above the Republican 20.2 average. Although Democratic presidents still ranked higher (a lower placement number) than Republican presidents, the voters of the time thought more highly of Republican presidents than did the experts. And if we remove Tyler and Andrew Johnson, who were really Democrats in Whig or Republican clothing, the parties of the right's average rank falls to 19.2 in the SVP, just one place below the Democrats.

That's all: **End of game.**

Neither party has won the game of politics—nor, from the author's point of view, would it be desirable if one did—but there have been three times when a political party temporarily took a commanding lead by knocking its opponent off the playing field for a couple of decades. James Madison, Abraham Lincoln, and Teddy Roosevelt all captured both the right and the left side of the political agenda, leaving the opposing political party befuddled and meandering about in circles. In fact, the Federalists broke up in the early nineteenth century, and beginning shortly after mid-nineteenth-century the Democrats began their long trek in the political wilderness.

If winning the game is what the **Game** is about, then probably those 3 should move up to the top of the list. But there may be more to the **Game** than merely knocking your opponent off the playing field. The **Game** may be about moving the nation further along in its quest for either a higher standard of living or a fairer and more satisfying social structure. And the absence of a credible opponent may hinder rather than help the nation in arriving there.

In addition, there were four key players who never made it to the presidency but played a key role in calling attention to their party's proud tradition when the party was on the ropes. In the early nineteenth century it was the Whig Henry Clay who played that role by inspiring his party of the right (and the future conservative party) to become the agent of industrialism. In the late nineteenth century William Jennings Bryan performed that role by reminding the Democratic Party of their allegiance to the nation's underclasses. Also, when a mammoth Democratic Party roamed the political landscape in the mid–twentieth century, nearly reducing the Republicans to impotence, it was Barry Goldwater, the GOP candidate for president in 1964, who reminded the Republican Party where its roots were planted. Clay and Bryan became spiritual fathers to their party's (or successor party's) next great pattern-setter. Goldwater, however, did not present a fresh vision and, thus was not really Ronald Reagan's muse. The Republican candidate of 1964 mostly wanted to dismantle the New Deal and go forward into a Republicanism of the past.

Also, Alexander Hamilton deserves a place on this short list. Even though never a candidate for president, he first introduced the tradition that would inspire the Federalist Party and all subsequent parties of the right.

———∞∞∞———

Conclusion . . . "Catching On"

"This We Know"

1. Sometime around ten thousand years ago hunters and gathers began to settle in the fertile valleys and build an agricultural civilization. This Agricultural Revolution was accompanied by a transformation in social organization during which society became highly stratified and the family its basic unit.

2. This dual revolution ended approximately five thousand years ago. There were four main civilizations, with several satellite societies revolving around the main centers, and all proceeding down similar paths.

3. Up until about two hundred years ago, these civilizations did not change much outside of becoming more complex, especially in developing a morality—a conscience. The West also developed a "rule of law" and a "sanctity of human life" ethic.

4. In the late eighteenth century, after several centuries of increasing scientific knowledge, culminating in Newton's "law of gravity," the West broke through and began a new Industrial Revolution.

5. It, like the earlier Agricultural Revolution, is a dual revolution progressing along both an economic and a social front.

6. The two-hundred-year history of the New World has been characterized by a continuing struggle between two competing ideologies, each exhorting their nation to focus on a different front, economic growth or social rebalancing.

Since the American republic was founded there have been nine mini-revolutions, and each continued in force until a new paradigm was in place. The tectonic plates did not stop shifting until there were new rules, fresh modes of behavior, and a profound transformation in the way the American people viewed reality.

Yet paradigms alternate: one type model is followed by a mini-revolution in the direction of the other type. This means we live in a world of **discontinuity**! But it is also a world in which predictions and expectations as to the future are based mostly on assumptions that what has been occurring in the recent past will continue. Because of this disconnect, we, as a group, are continually **surprised.**

In the 1920s a prosperous future for middle-class Americans seemed just around the next corner. John J. Raskob, chairman of the finance committee of the General Motors Corporation, vice president of E. I. Du Pont de Nemours & Company, director of the Bankers Trust Company, and chairman of the Democratic National Committee, explained how easy it was to accumulate wealth in an article in the *Ladies Home Journal* titled "Everybody Ought to Be Rich." And people believed. Then they turned that corner. Waiting for them, instead of the Goddess of prosperity, stood the mugger of depression.

In the late 1970s a baffling inflation had imbedded itself into American economic life and was paralyzing the nation's financial markets. Japan's economic forces were gobbling up the world economy, and a bloated U.S. federal government was usurping more and more control over people's daily lives. Serious people plausibly speculated that the nation was in terminal decline and thought the country was headed toward some sort of state social-ism. What followed: an American "free-market" renaissance—just the opposite of what most Americans had been expecting!

Do you remember what the investment world looked like in 1980? The majority of people have long forgotten, but for the record, the most popular view was one of growing energy short-ages and galloping inflation. According to the fashionable gurus of the time, Howard Ruff and Douglas Casey, whose best-selling books were being read by millions, the world was running out of oil supplies, the oxygen of industrial life, and inflation, already in double digits, was headed much, much higher. According to them, the price of oil was destined to soon reach $100 a barrel and the recommended heavy lifters for all portfolios should be gold and silver. As for stocks: Forget it! They were a dead asset with lim-ited upside potential at best. In fact, a year earlier *Business Week*'s cover article loudly proclaimed "The Death of Equities." So what happened? Fast forward to the end of 1998, nearly 18 years later: Oil trading for about $11 a barrel, almost 75 percent below its 1980 price level and nearly 90 per cent below its expected price; gold $290 an ounce, down about 65 percent from its price 18 years earlier; silver did even worse, trading at about $5 an ounce, approximately 90 percent below the peak 1980 price; and as for the "dead" asset, equities, the S&P "500" was trading at about 1230, or up about 1150 percent from its 1980 low. Those widely accepted forecasts achieved a perfect score: dead wrong on all four counts.

Throughout the 1980s Japan's miracle economic troops were on the march, demolishing all before them. Americans were bom-barded, almost daily, with new books claiming Japan was des-tined for world economic supremacy. However, most authors were kind enough to explain the Japanese business model, which was operating by different rules from the Western economies, along with an urgent call for America to hurriedly adopt it. How did the highly touted Japanese model do? At the end of 1998, while world stock markets, in general, were selling at more than three times their 1990 levels, stock prices in Japan were trading approximately 65 percent below their 1989 year-end peak. And for Japan the 1990s had become the "lost decade": 10 years of economic stagnation, during which time property markets collapsed, bad loans crippled their banking system, and pension funds began running short of money to pay retirees. By century's end no one was praising the Japanese model.

In the mid-1980s Americans were caught up in budget deficit mania. A sea of red ink, stretching as far out as the eye could see, was surely going to bankrupt the country . . . unless the Reagan tax cuts were reversed. During the 1984 presidential campaign, Walter Mondale told cheering Democrats that there had to be a "new realism" in government. "Let's tell the truth," he said. "Mr. Reagan will raise taxes and so will I. He won't tell you. I just did." Reagan won and did not raise them. In fact, he lowered them . . . again. Taxes would not be raised until the 1990s, and then the upward adjustment would only partially offset the prior Reagan cuts. Although government debt from 1980 to 1992 quadrupled, the American economy didn't implode. Instead it surged to unprecedented heights far surpassing Japan's "miracle" economy. And who would have thought that from late 1982 until the end of 2000, a period of 18 years, the nation's economy would experience only one eight-month recession? Never before had the country had such a long run of economic good fortune. And as for government deficits as far as the eye could see, well, by the end of the century they had become surpluses extending as far as the eye can see. (Since then we have gone back to a red ink federal budget.)

Oh yes! Not to forget the widely predicted post–World War II depression, which achieved broad acceptance just as the American economy and stock market were beginning a 25-year period of prosperity and rising share prices. All of these "consensus" forecasts were laughingly wide of the mark. No wonder America's most respected authority on business management, Peter

Drucker, has thrown up his hands, proclaiming, "Forecasting is not a respectable activity . . ."

The problem is: Forecasts based on continuity don't work in a world of discontinuity (shifting paradigms). But why should paradigms alternate? To understand how our world works we need look no further than to financial markets, that is, the stock market. The stock market, because it reflects bull markets followed by bear markets (chilling declines in corporate values), registers discontinuity every few years or so. Consequently, it serves very well as a microcosm for what goes on in the broader society.

By definition, bull markets are periods, usually several years in duration, wherein share prices are on a continually rising slope, rallying from peak to peak and then on to another peak. To be sure, along the way there are corrections, givebacks of some of the previous rise. But the price dips are mild, as are levels of investor pain. They do not change people's psychology, which is to view sell-offs in stock prices as opportunities to buy. And they are! Normally investors can count on another wave up to new high-water marks, vindicating all who bought the dip, as well as shareholders who hung on throughout the correction. As long as the upward trend in share values remains intact, large numbers of wanna-be stockholders will line up in the wings awaiting their chance to take advantage of price falloffs.

A rationale develops to make sense of the continuous rise in stock prices and spell out why it should continue. Although each bull market has its own thesis, there is a remarkable consistency about them, in that all posit a belief that a "prosperous tomorrow"—or the current trend of events—will continue. The rationale that a vast Internet Revolution was about to rewrite the rules of business is probably about as good as you can get. These axioms, whether correct or not, are very important because they not only justify the way many people are already behaving but also provide new crops of investors (those lining up in the wings) with the courage to join in. It becomes easier to recruit new investors.

But stock market trends do not last forever. Discontinuity, remember! Sooner or later one of the corrections is bound to get out of hand. Following a normal dip, share prices will appear to be recovering and on their way to new market highs . . . but do not make it. Instead, prices roll over and continue on down past the correction low, leaving those who bought the dip holding the bag. Losses accumulate and stockholders begin to feel pain, real pain. As prices recede to lower levels, investor psychology changes. Many disappointed shareholders become sorry they didn't dump their stocks earlier and change their behavior. Instead of buying the dips, they begin selling off their holdings on the rallies. Bull market has turned to bear, as all bull markets eventually do—even the granddaddy of them all, the Roaring Bull of the 1990s. And a growing number of disappointed investors wave good-bye to the belief in a "prosperous tomorrow."

Actually, bull and bear markets are a reflection of a change in people's behavior. Bull markets occur when people "**catch on**" to the fact that their nation's businesses are poised for big increases in sales and earnings and invest, hoping to cash in on the improving business conditions. A crowd of enthusiastic investors, believing in a "prosperous tomorrow," bid up the prices of stocks, paying ever-increasing premiums to "join in."

A bear market occurs when investor hopes for a rosy economic future do not pan out. Many shareholders are caught off guard and sell off their holdings. As stock prices recede, other fretting investors take notice and, fearing the faltering economy will bring about even lower prices, join in the selling stampede, which, in turn, further reduces share prices. As investors "drop out," stock prices are no longer able to command the premiums they did during prosperous times.

Most investors accept the fact that investment markets

undergo bull and bear phases. However, they attribute their losses to having guessed wrong, to thinking business was going to improve when, in fact, it slumped. **Not completely so!** Something else is going on, and this part is important.

What happens is that during an upward trend in stock prices increasing numbers of people become convinced that owning stocks is less risky and wish to "join in." Their purchases provide the fuel to send stock prices higher, and this, in turn, gives the economy another shot of adrenaline. Business leaders are quite cognizant of what is going on in the stock market. A robust stock market gets their "animal spirits" flowing, and they undertake new investment projects in order to increase their sales. These might entail acquiring more machinery, adding more stores, or bringing new products to market. Naturally, additional workers will be required. As the job market improves; workers feel better about their prospects and join in the general optimistic economic outlook. They increase their purchases, and some might also try to make an extra buck or two by taking advantage of the good times, either buying stocks or participating in a start-up business.

Each of these activities feeds off the other. More investors, willing to pay larger premiums, push stock prices even higher, which, in turn, leads to improved business prospects, and that, of course, draws in still more investors. This circuitous process serves to ensure both an upward trend in share prices and an even faster pace of business expansion. The change in investor behavior, which was the result of a brighter economic outlook, leads to a further improvement in business prospects. And we can count on these changes in the way people act to help bend future events in the same direction (say, increased prosperity) as the current one. So far, so good.

But . . . **when too many people have "joined in," the very event the "joining in" was predicated upon is undermined.** An economy's ability to function, like the health of an ecological system, is dependent on a delicate balance, and if the weight at one end of the scale becomes too great the nation's business sector is apt to end up in a condition broken and dissolute. Too many people joining in will tip the scale. Imagine a closed ecological system with just two types of animals, say caribou, who live off the natural vegetation of the land, and wolves, who feed off the caribou. A lot of wolves dining on their prey will deplete the caribou population. But this will also diminish the predator's food supply, and in a short time the wolves too begin to die out. But before they do, the caribou population, absent predators in large amounts, will recover, and this, in turn, by providing an increased food supply, will allow the wolves to begin multiplying once more. When an ecological system gets out of balance, it self-corrects, which prevents it from destructing. So too with the economy and stock market!

When the stock market and the economy are racing ahead, people's emotions are in the driver's seat, overruling their rational processes. This also includes many of the nation's very smart business and banking leaders, who have become so anxious to join in the rush to prosperity, they overlook that very important matter of "balance." The business and financial elite along with the rest of the nation put on rose-colored glasses, buy into the "prosperous tomorrow" thesis, and throw caution to the wind. They pursue an even higher level of expansion, acquiring more machinery, adding more stores, and bringing more new products to market. Again this requires more workers, but . . . soon the nation has run out of potential new employees. The nation's businesses have pushed up against their natural constraint. The wolves have gobbled up far too many of the caribou.

The economy will be grossly out of balance. People's economic expectations will be too high in relation to what the economy can deliver. This presents problems, many of which defy statistical measurement. There are simply not enough workers, not enough cheap resources, and not enough low-cost capital available to allow the economy to respond to promising new opportunities without unduly undermining the positions of the more mature businesses. At the same time, consumers and businesspeople, viewing their economic outlook as nearly risk-free, will be overborrowing and overspending to the hilt, and this further endangers the economy. If businesses are going to continue to be able to deliver fast-paced growth, it becomes imperative to change human behavior so that economic balance is restored.

When the economy is at what economists term "full employment," in order to attain a further level of expansion the emerging businesses must pay up for workers, attracting them away from the more mature industries, who are struggling to maintain their position in the American economy. As this process goes on, a wave of inflation may ensue. Some of the older industries, which can no longer afford to pay the higher prices for labor and other scarce materials and still make a profit, start falling on hard times. Pockets of weakness begin to appear. Some workers lose their jobs, and it takes the edge off an economy that just yesterday appeared so robust. The additional purchasing power the new wave of expansion was predicated on evaporates. Many of the newer projects that were unprofitable but supported by a belief in a "prosperous tomorrow" are scuttled. More employees receive pink slips. As news of unanticipated trouble surfaces, behavior begins to change. Large numbers of people shun their rose-colored glasses, stop believing in the "prosperous tomorrow" thesis, and this removes another prop to a bloated economy and stock market. Soon a bear stock market along with a business recession are riding together throughout the American landscape, like two horsemen of the apocalypse, spreading havoc and destruction. Hundreds of thousands of people who had climbed their way onto lofty economic perches fall and hit the ground with a thud. While it takes a while for perceptions of less risk to induce a change to a more adventuresome behavior, once people experience a great deal of unanticipated pain, perceptions of danger spread like wildfire and at their heels comes a shift to a cautious behavior, which will persist for quite a while.

To sum up: a "catching on–joining in" process that goes on is both good and bad for business and the stock market. At its inception and early stages, when people first begin catching on to business improvement, it fuels business expansion, while in its later stages it produces imbalances, which must be corrected. The same process that operates on the upside also occurs on the downside. The imbalances in that case are an army of unemployed workers, a multitude of unexploited promising and profitable business opportunities, and an abundant supply of low-cost investment capital waiting to be put to use. When those conditions are present, they build in an immunity to further economic hardship and set a foundation for a long period of good economic times.

The same phenomenon of catching on and joining in occurs in man's social environment, which also responds to changes in human behavior. In general there are two overriding forms of human social behavior and, at any given time, one or the other is dominant.

Each is predicated on a different mass perception of risk. In the first type, when danger seems slight, people become adventuresome and aggressively pursue risk. In the other, which occurs when risk looms large, they become cautious and seek safe harbors. Each type political paradigm, economic growth and social reform, is predicated on one of those two forms of mass human behavior. But when one type of human behavior becomes too great it sets up the conditions that will bring about a shift to the other type behavior.

The economic growth type model is spurred on by a desire to play the money game and become a part of a great rush to prosperity that is occurring. It requires people being more comfort-able with taking risks and willing to become entrepreneurs and shareholders. As regulations are removed and taxes are cut, the economy takes off. More people take notice of the expanding opportunities and become believers in tax cuts and less regula-tion. It becomes a "New Era" or "New Economy" wherein politi-cians who offer more of the same connect with the growing crowd of believers in a "New Economy" and are more likely to win office. During this time people become receptive to those ideas that represent risk taking, such as privatizing Social Secu-rity. Even a Democrat, if he is to attain the White House in times like this, must be somewhat favorable to this viewpoint. And this process of more tax cuts and even less regulation continues until imbalances develop to topple the edifice, similar to what hap-pened in the late 1920s.

The social rebalancing type of political model gains credence because it plays to a desire to avoid pain and fashion a more secure world. Risk avoidance is the dominant behavioral mode at this time. People become quite cautious and are drawn to pro-posals that promise security and stability. In this climate a soci-ety regulates in order to make things safer; more people are promoted into the mainstream so as to right the social imbalance and defuse the anger of those groups who had taken the brunt of the pain. Furthermore, government is likely to invest in infra-structure, such as roads, bridges, subway systems, and water systems. And sure enough, these measures work! People catch on that a recovery is in process. They become convinced that a government-inspired social rebalancing is the way to go and back politicians who are in tune with that mindset. Republicans, if they are to reach the highest office in the land during these times, will also be relatively sympathetic to this point of view. And this set of events continues until social expectations have become too great in relation to what the government can deliver.

At that point the social system will be in serious imbalance, much as what occurred in the late 1960s and 1970s and, for that matter, in the 1850s.

In both cases, people's behavior is determined not only by a logical evaluation of all the relevant facts but more so by **how they perceive risk.** When danger appears to be low, people generally prefer a market-based economy. On the other hand, the public will opt for government intervention when risk looms large. Perceptions of risk are key. But those mass perceptions of danger don't just happen. They are based on recent events. Specifically, repeated instances of success, such as economic prosperity, create mass perceptions of lessened risk. On the flip side, an event that produces great trauma, for instance deep and protracted economic hardship, produces mass perceptions of danger. These repeated economic successes or painful business retrenchments are the powerful incentives or disincentives that, by affecting perceptions of risk, motivate people to change their behavior.

Keep in mind, in both cases, once perceptions of risk change, different modes of behavior soon follow. People "catch on" to an emerging new political model, and this catching-on, joining-in process once started will continue, spawning more of the same, until too many have joined in. Men and women don't stop their behavior of greater risk taking until they experience *a lesson of pain*. On the other hand, people are not inclined to shed a cautious mode of behavior and begin taking more chances until it becomes apparent that it has become easy for bold risk takers to ring up enormous profits—*a lesson of pleasure*. Each type paradigm replaces the other type model, but only after the latter one becomes out of balance.

A long period of prosperity provides a lesson of unanticipated pleasure. It changes the way many people see their world. It appears less risky to them and many of these early "catcheronners" **change their behavior** to adventuresome risk-taking, in hopes of pursuing pleasure. Some propose a rationale, compatible with the new risk perception, to explain the change. It both justifies the emerging behavioral pattern and provides courage for others to "join in." A large and growing crowd is now acting in a way that supports and helps bend future events in the direction of previous ones. What had been a rationale to explain what is going on becomes a belief system, which provides the psychological component of "confidence." Others, who had been sitting on the sidelines, witness a continued stream of prosperity and finally "catch on" and "join in," tipping the scale so that the bias to see less risk than really exists becomes quite pronounced. Because so many place heavy bets on continued prosperity a modest economic contraction, an event that normally unleashes only a modest amount of pain, will be unanticipated, catching large numbers of people off guard, and will be perceived as a lesson of pain setting off the same process in reverse. (See table 23.)

TABLE 23

A Law of Social Gravity

Step	
I	A lesson of unanticipated pain or pleasure = a stream of prosperity or economic retrenchment.
II	Changes the way many people perceive their world. They see more or less risk.
III	People begin the process of catching on and shift their behavioral pattern to match the new risk perception. They become risk takers or cautious risk averters
IV	A rationale, compatible with the new risk perception, surfaces that provides justification for the shift in behavior and courage for others to join in.
V	This new way people are acting helps bend future events in the same direction (more of the same occurs), which, in turn, proves the rationale correct so that it becomes a belief system, and this provides confidence.
VI	Others who needed more evidence catch on and join in until the scale has tipped too heavily on the side of low or high risk.
VII	People act accordingly, becoming too heavily committed to a continuance of prosperity or cutting economic commitments to the bare bones. The stage is set so that a small deviance from the string of events catches many people by surprise. It is unanticipated and becomes a lesson of pain or pleasure opposite to what had been expected and sets off the same process in reverse.

Economic retrenchment now provides a lesson of unantici- pated pain and changes the way many see risk. They see more risk and that leads to a change in behavior to cautiousness or risk avoidance . . . and so on.

During the past 140 years American society has alternated between favoring a "free" market and preferring government intervention in economic matters. There is also evidence an alter- nation between these same two forces, government intrusion and a free marketplace, has been occurring on a still much larger can- vass and over a greater length of time, spanning centuries. According to the Belgian historian Henri Pirenne, since the West awoke from the Dark Ages at the dawn of the eleventh century and began to cast aside a feudal system, long periods—say of about one hundred to two hundred years—of market freedom were followed by long periods wherein government assumed con- trol over the economy.

The Law of Social Gravity

This alternation from one type of paradigm to the other is a law of social gravity, somewhat similar to Newton's law, and men and women best heed it, as they are governed by it. In the Western world humans display a herd-like behavior that operates accord- ing to a "catching on" process and oftentimes defies the rules of logic. People catch on to some important event and attempt to join in (or drop out). In so doing they become believers that it will persist, and change their behavior so as to either take advantage of it or avoid it. But the "catching on" process continues beyond the point where it pays to catch on. We become part of a huge crowd of people doing likewise and thus help tip the scales, so that the event we hoped to exploit is unlikely to take place. There is no way for the ordinary "joiner-in" to escape the big **surprise**. This is the **"Great Paradox,"** which can be shortened to: **When**

most people believe something will surely happen, it is least likely to.

This paradox is a large part of the forecasting problem. Typically predications of the future implicitly incorporate past behavioral patterns in the formulations. However, when those predictions are widely followed they will very likely help create new and different behavioral patterns, which will affect the outcome in ways that had not been accounted for.

Question: Why cannot a people intelligent enough to make spaceships capable of traveling to distant planets learn where the straight path of equilibrium is and stay on it? Why can't human beings figure out a way to avoid the discontinuity that catches so many off guard and shatters their lives?

The most common form of human behavior is to try to "catch on" to what works and attempt to take advantage of it—or avoid impending danger. The trouble is: There is no way of knowing when what has worked is no longer working—until *after* the fact. At what point is the economy in balance between producers and consumers, between inflation and growth, between innovation and stability? This we do not know. There is no "just right" signal, at least not one that most people can agree on.

To see how difficult it is for people to find the right time to shift behavior, before a lesson of pain or pleasure has been sent, let's return to the world of investments. Professional investors consider themselves more sophisticated than the "man on the street" and often think they can maneuver from bull to bear and back again to bull ahead of the crowd. But . . .

The 1990s proved that bull markets can last way beyond what those professionals had thought probable or even possible. (So too can bear markets, as investors in Japan have discovered.) During what was to prove to be the greatest bull market of modern times, many, if not most, of those supposedly sophisticated investors, believing in a financial law of gravity, sold out what seemed to be overvalued stocks and spent the remainder of that unprecedented bull market, which in many cases would be years, sitting on the sidelines. By the time the bull market peaked, many of those financial seers had lost their jobs, along with their reputations.

Although we cannot know in advance where equilibrium is, we can certainly tell when things have gotten "out of whack." Let some unanticipated event register *a lesson of great pain or pleasure* on a social group and "we know."

This law of social gravity pushes us too far in one direction and then back again too far in the other. Two complementary and balancing forces alternate as to which dominates, and this renders a social system stable and able to regenerate itself for very long periods of time. Contrary to what most people might think, this type system is in long-term **equilibrium.** The path to equilibrium may not be straight but, rather, one that veers off course in first one direction and then the other in an attempt to seek a "right" level. And our friend, equilibrium, probably resides somewhere around the mid-point between the two extremes.

There is a socio-biological process operating in our world, which is triggered by the important lessons of pain and pleasure. About two hundred years ago the British philosopher Jeremy Bentham wrote: "Nature has placed man under the governance of two sovereign masters, pain and pleasure. It is for them to point out what we shall do." And they do . . . by altering risk perceptions, which lead crowds of people to change their behavior and thereby allow a society, an economy, and most types of social systems to correct themselves. It allows humans to adjust their views and actions so that they conform to what is occurring out there in the real world. It allows a society to push forward when opportunity beckons and, when calamity strikes, to circle the wagons so as to avoid further danger. But it also ensures that, at times, human behavior will alter events, thus influencing reality.

Humans are part of the process and thus have a hard time seeing how they affect that process. The two most generalized modes of human behavior are approach and avoidance: pursuing opportunity and avoiding danger. The majority of people implicitly emphasize one or the other. But in most cases some rationale, some belief system, is necessary to point people in one direction or the other. They need to believe. These beliefs, while providing people with the courage to select a form of behavior, also carry a disclaimer in fine print, unseen to the human eye, which is: when too many others also believe, all bets as to the viability of that belief are off. The trick, of course, is figuring out what constitutes too many.

How Do Men and Women Fit into the Equation?

Those who "catch on" quicker, during a mini-revolution, before the majority, usually get an earlier and better idea of what to expect and the direction of likely change for many years to come. It puts them on the favorable side of the learning curve, allowing them, if they so choose, to shift behavioral gears and join in or drop out ahead of the pack. For instance, in the early 1980s those who recognized a new economic growth paradigm was beginning would have been quicker to grasp the enormous economic and financial opportunities on the horizon. They might have attempted to capitalize by seeking entrepreneurial opportunities. Or they may have tried to partake in the mouthwatering investment opportunities that were opening up, especially in the stock market.

Catching on early appears to be the elusive comparative advantage economists search for. But shifting gears is easier said than done. Typically most people adopt a risk perception and corresponding mode of behavior that is compatible with their paradigm. And in so doing they become wedded to it. The result: They will be behind the curve in learning the new rules, resistant to acquiring the new skills, and tardy in modifying their principal mode of behavior. And as they believe what worked in the past will keep on working, their commitments and their strategies will become hopelessly out of step with the new tone of American political and economic society.

However, one huge group of people, in general, has an easier time catching on early to an emerging political model. The young, in not having adapted to the older political model, have a natural advantage. With less to unlearn, it is simpler for them to catch on to the new rules and learn the new skills, especially those geared to the increasingly more complex technological changes, which are in tune with the new paradigm. Typically, when paradigms shift, the young and the mature members of society find themselves on opposite ends of a risk-perception continuum. Neither is able to see things from the other's perspective, and both groups favor different behavioral patterns. This, of course, exacerbates the generational gap.

Some biblical scholars attribute the Jews' 40 years of nomadic wandering in the desert, following their exodus from Egypt, to the notion that God didn't want to build a new religious-based society on the foundation of a people with a slave mentality. Waiting for the oldsters to die out ensured that a fresh generation, with presumably different behavioral patterns, would be in charge of fashioning the new society.

There is also another very important consideration, which normally is even harder to master. That is, learning when having caught on is no longer an advantage. As time goes on and more and more people have caught on, early paradigm recognizers are in jeopardy of losing their edge. And many do! Finally there comes a time when joining in may, in fact, prove to be a disadvantage. Latecomers become scale tippers. But deciding when to stop believing in the paradigm, before a clear sign of change has been given, is a difficult matter indeed.

Yet attempting to catch on may not be for everyone. Some people do not want to catch on. These are usually the true believers in a particular viewpoint, and those people play an important role also. Just as it is necessary to have people who catch on and shift their strategy so as to right the ship of state, it is also incumbent that some remain behind to show the flag for the opposing viewpoint so that it remains a vibrant option for those on the other side to return to. Furthermore, if these resisters hold on to their viewpoint long enough, they may appear "heroes" to the crowd when it comes rushing back. Some caribou had to remain alive so the multiplying process could begin again, once their time came.

A speculative thought to leave you with: Perhaps we, humankind, are part of a grand scheme playing out biologically designed roles in a great social organism. Like armies of sperm dispensed to do a job that only one or two may succeed at, humans, in the millions, are sent out into the world either to find and help build new pathways to growth or to help society rebalance itself. If that be humankind's assigned role and we are to play our part, men and women may not be the "masters of their own fate" they deem themselves to be.

Bibliography

Frederick Lewis Allen, *The Big Change*. Perennial Library/ Harper & Row. 1952.

Robert J. Art and Kenneth N. Waltz, *The Use of Force*. Roman and Littlefield Publishers, Inc. 1999.

Louis Auchincloss, *Theodore Roosevelt*. Times Books/Henry Holt & Co., 2001.

Louis Auchincloss, *Woodrow Wilson*. A Lipper/Viking Book. 2000.

Thomas A. Bailey, *A Diplomatic History of the American People*. Prentice-Hall. 1980.

Bernard Bailyn, David Davis, David Donald, John Thomas, Robert Dallek, and Gordon Wood, *The Great Republic: A History of the American People*. Little, Brown and Co. 1977.

William Barney, *The Passage of the Republic*. D.C. Heath & Co. 1987.

Philip Bobbitt, *The Shield of Achilles*. Borzoi/Alfred A. Knopf. 2002.

Paul Boller Jr. *Presidential Campaigns*. Oxford University Press. 1996.

Alan Brinkley and Davis Dyer, eds., *The Reader's Companion to the American Presidency*. Houghton Mifflin Co. 2000.

Henry Steele Commager, *The Empire of Reason*. Anchor Press/Doubleday. 1977.

William Degregorio, *The Complete Book of U.S. Presidents*. Wings Books. 1984.

Robert Divine, T. H. Breen, George Fredrickson, and R. Hal Williams, *American Past and Present*, Vols. I and II. Longman/Addison Wesley Longman. 1999.

David Donald, *Lincoln Reconsidered*. Vintage Books/Random House. 1947.

Joseph J. Ellis, *American Sphinx: The Character of Thomas Jefferson*. Vintage Books. 1996.

Joseph J. Ellis, *Founding Brothers*. Borzoi/Alfred Knopf. 2000.

Robert William Fogel, *The Fourth Great Awakening*. University of Chicago Press. 2000.

David Fromkin, *The Way of the World*. Alfred Knopf. 1998.

David Frum, *How We Got Here: The 70's*. Basic Books. 2000.

Francis Fukuyama, *The Great Disruption*. The Free Press. 1999.

John Lewis Gaddis, *We Now Know: Rethinking Cold War History*. Oxford University Press. 1997.

John Gray, *False Dawn*. The New Press. 1998.

Louis Hartz, *The Liberal Tradition in America*. Harvest Book/Harcourt Brace & Co. 1955.

Carlton Hayes, *A Generation of Materialism: 1871–1900*. Harper Torchbooks, Harper & Row. 1941.

Robert Heilbroner, *The Making of Economic Society*. Prentice-Hall. 1962.

John Hicks, *A Short History of American Democracy*. Houghton Mifflin/Riverside Press. 1949.

Don Higgenbotham, *George Washington Reconsidered*. University Press of Virginia. 2001.

Gertrude Himmelfarb, *One Nation, Two Cultures*. Alfred A. Knopf. 1999.

Richard Hofstadter, *The American Political Tradition.* Alfred Knopf. 1948.

Michael J. Hogan, *America in the World.* Cambridge University Press. 1995.

Michael F. Holt, *The Rise and Fall of the American Whig Party.* Oxford University Press. 1999.

Samuel P. Huntington, *The Clash of Civilizations and the Remaking of World Order.* Simon & Schuster. 1996.

Paul Johnson, *A History of the American People.* HarperCollins Publishers. 1997.

Robert F. Kennedy, *Thirteen Days.* W. W. Norton & Co. 1969.

Russell Kirk, *The Conservative Mind.* Regnery. 1953.

Irving Kristol, *Two Cheers for Capitalism.* Basic Books. 1978.

Paul Krugman, *The Accidental Theorist.* W. W. Norton & Co. 1998.

Bernard Lewis, *What Went Wrong?* Oxford University Press. 2002.

Samuel Lubell, *The Future of American Politics.* Harper Colophon Books. 1951.

Ernest R. May and Philip D. Zelikow, *The Kennedy Tapes.* Harvard University Press. 1997.

Herbert McClosky and John Zaller, *The American Ethos.* Harvard University Press. 1984.

William H. McNeill, *Plagues and Peoples.* Doubleday. 1977.

James M. McPherson, *To the Best of My Ability.* Agincourt Press Production/Dorling Kindersley. 2000.

Walter Russell Mead, *Special Providence.* Borzoi/Alfred A. Knopf. 2001.

John J. Mearsheimer, *The Tragedy of Great Power Politics.* W. W. Norton & Co. 2001.

Edmund Morris, *Theodore Rex.* Random House. 2001.

Jeffrey B. Morris and Richard B. Morris, *The Encyclopedia of American History.* HarperCollins, Publishers. 1996.

Samuel Eliot Morrison, *The Oxford History of the American People*, Vol. II. Meridan/Penguin Group. 1994.

Samuel Eliot Morrison, Henry Commager, and William Leuchtenburg, *The Growth of the American Republic*, Vols. I and II. Oxford University Press. 1930.

Douglass North, *The Economic Growth of the United States 1790–1860*. W. W. Norton & Co. 1966.

Douglass North, Terry Anderson, and Peter Hill, *Growth and Welfare in the American Past: A New Economic History*. Prentice-Hall. 1983.

Geoffrey Perret, *Ulysses S. Grant*. Modern Library/Random House. 1999.

Merrill Peterson, *Adams and Jefferson*. Oxford University Press. 1976.

Kevin Phillips, *Arrogant Capital*. Little, Brown and Co. 1994.

Kevin Phillips, *Wealth & Democracy*. Broadway Books. 2002.

Michael P. Riccards, *The Ferocious Engine of Democracy*, Vols. I and II. Madison Books. 1997.

Arthur Schlesinger Jr., *The Cycles of American History*. Houghton Mifflin Co. 1986.

Jean E. Smith, *Grant*. Simon & Schuster, 2001.

Robert Sobel, *Panic on Wall Street*. Macmillan & Co. 1968.

Melvyn Stokes and Stephen Conway, *The Market Revolution in America*. University Press of Virginia. 1996.

James L. Sundquist, *Dynamics of the Party System*. Brookings Institute. 1983.

Lionel Tiger, *The Decline of Males*. St. Martin's Griffin. 1999.

Rexford Tugwell, *How They Became President*. Simon & Schuster. 1964.

Mark J. White, *The Kennedys and Cuba*. Ivan R. Dee. 1999.

Theodore H. White, *America in Search of Itself*. Harper & Row. 1982.

Garry Wills, *James Madison*. Times Books/Henry Holt & Co. 2002.

Gordon S. Wood, *The American Revolution*. The Modern Library. 2002.

Bob Woodward, *Shadow*. Simon & Schuster. 1999.

Index